W9-ABB-941

THE POLITICS OF AGENDA SETTING

For Jo, Justin and Ella

The Politics of Agenda Setting

The car and the shaping of public policy

NICK ROBINSON
University of Leeds, UK

Ashgate

Aldershot • Burlington USA • Singapore • Sydney

Published by
Ashgate Publishing Limited
Gower House
Croft Road
Aldershot
Hampshire GU11 3HR
England

Ashgate Publishing Company
131 Main Street
Burlington VT 05401-5600 USA

Ashgate website: http://www.ashgate.com

HE
243. 172
.A2
R63
2000

British Library Cataloguing in Publication Data
Robinson, Nick
 The politics of agenda setting : the car and the shaping of
 public policy
 1. Transportation and state - Great Britain
 I. Title
 388'.0941

Library of Congress Control Number: 00-134011

ISBN 0 7546 1142 6

Printed and bound by Athenaeum Press, Ltd.,
Gateshead, Tyne & Wear.

Contents

List of Figures and Tables

Figures

Tables

Acknowledgements

I would like particularly to thank Jim Bulpitt, Wyn Grant and Jeremy Richardson, from whom I have learned so much. I would also like to thank the following who commented on the various drafts which finally made up this book: Peter Burnham, Roger Duclaud-Williams, Ed Page, Matthew Paterson and Wayne Parsons. In addition, the University of Warwick provided generous financial support for the initial stages of this project. Thanks also to my former colleagues at the University of Derby for their support.

I owe a substantial debt to the numerous individuals who agreed to be interviewed and gave generously of their time and expertise, a number of whom cannot be acknowledged within the text due to the sensitivity of the information which they provided.

I would also like to thank Roger McGough and his agency, the Peters Fraser & Dunlop Group Limited, for permission to reproduce 'Five-car family', from Roger McGough (1992), *Defying Gravity* (Harmondsworth: Penguin) on pages 77-78 of this book.

Last but not least, I must acknowledge the support of my family. My partner Jo Townsend has been a veritable rock, undertaking meticulous proof-reading and being simply wonderful throughout, while my two year-old son Justin has given me a sense of perspective and provided endless fun.

List of Abbreviations

AA	Automobile Association
BBC	British Broadcasting Corporation
BRF	British Road Federation
CBI	Confederation of British Industry
CCT	Compulsory Competitive Tendering
CfIT	Commission for Integrated Transport
CIT	Chartered Institute of Transport
CPRE	Council for the Protection of Rural England
CTP	Common Transport Policy
DG	Directorate General of the European Commission
DoE	Department of the Environment
DoETR	Department of the Environment, Transport and the Regions
DoH	Department of Health
DTI	Department of Trade and Industry
DTp	Department of Transport
EC	European Community
ECJ	European Court of Justice
ECMT	European Conference of Ministers of Transport
ecu	European Currency Unit
EEC	European Economic Community
EMU	Economic and Monetary Union
EPEFE	European Programme on Emissions, Fuels and Engine Technologies
ERDF	European Regional Development Fund
EU	European Union
FoE	Friends of the Earth
HCSC	House of Commons Select Committee
HCTSC	House of Commons Transport Select Committee
HLSC	House of Lords Select Committee
LRT	Light Rapid Transit
NAQS	National Air Quality Strategy
NRTF	National Road Traffic Forecasts

OECD	Organisation for Economic Co-operation and Development
PFI	Private Finance Initiative
RAC	Royal Automobile Club
RCEP	Royal Commission on Environmental Pollution
RFP	Roads for Prosperity
RHA	Road Haulage Association
RSPB	Royal Society for the Protection of Birds
SACTRA	Standing Advisory Committee on Trunk Roads Assessment
SEA	Single European Act
SEM	Single European Market
T2000	Transport 2000
TEN	Trans-European Network
TEU	Treaty on European Union
TPP	Transport Policies and Programmes
TSG	Transport Support Grant
UNICE	Union of Industrial and Employers' Confederations of Europe
WMPTA	West Midlands Passenger Transport Authority
WTO	World Trade Organisation

1 Introduction

This book argues that in the 1990s transport emerged as an issue of high political salience as the motor car increasingly came to be blamed for a combination of economic and environmental problems including rising congestion, noise, land-use impacts and a deterioration of air quality and traffic safety standards. As a result, the politics of the car has become a crucial issue confronting every government world-wide: arguably, it is tangential to all government decision making. Access to the car has had an important effect on issues such as hospital and education provision; planning decisions shaping the character of city centres throughout the world, and the development of out-of-town shopping (with equity implications for those without access to a car). Furthermore, the car is a key aspect of family spending with many citizens now almost totally dependent on the car. Such issues raise significant paradoxes for government: how can they gain the benefits of the car – the jobs, convenience, economic benefits etc – while ameliorating the costs – the environmental and planning effects and the costs in human life resulting from traffic accidents. Yet transport is an issue which has invited little comment from political scientists, remaining in the main the preserve of economists, geographers and town and country planners (Grant, 1995, pp. 4-5).

The primary rationale for this book is, therefore, to add to the contribution of political science to the study of the politics of transport. This is a particularly worthwhile exercise as the studies of UK transport policy which have been undertaken by political scientists thus far have tended to focus on discussion of the political conflict surrounding the pre-eminent power of the road lobby (see for example Hamer, 1987, Dudley, 1983 and Finer, 1958). Such studies have generally emphasised the static nature of transport policy in the post-war era, as the road lobby has combined skilful lobbying with luck 'to link its demands for resources to a more generalised belief that: (i) growth was desirable, and (ii) it was connected to the need for good infrastructure' (Dudley, 1983, p. 104). However, in the 1990s the transport issue gained higher political salience and the policy agenda increased in dynamism, thus posing a significant

1

challenge to the position of the road lobby. This book aims to reflect both on the reasons for these changes and their implications.

The second key aim of this book is to apply intellectual innovations from the study of agenda setting to the transport case. The 1980s and 1990s have seen a number of theoretical innovations in this area: in particular, the work of Kingdon (1984 and 1995), Sabatier and Jenkins-Smith (1993a) and Baumgartner and Jones (1991 and 1993) have all provided a much needed impetus to the study of agenda setting, helping to encourage a holistic conception of the policy process by political scientists. Such intellectual innovations increase the need to evaluate theoretical models of agenda setting through detailed case studies. It is the aim of this book to begin this task.

Throughout the late 1980s and 1990s the network approach was the dominant methodology adopted to study policy making by UK academics (see for example Atkinson and Coleman, 1992, Rhodes, 1990, Smith, 1993 and Wilks and Wright, 1987). Now, however, 'it is time to take stock: to see how much we have learned from this approach, to judge whether it can develop into a genuine and fruitful theory of the policy process or whether a more fundamental theory is required' (Dowding, 1995, p. 136). This book shares Dowding's aspiration; its third aim, therefore, is to provide a rigorous critical evaluation of the validity of the network approach in accounting for the increased political salience of the transport issue in the Major and Blair eras.

The final aim of this book is, more generally, to add to the literature on politics in the Major and Blair eras. As Bonefeld et al (1995) have argued, 'very little attention has been given to the administrations of John Major, and this despite the fact that he is one of the longest serving premiers in Britain this century' (p. 1). With its detailed study of the politics of transport in the Major era this book aims to go some way to correcting that shortfall, with the postscript bringing the reader up to date with developments since Major. Furthermore, Bonefeld et al point out that the studies of the Major era which have been undertaken tend to focus on a comparative evaluation of levels of continuity or change between the Thatcher and Major governments. The problem with such a focus is that 'concentration on the issue of continuity versus discontinuity tends to lead to the not too surprising conclusion that forces for continuity are powerful' (1995, p. 2). However, a consideration of transport policy in the 1990s reveals considerable discontinuities with the Thatcher period: this book therefore also challenges the conventional view that continuity between the Thatcher and post-Thatcher eras was considerable.

A Question of Questions

This book investigates three major research questions concerning the relationship between the politics of the car and the dynamics of political change. All are central to the evaluation of the competing models of agenda setting which is the aim of this book.

The first key question which this book addresses is that of providing an explanation for the increasing political salience of the transport issue in the Major era. Theoretical explanations of agenda setting can be classified as either actor centred, problem centred, external (or systems) based or non-decision making models, each focusing on different explanations of political change. In seeking a convincing explanation of developments concerning the car in the Major and Blair eras, this research therefore aims to draw on these models and to evaluate which, if any, of them can provide such an explanation.

Second, non-agenda setting models emphasise that governments have certain policy imperatives which they will always aim to protect through the exercise of control over the agenda setting process. Benson argues that the policy agenda is 'shaped by "deep rules" which operate to ensure that some demands are excluded from the decision-making process, and which limit the choices and behaviour of policy-makers' (Parsons, 1995, p. 149 summarising Benson, 1982, pp. 159-64. This process is described in detail in Chapter 2, which reviews the models of agenda setting). Consequently, controversial issues are managed from the agenda by government on behalf of policy insiders if they challenge these 'deep rules' (or if in policy terms they challenge the state's policy imperatives) (Benson, 1982, p. 162). Therefore, the second crucial question considered in this book is the extent to which transport policy in this period has been shaped by government policy imperatives. Is there any evidence that the policy agenda has excluded issues which are incompatible with these imperatives? To what extent have the challenges to the status quo in the Major era been sustained? Is there evidence of successful manipulation of the agenda by dominant interests, or has the Major era bequeathed to the Blair government a legacy of lasting volatility in the transport agenda?

Finally, this book examines the capacity of network theory to explain policy change in the Major and Blair eras, asking to what extent transport agenda setting in this period can best be explained by a focus on policy networks. Is political conflict over this issue best characterised by a division of actors into insiders and outsiders, based on their relationship to a core policy community? And assuming that the network approach provides a useful framework for the analysis of the politics of the car, how much operational autonomy does the core policy community have from central government? Accounts of the politics of the car, as I have argued, have tended to take a network approach, albeit with varying views of the extent to which networks have acted with autonomy. This book therefore aims to determine the validity of the network approach in this case, and to examine the level of autonomy possessed by the transport policy community, its impact on the agenda setting dynamic and the extent to which it has changed over time.

An Overview of the Book

The remainder of this book is divided into six substantive chapters, a conclusion and a postscript, which together provide an evaluation of the politics of the car in the Major and Blair eras. Chapter 2 provides the theoretical framework for the study of agenda setting in this period. It offers a critical review of the existing literature on agenda setting and argues that the models can be classified under one of four headings: actor centred; problem centred; external (or systems) models, and non-decision making models. Chapter 2 describes these models in general terms; the evidence for their ability to account for developments in the Major era and beyond is discussed throughout the remainder of the book.

Chapter 2 also reflects on the policy network approach and its relationship to agenda setting. In particular, it argues that while networks provide a useful method of classifying actors, the approach can lead to problems when attempting to explain agenda setting. In particular, a network approach has difficulty in incorporating external or systems events, tending to assume that agenda setting is explained only by changes in the balance of power between actors inside and outside the network. The network approach implies that policy communities have considerable autonomy from central government; however in the remainder of this book I argue that network autonomy in the UK is in fact highly conditional on the acquiescence of central government.

Events in the Major and Blair eras cannot be effectively evaluated without first placing them in their historical context. In Chapter 3 I argue that, on the surface, considerable parallels seem to exist between the conflicts over the transport issue of the 1970s and the 1990s. Both are periods of increasing concern over the environmental impact of motor vehicles; the trunk roads programme was the subject of increasing conflict as the opponents of roads launched a number of protests which captured the attention of the media; exogenous events provided the government with a justification for cuts to the road budget, and a broad-based 'review of policy' was undertaken, which ultimately served to stall the agenda. The increased salience of the transport issue in the 1970s appeared to pave the way for the reallocation of resources from road building to public transport, but in hindsight the 1980s saw a return to a significant road building programme, together with an increased emphasis on market instruments and a reduction in state funding for public transport. Overall, Chapter 3 provides a warning that in the long term the outcomes of the agenda setting process can be highly unpredictable. It also provides an initial indication of the importance of government action to manage the agenda in protecting the road lobby from challenges to their pre-eminent position.

The substantive argument within the book is contained in Chapters 4-7, which adopt themes from the agenda setting models discussed in Chapter 2 in order to explain, and examine the effect of, the increased political salience of the transport issue in the Major era. First, in Chapter 4, I adopt ideas from problem centred accounts of agenda setting and argue that during the Major period transport increasingly came to be seen as a policy problem. In the last ten to fifteen years the problems associated with road transport such as congestion and vehicle related air pollution have become more serious. In addition, knowledge about the environmental effects of road transport has increased immeasurably: this has helped to identify a series of new policy problems such as global warming.[1] These new policy problems have in turn created an impetus towards new solutions which the anti-roads groups have been able to exploit. As Kingdon (1995) argues, problems tend to develop as a result of events, independently of the actions of groups. This has proven to be true in the transport case.

Of all of these problems I argue that the most significant has been congestion. In particular, I argue that the Thatcher government created a significant policy problem for its successor through the creation of what Dunleavy has termed a 'policy disaster' (1995). In 1989, the government produced the *National Road Traffic Forecasts* (DTp 1989a) which predicted that traffic levels would grow by between 83% and 142% by the year 2025. Thus government was itself instrumental in defining the serious nature of the problem of congestion. In response to these figures, the government then launched an expanded roads programme, *Roads for Prosperity* (Cm 693), presenting it as the solution to the problem. However, it immediately became clear that the scale of the problem outlined in the government's traffic projections was such that it could not be solved by the proposed programme. The anti-roads groups benefited from this disparity, being able to argue that it was virtually impossible for any road programme to accommodate the government's own projections for road traffic growth. Thus the government's own forecasts, and its proposed solution, unwittingly aided the opposition of the anti-roads groups.

Chapter 4 concludes that although increasing concern with congestion and pollution has led to a conceptualisation of transport as a policy problem, this has had only a mixed impact on the transport agenda as central government has successfully promoted a number of policies designed to reduce the *environmental impact* of motor vehicles and thus lower the salience of the transport issue. Government intervention has depoliticised the transport agenda in relation to issues such as vehicle emissions in the short term. However, this has left the fundamental transport 'problem' of reconciling twentieth century lifestyle and mobility choices with ecological sustainability unresolved, as the Major government avoided the true implications of conflict over policy in this area.

Chapter 5 adopts themes from the actor centred approach to agenda setting in order to focus on changes in the relationship between insider and outsider groups and their effect on the agenda setting process. In the literature on the politics of the car the change in this relationship is viewed as being of primary significance: actor centred models argue that the anti-roads groups became increasingly adept at gaining access to government, while the road lobby was increasingly fragmented as divisions emerged between the construction and manufacturing sectors and the road users. In this chapter the impact of these changes is viewed more narrowly, for a number of reasons. First, the government itself has policy imperatives based on the realisation of an efficient network of trunk roads which it believes is central to the promotion of economic efficiency and personal mobility. Second, the fragmentation of the road lobby in the Major era has been overstated; this lobby in fact remains united around a shared belief that mobility is essential for economic development. Actor centred accounts have, I argue, confused the development of dialogue between 'moderate elements' of the road lobby and anti-roads groups for changes in the core beliefs of these groups. Finally, I argue that actor centred accounts of agenda setting have misrepresented the importance of the alternative policy arenas which were available to the anti-roads groups in the Major period. In particular, I examine the significance of the media's relationship to the direct action protests, arguing that while the media has changed the policy image of transport from that of a dull technical issue to a highly emotive one, it has done so at the cost of marginalising both the more moderate anti-roads groups (such as Transport 2000) and the solutions which they have to offer. I also examine the impact of Parliamentary politics in the Major era, considering the Parliamentary arena as a potential site for change. The Major government's small majority after 1992 enabled MPs, particularly from the South East of England, to oppose road schemes which affected their constituencies, forcing the cancellation of individual road schemes and reductions to the road programme generally. However, I argue that this opposition was largely pragmatic, being without consequence for the ideology of the Major government, which continued investment in the road programme in the Midlands and Northern England where opposition was minimal.

Neither of these national arenas, therefore, offered the kind of alternative sites for change to the anti-roads groups which are envisaged by actor centred models of agenda setting. In Chapters 6 and 7 I go on to examine two alternative arenas with the potential to exert significant exogenous influence on national decision making: the European Union (EU) and local government. In the policy making literature local government and the EU are frequently seen as alternative arenas which groups will attempt to infiltrate in order to exert pressure on national policy making. This book evaluates the extent to which this is the case.

In Chapter 6, I argue that the EU has become increasingly important as an alternative venue for policy making. EU initiatives to strengthen the Community's regulatory framework were supported by the Major government because their aims of facilitating the development of the single market programme and promoting technical solutions to the transport problem accorded with that government's own initiatives. However, the EU has had less success in its efforts to develop an activist environmental or infrastructure policy. Proposals to develop policy in the domain of 'high politics' have failed due to the opposition of a number of national governments (including the UK) and a lack of fiscal resources.

Overall, the imbalance between the development of regulatory policy and activist policy in the EU has served to further limit the environmental movement's challenge to the road programme in the UK. The EU's regulatory strategy works to reduce the political salience of the transport problem by creating a technical framework for its solution: in consequence issues of sustainability, land-use and mobility are largely removed from the political agenda. And further, the EU's plans to develop a strategic network of European roads has been used by national governments to try to undermine the opposition of national road protests. However, this aspect of the government's political strategy has seriously backfired, resulting in a policy disaster similar to that surrounding the 1989 *Roads for Prosperity* programme.

In turn, Chapter 7 examines the difficulties experienced by local government in its attempts to overcome the dominance of central government over the agenda setting process. The increased political salience of the transport issue has led central government to acknowledge that responsibilities for traffic restraint, the provision of alternatives to the car and monitoring air quality are best placed on local government, but there has been no creation of an accompanying funding mechanism enabling it to act on these responsibilities. Thus local authorities have become the victims of an agenda driven by the priorities of the centre, in which they are confronted with political pressure for action but remain deprived of the resources to enable this.

In Chapter 8, which concludes this main part of the book, I return to the questions which provided the initial rationale for this investigation: namely to examine competing models of agenda setting; to evaluate the literature on non-decision making; and to evaluate the network approach.

First, I conclude that no single model of agenda setting provides an explanation of developments in the Major era, but nor is any one model totally inappropriate. Policy making became increasingly complex in this period: opposition to the road programme become more sophisticated and transport increasingly came to be seen as a policy problem. Yet the agenda in the Major era remained relatively stable. Overall, I conclude that a consideration of the transport agenda setting process demonstrates aspects of all four models. This is because the transport agenda setting process operates in, and is constrained by, a policy making environment which is dominated by the policy imperatives of the state. Consequently, the problem and actor centred models provide an explanation of agenda setting when the policy imperatives of the state are not threatened, while non-decision making models provide an explanation of cases in which those imperatives are threatened. Exogenous or systems models are also important, as they emphasise that the external environment provides a major source of stability for policy subsystems. However they are less useful as an explanation of political change, as the EU itself (the principal arena through which exogenous forces assert themselves upon the UK government) has had little effect when it has advocated policies which the UK government has opposed.

Second, non-decision making matters. The reason for this is that the agenda setting dynamic demonstrates two contradictory aspects in the Major period. On the one hand the opposition to the roads programme became increasingly sophisticated, and transport is now clearly seen to be a policy problem. On the other hand the underlying policy imperatives of the state have ensured that many aspects of the transport issue remain within the pre-decision stage of decision making. Two key policy imperatives can be identified: the desire to promote liberty and mobility, and the pragmatic realisation by the centre that the costs of implementing significant change to policy will be immense. For example, countries such as the Netherlands which have developed public transport networks and high levels of bicycle usage still suffer from increasing traffic levels. Thus it is clear that the only way in which government policy can be expected to have any significant impact on behaviour in the transport sphere is by actually restricting car usage, a move which would carry with it enormous political and ultimately electoral costs, and which also contradicts the policy imperatives of the state.

The final contention within the conclusion is that although a policy networks approach provides a useful method for classifying actors, it does not provide an adequate theoretical framework for a discussion of agenda setting. This is because, historically, transport insider groups have derived their status from the support of the government and not from their activities within the core policy community. Thus, the pro-roads groups have historically been the beneficiaries of what Dowding has termed 'systematic luck', with their status as policy insiders secured on the basis of central government support rather than as a result of their lobbying activity.

Finally, the Postscript (Chapter 9) provides an overview, and analysis, of the policy initiatives undertaken by the Labour party since its election in 1997 in order to re-examine the substantive conclusions within the book and reflect on the pattern of governance in the Blair era.

The Blair government's principal policy initiatives concerning the car were outlined in the transport White Paper, *A New Deal for Transport*, with a transport bill scheduled for ratification in the year 2000 providing the required primary legislation. In common with the pattern of the Major era, these initiatives have emphasised levels of both change and continuity.

On the one hand, policy change has been considerable and is demonstrated by a number of initiatives: the setting up of the Commission for Integrated Transport charged with the development of solutions to transport problems; the proposed implementation of hypothecated urban road pricing; a shift in the balance of the road budget from increased capacity construction to road maintenance encompassing environmental improvements such as low noise surfaces, and the increased provision of alternatives to the car in order to try to change travel behaviour.

On the other hand, the Blair administration has demonstrated considerable policy continuity in this area: a focus on technical fixes in order to manage/reduce vehicle emissions remains, with the Blair government further promoting the development of policy at the EU level within the Auto-Oil framework, in spite of the fact that such a focus undermines lifestyle solutions designed to reduce usage of the car. Furthermore, inconsistency in the nature of the planning process has remained, with rhetoric regarding the need to reduce the need to travel being offset by support for further housing developments in green field sites. Continuity is also emphasised by the nature of central-local relations, with the Blair government (as the Major government before it) proposing that local authorities implement unpopular measures such as road pricing and work-place parking charges. Thus the Blair government, like the Major government, still aims to manage the policy agenda in response to perceived opposition to unpopular proposals from voters.

Finally, the postscript suggests that the model of agenda setting which has been developed within this book remains effective in explaining the nature of policy change in the Blair era. As I have argued in the bulk of the book, policy change and the formulation of policy proposals are constrained by the policy imperatives of the state. Furthermore, alternative arenas, such as the EU or local authorities, are exploited by the government when to do so suits its purpose. Thus, policy change in the Blair era (as in the Major era) remains limited, being constrained by the policy imperatives of the state which limit the capacity of government to undertake radical action in this area.

Note

1   Although transport is only one of a number of sources contributing to global warming, it is the fastest growing sector. Thus the growth in the knowledge of the effects of transport on the environment and concerns over the implications of global warming are closely related (Button, 1995, p. 176).

2 Agenda Setting: A Review of the Literature

An Agenda Survey: Justifications for Theoretical Investigation

> When the city of Gary, Indiana, was being put together just after the turn of the century, its low skyline was already streaked with industrial smoke. Before Gary had a city hall, or a public school, or paved streets, it had a steel mill. Before the steel mill, there was an uninhabited stretch of sand dunes and boggy meadows where the city of Gary now stands ... Today, thanks largely to Judge Gary and his corporation, there is a city of more than 180,000 on a site that late nineteenth-century entrepreneurs considered one of the 'most desolate available in the United States'. The town has the largest steel mill in the world, an impressive domed city hall, about twenty public schools, many miles of paved streets, and it often lies under a heavy blanket of dirty air ... In 1962 the U.S. Public Health Service, ranked sixty American cities according to the dirtiness of the air. Gary stood at the head of the list. (Crenson, 1971, pp. 35-36)

When Victor Hugo stated that 'greater than the tread of mighty armies is an idea whose time has come' he made a statement of fundamental importance (cited in Kingdon, 1984, p. 1). As Schattschneider has argued, understanding the process of agenda setting is central to building a broader understanding of political concepts such as power and policy making: 'Political conflict is not like an intercollegiate debate in which the opponents agree in advance on a definition of the issues. As a matter of fact, *the definition of the alternatives is the supreme instrument of power*; the antagonists can rarely agree on what the issues are because power is involved in the definition. He who determines what politics is about runs the country, because the definition of alternatives is the choice of conflicts, and the choice of conflicts allocates power' (1960, p. 68, emphasis in original).

Equally important to the study of politics is evaluation of the non-emergence of issues and ideas. In studies such as Crenson's (1971) it is fundamental: why, he asks, is it that in the city of Gary, which had a

11

clearly indentifiable perpetrator, did the local agenda not respond to the problem, when environmental concerns were high on the policy agenda nationally? Was the politics of non-decision making in Gary a reflection of limited public interest or of manipulation of the policy agenda? (1971, Ch. 2). Crenson's study argues that if power is involved in the selection of alternatives then it must also be instrumental in the restriction of alternatives. Given the importance of the issues, it is paradoxical that the literature on agenda and non-agenda setting is relatively limited.

But in spite of the limited volume of the literature on agenda setting a number of important questions still emerge. Why do some issues rise on governmental agendas while others are neglected? Who, or what, is important in this process? How is the agenda set? Is there a discernible sequence of events (or series of conditions) or is the process essentially random? Can agenda setting be readily manipulated by powerful interests or is it an imprecise process? Once an item rises on the agenda how is an alternative selected to attend to it? (see Kingdon, 1984, Walker, 1981, Durant and Diehl, 1989). The aim of this chapter is to review the theoretical writings on both the agenda and non-agenda setting processes in order to clarify these questions. Thus it begins with a discussion of the terminology associated with agenda setting. Following this, it examines a number of models of agenda setting: those based on actors, problems and developments in the systemic sphere. Finally, it reviews the literature on non-decision making, focusing in particular on the ideas associated with Lukes' work on power in three dimensions (1974).

Problems, Paradoxes and Definitions: Clarifying and Confining the Agenda Concepts

> Let no reader begin with the illusion that the journey is easy. In contrast to many areas of study in the social sciences, this one is particularly untidy. Subjects drift onto the agenda and drift off, and it is difficult even to define agenda status. When a subject gets hot for a time, it is not always easy even in retrospect to discern why. The researcher thinks one case illuminates the process beautifully, only to discover another case study that behaves differently. Conceptual difficulties often rise up to ensnare the traveller. (Kingdon, 1984, p. 2)

In his highly influential study of the agenda process, John Kingdon provides a directory of terms which it is convenient to adopt here. He identifies the policy making process as an exercise which can be separated into four stages: setting the agenda; the specification of the alternatives from which a choice is then made; the making of that choice, and finally its implementation. The agenda process is concerned with the first two of these stages (1984, p. 3):

> A governmental agenda is a list of subjects to which officials are paying some serious attention at any given time. Thus an agenda-setting process narrows the set of subjects that could conceivably occupy their attention to the list on which they actually do focus. ... Apart from the set of subjects or problems that are on the agenda, a set of alternatives for governmental action is seriously considered by governmental officials and those closely associated with them. (1984, p. 205 and p. 4)[1]

According to Kingdon, if, for example, the environmental impact of transport became a prominent agenda item then officials could consider a number of *alternatives* for action related to it (see Kingdon 1984, p. 4 for an example concerning the cost of medical care). Such alternatives might be to reduce the damage of behaviour without changing it in any way by, for instance, reducing the pollutants in petrol; to offer alternative forms of travel (aiming to influence behaviour) by, for example, improving public transport or building more cycle paths; or to take restrictive action (forcing changes of behaviour) by, for example, closing areas of cities to motorised vehicles. 'Out of the set of all conceivable alternatives, officials actually consider some more seriously than others. So the process of specifying alternatives narrows the set of conceivable alternatives to the set that is seriously considered' (1984, p. 4).

Kingdon's work is also important as it emphasises that the process of agenda setting can show considerable variation across policy sectors (see also Atkinson and Coleman, 1992, p. 157). 'Obviously, there are agendas within agendas. They range from highly general agendas, such as the list of items occupying the president and his immediate inner circle, to rather specialised agendas, including the agendas of such subcommittees as biomedical research or waterway transportation. Subjects that do not appear on a general agenda may be very much alive on a specialised agenda' (Kingdon, 1984, p. 205).

This variation poses considerable problems for the researcher aiming to develop a universal model of the agenda process. The problem is further compounded by the observation that different issues (even within the same policy sector) may be susceptible to a different agenda dynamic. Schattschneider also offers a useful distinction between issues on the basis of whether they are 'public' or 'private'. He argues that the definition of an issue as either public or private reflects the interests of the most powerful groups and institutions in society and, further, that one of the pre-eminent sources of political conflict is over the definition of issues (1960, pp. 22-28).

Private or special interests in Schattschneider's terms (or issues in the terms adopted here) are those which are closely controlled by a restricted strata of society. They remain private much as private property remains private. The protectors of the 'rules of the game' have much to gain by maintaining this control over issues. In contrast, public interests are those in which the whole, or large majority, of the community have a stake. These issues have become public either because the dominant groups in society have failed to retain control over them or because they have chosen not to restrict them to the private sphere. Public issues are important as without a consensus surrounding them 'no democratic system can survive' (1960, p. 23). The distinction between private and public interests is important for discussions of agenda setting and an exploration of Schattschneider's argument forms an important element of the remainder of this analysis.

A further distinction between agenda processes results from whether the issue is perceived as operating in the domain of 'high' or 'low' politics. According to Pross, issues of high politics operate through a distinct process. Such issues 'are considered too important to the country at large to be left in the hands of a small number of government agencies and their associated interests. They have to be resolved by the political leadership after full dress debate in the media, in Parliament, and often at intergovernmental meetings' (1992, p. 165). This distinction between high and low politics proves to be particularly important in the transport case and is a theme to which I will often return throughout this book.

The tendency for a different process to operate in different circumstances could pose real problems for the political scientist who seeks a comprehensive model to explain political behaviour and the agenda setting process. However, although the factors which influence the setting of the agenda may often seem unique, it is easy to overstate these differences. Agenda setting and the process of alternative specification often have common characteristics which are drawn upon in the literature.

Models of the Agenda Process

In common with state theory and the policy making literature in general, there is no orthodox view of the agenda setting process in the liberal democratic state, and a number of approaches can be identified within the literature. In order to aid clarification I have classified the models of agenda setting under one of four headings. First, what I have termed the *problem centred model*, in which the agenda is set by the evolution of a problem which demands some form of response. Second, the *actor centred model*, where the agenda is set either by the actions of actors within the core decision making process (i.e. insiders) or by those outside it via the application of pressure for political change. Third, what I have referred to as the *exogenous model*, in which the agenda is set by exogenous or systemic developments which occur outside the policy subsystem, such as changes to 'macroeconomic conditions or the rise of a new systemic governing coalition' (Sabatier, 1993, p. 20). And finally, the *non-decision making model*, where patterns of agenda setting reflect insights from theories of non-decision making.

The Problem Centred Model of Agenda Setting

Not all social problems rise to agenda prominence. To problem centred theorists it is the qualities of the problem itself which determine whether or not it is able to rise to formal agenda status. Downs has argued that for any issue to have the potential for agenda prominence it requires three essential characteristics: it must have exciting or crisis qualities; the problem must be seen to be detrimental to a large number of people, and the proposed solution can not be incompatible with the interests of the majority (1973, pp. 66-67).

Kingdon has a similar list of characteristics which he uses to highlight the distinction between a condition and a problem. 'We put up with all kinds of conditions every day, and conditions do not rise to prominent places on policy agendas. Conditions come to be defined as problems, and have a better chance of rising on the agenda, when we come to believe that we should do something to change them' (1984, p. 207). For Kingdon, the distinction between conditions and problems is also predominantly based on the characteristics of the issue, but he adds a further series of factors: that conditions which violate central social values will become problems; that conditions may become problems when they are seen as inadequate in comparison to other policy sectors or countries; that conditions may become problems in response to changes in the way in which they are defined (p. 207). Thus, for a condition to become a problem it has to possess certain characteristics. I will now examine the most significant of these.

Problem Centred Accounts of Agenda Setting: The Conflict Over Policy Image

> Problem definition is a process of image making, where the images have to do fundamentally with attributing cause, blame, and responsibility. Conditions, difficulties, or issues thus do not have inherent properties that make them more or less likely to be seen as problems or to be expanded. Rather, political actors deliberately portray them in ways calculated to gain support for their side. [Political actors do not, in fact, accept the definition of the problem that is advanced by] ... science, popular culture or any other source. [Rather they] ... compose stories that describe harms and difficulties, attribute them to actions of other individuals or organisations, and thereby claim the right to invoke government power to stop the harm. (Stone, 1989, p. 282)

According to accounts such as Stone's, problems are constructed following conflict between actors over the policy image of issues. She argues that one of the key weapons that outsiders can utilise is to redefine a problem as an intentionally created harm. 'Books and studies that catalyse public issues have a common structure to their argument. They claim that a condition formerly interpreted as accident is actually the result of human will, either indirectly ... or directly; or they show that a condition formerly interpreted as indirectly caused is actually pure intent' (1989, p. 289). Studies such as Crystal Eastman's *Work Accidents and the Law* (1969) and Ralph Nader's *Unsafe at Any Speed* (1965) have redefined the accident at work issue and the vehicle safety issue respectively, shifting the perception of the issue away from personal to commercial negligence. The resulting potent image of a powerful interest deliberately willing harm on a defenceless majority provides the catalyst for policy change (Stone, 1989, pp. 289-90).

Group conflict, according to these accounts, is extremely important in shaping the perception of issues: 'Public policies are generally discussed in a positive or negative light, and we can call this the policy image ... How public policies are discussed in public and in the media is the policy image, according to the terminology we use here. We simply differentiate between images that are favourable to proponents of a given policy and those that are detrimental. For nuclear power, these distinctions are simple: positive images are growth, jobs, high-technology solutions; negative images are mushroom clouds, waste, leaks and the like' (Baumgartner and Jones, 1991, p. 1046). Thus, policy image can have either a powerful positive or negative impact for groups which are trying to retain control over the policy agenda. Even apparently stable networks such as the American nuclear network can be significantly destabilised if the policy insiders lose control of the policy image and popular opinion becomes hostile to it.

The potential power of visible imagery and its effect on the political agenda is well illustrated by the growth in concern over the nuclear weapons issue in the 'western world' in the early 1980s. The terrifying images of mushroom clouds and fears of global annihilation through nuclear war were instrumental in the development of many social movements that occurred at this time (Joppke, 1991, p. 50). As Walker has argued, the 'more graphic and easily understood the evidence of trouble, the more creditable the sources of information upon which the case is based, the more appealing the aspiring agenda item becomes' (1977, p. 431).

However, visibility need not be linked to such a dramatic event as potential nuclear conflict. It can result from changes to a social indicator, demonstrations of public disquiet or the commemoration of a historic event (Pross, 1992, p. 169). For Pross visibility is essential to capture the media's attention (1992, pp. 168-170), while for Walker it is legislatures who are the key audience (1977, p. 433). The mechanics, however, are the same: visibility is a key requirement if an item is to engage the interest of an actor or institution who will subsequently act on it (Hogwood and Gunn, 1984, p. 68).

Closely linked to visibility are issues which have an emotive or human interest angle. Although emotive issues are often highly visible, as the nuclear issue illustrates, they can also take an invisible form. An example of the power of invisible, emotive symbolism is well illustrated by the public reaction in America to the McCarthyite witch-hunts of the 1950s. This change in national mood led to many actors putting forward ideas which would have seemed alien only a few years before. For example, 'a group opposing a certain book in the local library because it is "obscene" might contend that it is part of a "communist conspiracy" to put such books in libraries throughout the nation to corrupt young minds. Such an argument might [and indeed did] arouse fear and suspicion in the community and lead to an opinion change concerning library policy' (Cobb and Elder, 1972, p. 46).

For those who wish to control the dynamics of an issue, the manipulation of the public's perception of it is vital. Overall, conflict over the policy image of an issue is intense as although public opinion may change over time it tends to 'show a fascination with one aspect of the issue at the exclusion of the other, at any given time'. Even though individuals are often able to discern both the good and bad sides of an issue, 'public attention as it is reflected in media coverage tends to focus on one or other', and attention can shift from euphoria to dismissiveness in a short period of time (Baumgartner and Jones, 1991, p. 1046).

Problem Centred Accounts of Agenda Setting: Free-floating Policy Problems

A number of commentators focus their attention on problems which occur independently of the actions of actors (see for example Kingdon, 1984, pp. 94-95 and Cohen *et al*, 1972, p. 3). Such problems can be said to 'free-float'. The first category of free-floating problems are those which are often highly visible and emotive: the crisis. Crises often result either from what may be called 'acts of God' or from developments in the foreign policy sphere and often occur without any forewarning, forcing themselves to the top of the political agenda. Thus, policy makers have to react to crises quickly, with largely untried alternatives. This is quite different to domestic policy making in which the 'overused term "crisis" usually refers to a serious problem, but one where [the] consequences are not immediate and the government may take years to address the problem' following extensive consultation and widespread testing of policy alternatives (Durant and Diehl, 1989, p. 191).

As Downs has pointed out, there are other free-floating problems which 'are very difficult to dramatise at all. Examples are poor housing, inadequate public transportation, and the rising costs of medical service' (1973, p. 67). Yet items such as these, which lack intrinsically dramatic qualities, are still often significant issues on governmental agendas.

Still other issues arise on the policy agenda because they become 'solvable'. Solutions can result from a variety of sources. First, they may come from a gradual infusion of new ideas amongst the specialists in a given policy area, increasing receptivity to new alternatives (Kingdon, 1984, p. 18). Second, the development of new technology can create demands for policy change, especially if the problem was previously regarded as unamenable to human action (see Durant and Diehl, 1989, p. 191 for the impact of technical innovation on the foreign policy process). Third, financial changes can have an important impact on the operation of the agenda process and the alternatives up for consideration. Cost related changes can manifest themselves in two ways: by the discovery of a more cost effective alternative or by changes forced through economic austerity. At its most extreme, cost containment can become an ideology of its own, resulting in widespread change to agendas across the polity (Kingdon, 1984, p. 82. See Sharpe, 1985, p. 378 for the impact of government austerity measures on central-local relations following the election of the UK Conservative government in 1979).

The development of a potential solution to a policy problem causes considerable pressure for government action. Reiterating the overload thesis, Jordan and Richardson argue that: 'The electoral pressure is for any potential government to show an interest in all problems and to be confident that it can ameliorate the issue at hand. Put simply, the doctor who says he is not interested in the disease, or that it is incurable, anyway, is going to lose patients. Electorally, hyperactivity is popular' (1987, p. 25. See also King, 1975).

The Issue Attention Cycle

> Public perceptions of most crises in American domestic life do not reflect changes in real conditions as much as they reflect the operation of a definite and systematic cycle of heightening public interest and then boredom with major issues. This issue attention cycle is rooted in both the nature of certain domestic problems and the way major communication media interact with the public. (Downs, 1973, p. 63)

An important theoretical innovation within problem centred accounts of agenda setting resulted from the work of Anthony Downs, who argued that issues rise and fall in a stage-based policy cycle. This 'issue attention cycle', as Downs called it, is made up of five clearly separable stages, which occur in sequence across issues. The first is the *pre-problem stage*, in which specialists or interest groups are captivated by a problem which has yet to grab the public's attention. The perception of the problem is usually far worse at this stage than when it becomes a public concern (1973, p. 64).

The second stage is that of *alarmed discovery and euphoric optimism*, in which the public becomes aware of a problem and demands a response from government. Often public pressure and optimism results in over ambitious promises of quick fix solutions from political leaders (p. 64).

This results in the third stage, *realising the cost of significant progress*. At this stage experts, and later the public, realise that any serious attempt to solve the problem would require considerable financial costs and changes to the power relations between actors and institutions which the majority are unwilling to pay. 'The public thus begins to realise that the evil itself results in part from arrangements that are providing significant benefits to someone – often to a great many people'. There are some problems which can be resolved by a technical solution which does not challenge the social position of the majority, 'but, in reality, the very nature of our most pressing social problems involves either deliberate or unconscious exploitation of one group in society by another or the prevention of one group from enjoying something which another wants to keep for itself' (pp. 64-65).

The fourth stage, *gradual decline of intense public interest*, almost inevitably follows. Public interest declines as the personal sacrifices which are required for any serious attempt to solve the problem become clear. A combination of hostility, boredom, and discouragement force the issue to stage five, *the post-problem stage* (a process accelerated by the fact that a competing issue is almost inevitably entering stage two).

This final, post-problem stage can be thought of as 'a sort of prolonged limbo' (p. 65). It differs from the pre-problem stage however in two key ways. Firstly, when the problem was at the peak of the issue attention cycle a number of policies, institutions or programmes may have been created which aimed to solve it. These are likely to have an enduring impact on the issue, ensuring that it is attended to even when it is not of public concern. Secondly, once a problem has completed an issue attention cycle it is likely to sporadically reoccur, either attached to another problem or propelled there by one of the vested interests which were created when the problem previously enjoyed high political salience (pp. 65-66. See Walker, 1977, pp. 432-37, for a discussion of this in relation to road safety legislation in the USA).

Although Downs' model is important from a problem centred perspective, he does not aim to provide a universal model of agenda setting (1973, p. 66), restricting it to issues which Joppke has termed collective issues.[2] 'Collective issues such as technological risk and environmental pollution pass through cycles in public attention, which are determined by a complex interplay of cultural, political, and conjunctural factors. Social problems are not simply "out there" but are constructed – especially those which are not promoted by well-defined interest groups. The related social movements feed upon external processes of agenda-setting, which they reinforce but are unable to control' (1991, pp. 45-46).

These issues have the following characteristics: that a sufficient minority are affected to mobilise the cycle in the first place (instigating stages 1 and 2); that this minority have a strong enough stake in perceived change to challenge the status quo (affecting stages 3 and 4); and that the issue itself is sufficiently exciting to instigate an issue attention cycle in the first place but not so important that it acquires permanent status on the government's agenda (i.e. it must be possible to complete the cycle) (Downs, 1973, p. 66).

The problems with these criteria are threefold. First, Downs' model does not adequately account for a number of issues which arise on agendas and affect only a limited number of people, or which *do* fundamentally challenge the stake of the dominant groups in society, or which lack exciting properties. Second, the issue attention cycle has difficulty in explaining why certain issues never seem to leave the agenda and why a number of agendas exhibit long term stability. Third, as Parsons has argued, Downs' model does not adequately distinguish between the role of insider and outsider groups in the setting of the policy agenda: 'The formation of issues in the context of more limited policy "communities" and "networks" may strongly suggest that the role of policy elites is far more significant than the opinions of Joe or Josephine public' (1995, p. 119). Therefore, the issue attention cycle places too great an emphasis on the role of outsider groups, which emphasis, as I shall argue below (pp. 26-28), has a number of significant limitations.

Overall, the discussion of problem centred models of agenda setting in this section has emphasised that the way in which an issue is defined will have a significant bearing on its capacity to gain access to the agenda. I have also illustrated that many issues require the skilful management of actors operating within the policy process if they are to be defined as policy problems and gain access to the agenda setting process. However, I have not, as of yet, dealt with the role of actors in any systematic manner and therefore the aim of the next section will be to explore the role of actor centred accounts of agenda setting.

Actor Centred Approaches to Agenda Setting

> Some actors bring to the policy process their political popularity; others, their expertise. Some bring their pragmatic sense of the possible; others, their ability to attract attention. (Kingdon, 1984, p. 81)

Actor centred accounts of agenda setting argue that agenda setting is principally conflict-based, with political change resulting primarily from changes in the balance of power between insider and outsider groups. These models characterise actors in terms of their relationship to a policy making core.

Insider groups have a privileged position in the policy process which enables them to have a 'significant influence' on consultation, and ultimately, policy formulation (Maloney, Jordan and McLaughlin, 1994, p. 19).[3] Outsider groups, in contrast, have goals which cannot be readily accommodated by decision makers. Consequently, they are outside the consultation process and their influence on policy making will be conditional on their ability to pressure decision makers through 'publicly active' campaigning (Maloney, Jordan and McLaughlin, 1994, p. 32).[4] Distinguishing between the included and the excluded 'encourages us not only to examine relations between those who enjoy inclusion, but also to examine the characteristics of those excluded. That the structure of power is shaped by modes of exclusion from any political process is an elementary truth' (Hancher and Moran cited in Atkinson and Coleman, 1992, p. 173).

The distinction between insider and outsider groups will prove particularly valuable in the transport case for identifying and contrasting the tactics used by the road lobby (historically insiders) and anti-roads groups (historically outsiders) in their attempts to influence the decision making process.

Maloney, Jordan and McLaughlin in their article, 'The Insider/Outsider Model Revisited', expand on the traditional conception of insiders and outsiders by offering a subdivision of actors into five categories which attempt 'to make distinctions about the degree of acceptance for a group by the relevant department': core insiders; specialist insiders; peripheral insiders; outsiders by ideology or goal, and outsiders by choice (1994, p. 30).

According to this typology, *core insiders* are those which are seen as important sources of expertise across a wide range of policy areas. In contrast, *specialist insiders* will be less frequently involved in consultation with civil servants, being called upon as 'authoritative sources of information' in specific policy niches (p. 30). Both these categories of groups will be involved in extensive consultation with government and their opinions will be highly valued by actors within the bureaucracy, unlike those of peripheral insider groups which 'pursue insider strategies but have little or *no impact* on the thinking of civil servants ... Consultation of these groups is largely a cosmetic exercise. In most cases it would cause the official concerned more problems to ignore the failed insiders than it would to extend them polite recognition' (p. 32. Emphasis in original).

The final groups of actors are those outside the formal mechanisms of consultation, namely *outsiders by ideology or goal* and *outsiders by choice*. The former status is 'usually "self-selected" by the group through its adoption of *goals* that cannot be accommodated in the consultative process': these groups are engaged in making demands which are not reconcilable through a process of incremental bargaining or compromise. The latter term refers to groups which choose not to be involved in the formal process of consultation for tactical reasons. Such groups often rely on a perception of outsider status in order to retain their identity and the commitment of their supporters (p. 32). As will be seen in later chapters, this distinction between groups proves particularly useful in the transport case.

The Issue Expansion Model

In the nature of things *a political conflict among special interests is never restricted to the group most immediately interested.* Instead, it is an appeal (initiated by relatively small numbers of people) for the support of vast numbers of people who are sufficiently remote to have a somewhat different perspective on the controversy. (Schattschneider, 1960, p. 27. Emphasis in original)

A number of scholars have approached the study of policy making and agenda setting from a conflict perspective. Such arguments are important as they provide a theoretical model which explains the mechanism by which agenda setting occurs even when the decision making process is dominated by insider groups. The pattern of conflict in this model is focused on gaining control of the scope, intensity and visibility of an issue.

Scope refers to 'the number of persons and groups who have actually aligned themselves in a conflict. At any point in time, scope will include those persons or groups who were initially involved, plus any persons or groups who have subsequently been drawn into the conflict ... The intensity of a conflict relates to the degree of the commitment of the contending parties to mutually incompatible positions. It will be directly linked to the "dearness" or value saliency, attached to the objects of conflict by those involved' (Cobb and Elder, 1972, p. 43). The visibility of a conflict 'indicates the number of persons or groups that will be aware of a conflict and its possible consequences. The visibility of a conflict will be a function of its scope and intensity, as well as its definition' (Cobb and Elder, 1972, pp. 43-44).

The extent to which agreement can be reached between the insider groups over the definition of the issues will have considerable bearing on whether the scope of a conflict is expanded or not. 'If the original disputants can agree upon a definition of the issues it is likely that the conflict will remain restricted and largely private to the original parties. In such a case the outcome of the conflict will be primarily a function of the relative strengths of the contestants' (Cobb and Elder, 1972, p. 51). However, Schattschneider has argued that often agreement on the definition of an issue is not possible between insider groups and in such cases pressure to externalise conflict becomes strong: 'Political conflicts are taken into the public arena precisely because someone wants to make certain that the power ratio among the private interests most immediately involved shall not prevail' (1960, p. 37).

Schattschneider's argument is that an group which is not having its interests well served within the policy network will intentionally aim to expand the issue and involve other groups in order to strengthen its own position. The tendency towards issue expansion may not end after a single cycle as any group which has lost its relative advantage may then seek to regain it by further expansion. Once the expansion dynamic has been set in motion, and more and more people become involved, 'the original participants are apt to lose control of the conflict altogether' (p. 4).

Issues become more vague, ambiguous, simplified and distorted as conflict expands. As a result, more and more actors can attach their own interpretation to events, thus intensifying conflict. 'The expanding scope of a conflict is likely to cause various symbols and values to be conjured up, posing a threat to popular beliefs and values. Also, the increasing scope of a conflict tends to polarise social relations, which in turn reinforces the intensity of hostility' (Cobb and Elder, 1972, p. 52).

The final stage in the process is the involvement of the government which is forced to act in order to regain control over the issue: 'In the schoolyard it is not the bully but the defenceless smaller boys who "tell the teacher". When the teacher intervenes, the balance of power in the schoolyard is apt to change drastically' (Schattschneider, 1960, p. 40). As the conflict expands uncontrollably, the government is forced to act as peacemaker and reallocate the responsibility for policy formulation and implementation according to the outcome of the conflict. Consequently, change in this dynamic can be rapid and fundamental, resulting in a considerable change to the existing political order.

The implication is clear: for insider groups, operating at the heart of the agenda process, control of the agenda process is most easily managed at the outset. Consequently, sub-governments or networks which maintain control over the agenda have a considerable incentive to ensure consensual decision making (Richardson and Jordan, 1979, p. 74), internalise conflict and ensure that all affected actors are conscious that participation in the network is a 'positive sum game' (Rhodes and Marsh, 1992, p. 186). Careful management of the internal relations between the insider groups is essential if the issue expansion process is to be avoided and control over the agenda dynamic is to be retained.

An important practical application of the issue expansion model can be found in Walker's study of the early development of auto-safety legislation in America. In 1966, the policy community of experts was internally divided over the best method of dealing with increasing public concern over rising rates of accidents and fatalities on the roads. Most of the actors within the policy community favoured the established policy solutions, such as an increased emphasis on driver training in high schools, better lighting and road signs and the extension of existing road safety campaigns. However, a small group of traffic engineers recognised that campaigns to change driving habits were unlikely to succeed. They focused their attention on minimising the effects of accidents after they had occurred, proposing improvements to the safety features of motor cars themselves, particularly through the addition of seat belts and changes in car design. Their campaign to instigate changes to road safety legislation by externalising their particular perception of both the problem and the necessary solutions to members of the legislature proved to be highly successful (1977, p. 433).

The focus of the issue expansion model is thus either on the dynamics which are invoked when compromise between insider groups breaks down, or on the situation where outsiders are able to destabilise the relationship between insider groups within a closed policy community. It remains an important contribution to actor centred accounts of agenda setting. However, there is one significant reservation with this model, in that it seems to assume that the government's role is in some way independent of self interest.

According to Schattschneider, the state intervenes to champion the role of the underdog: 'The role of the government as the patron of the defeated private interest sheds light on its function as the critic of private power relations' (1960, p. 39). But this model, which describes the government as a teacher intervening in playground disputes between bullies and victims, ignores the fact that government often has interests of its own in many policy disputes, which may favour the dominant group in a particular conflict (see pp. 32-36 below). As Nordlinger has argued, 'the preferences of the state itself are at least as important as those of civil society in accounting for what the democratic state does and does not do; the democratic state is not only frequently autonomous insofar as it regularly acts upon its preferences, but also markedly autonomous in doing so even when its preferences diverge from the demands of the most powerful groups in civil society' (1981, p. 1).

Outsiders and the Political Agenda: The Conflict over Policy Arenas

Dudley and Richardson's work on policy change and British trunk roads policy provides a particularly useful starting point for exploring the role of outsiders on the agenda setting process (1995, 1996a, 1998). They have produced a number of articles exploring the role of group conflict in the development of UK trunk roads policy which have been motivated by a desire to 'reconcile the tendency of established policy communities to create conditions of stability, or even inertia, with powerful dynamics which can produce significant change both in the network of actors involved and in policy itself' (1996a, p. 63).

They argue that, historically, roads policy has been dominated by a core arena involving an 'alliance' between the road lobby and Department of Transport, which has excluded the anti-roads groups (1996a, p. 64). However, since the 1970s the anti-roads groups have been able to overcome the institutional bias of the core arena by infiltrating arenas which the pro-roads groups have less control over: 'It is of crucial importance, therefore, to recognise that, although an interest may be apparently excluded from a core policy community, by selection of the correct arena for its activity, and effective transmission of its message, it may by indirect means have a significant effect on the policy network and policy itself' (1996a, p. 75).

A key method by which these groups have affected policy by *indirect means* reflects the interaction between the image of a policy and the arena in which it is discussed (Baumgartner and Jones, 1991, pp. 1045-47). Policies which are discussed in the core arena will be dominated by the institutional bias of the actors which are involved within that arena: they will dominate the nature of discussion and will be able, in normal circumstances, to maintain control over the image of policy. In contrast, when policy is discussed in an arena outside the core, outsider groups are able to exercise more influence over the nature of the conflict between actors and hence, the policy image of an issue (Dudley and Richardson, 1996a, pp. 64-65).

Dudley and Richardson have described a number of arenas which the anti-roads groups have successfully infiltrated in order to change both the discourse conducted between actors involved in, and the policy image of, the transport issue. Of particular importance to the opponents of roads have been, in the 1970s, the highway inquiry process (see 1998, pp. 6-15), and in the 1990s, the road construction sites (see 1996a, p. 78 and 1998, pp. 18-21) and the European Union (see 1996a, pp. 77-79). Thus, change to the policy agenda has resulted from the anti-roads groups' strategy of operating in alternative arenas using a variety of tactics, of which the most innovative has arguably been extra-legal activity in the form of occupation of the road construction sites.

Extra-legal, non institutional means such as violence by disaffected outsiders can be particularly effective for outsider groups aiming to gain access to alternative policy arenas. 'Such actions are usually taken when participants believe that they cannot gain access without recourse to extra-legal means' (Cobb and Elder, 1972, pp. 21-22). When an organised group, or one which is incapable of organisation, has been continuously denied access to the policy process it may feel forced to adopt extra-legal means. Often groups lack credibility in the eyes of policy insiders and cannot gain it through the established policy arenas. However, the infiltration of alternative policy arenas and the adoption of violent or direct action will help 'to establish the credibility of a group in the eyes of decision makers' (Cobb and Elder, 1972, pp. 55). Nieburg (1962) argues that once that credibility has been achieved, a 'group should be able to rely on the threat to commit further violence without actually committing disruptive acts. In fact, threats of violence rather than acts of violence are one of the most common means by which new or deprived groups gain entry into the legitimate political arena. If the group loses its credibility, however, a series of violent acts may be required to demonstrate to governmental leaders that the group still has the capacity to disrupt the system' (Cobb and Elder, 1972, pp. 54-55 paraphrasing Nieburg, 1962, p. 865 and p. 871).

In practical terms, however, the capacity of groups to alter the agenda through direct action or violence is highly unpredictable. While direct action can often prove effective in airing political grievances, it also often leads to the political isolation rather than inclusion of the group concerned. Direct action often results in tough counter-measures by government on behalf of insider groups, who regard such action as a challenge to the social order rather than a legitimate mechanism for policy change (Cobb and Elder, 1972, p. 166).

Dudley and Richardson's account of agenda setting hinges on two key premises: that the strategies of the outsider groups have opened new arenas to the anti-roads groups, creating opportunities for them to challenge the dominance of the pro-roads groups; and that these changes, in a causal sense, explain the transformation of the transport agenda in the Major era. It will be seen in Chapter 5 that the activities of the anti-roads groups indeed opened a number of new arenas of political conflict in the Major era, in particular through the interaction between the media and the direct action protests which were undertaken in the construction sites. However, Chapter 5 argues that these changes have not had as extensive an impact on the agenda setting process as Dudley and Richardson suggest because the anti-roads groups have had only an arm's length relationship with the policy making and agenda setting processes.

Sabatier's Advocacy Coalition Framework: A Synthesis of Actor Centred and Exogenous Accounts of Agenda Setting

Sabatier's advocacy coalition framework is another important contribution to the study of agenda setting, with its insights for actor centred analysis. However, the principal innovation within this model is to combine aspects of actor centred models of agenda setting with exogenous explanations of political change.

Sabatier's framework is based on four premises: that in order to understand policy change a time perspective of at least a decade is required; that policy subsystems (i.e. a given policy area) must provide the focus of inquiry; that in order to analyse a subsystem all levels of government must be included (i.e. local, national, and the EU in the UK case), and that public policies result from conflicts over belief systems (i.e. rival accounts of the world) (1993, p. 16).

He provides a series of justifications to support these premises. Firstly, in relation to the need to focus on a time frame of a decade or more, Sabatier argues that policy orientated learning occurs as a result of the 'enlightenment function' (p. 16). Enlightenment occurs as a result of reflection on all stages of the policy process, from conception to implementation. A time period of a decade is required to complete a cycle of formulation, implementation and reformulation.

Secondly, in focusing on the subsystem, Sabatier seeks to move beyond analysis which focuses on the effect of specific governmental institutions. In the advocacy coalition framework the policy subsystem is defined as a broadened version of an iron triangle which includes 'actors at various levels of government active in policy formulation and implementation as well as journalists, researchers, policy analysts who play important roles in the generation, dissemination, and evaluation of policy ideas' (p. 17). In a broad sense his view of a policy subsystem is close to Heclo's model of issue networks (1978), as opposed to the restricted policy community which is seen as more accurately reflecting the British political tradition (See Jordan, 1990 for a review and Judge, 1993, pp. 120-30 for a critique).

Sabatier's desire to focus on a 'policy subsystem' is ambiguous. He is right to argue that actors outside a traditional 'iron triangle' could have a considerable influence on the agenda over time and that as such they should be included in the analysis. However, it is not clear how he perceives the distribution of power within policy subsystems: whether he suggests that 'outsiders' wield similar power to insiders in a broad-based issue network (along the lines described by Heclo, 1978) or instead, that although the actors within iron triangles dominate the policy subsystem it is important to incorporate groups which appear to be peripheral to the process in order to capture the complexity of policy change over a decade or more. If the latter is accepted, then his perception of a policy subsystem will closely reflect his desire to ensure that external events are incorporated as factors affecting the stability of policy networks.

Thirdly, he argues that policy subsystems include actors from all levels of government. According to Sabatier, state level policy innovation and learning are important as, in the USA, many policies are adopted at the national level after periods of state level experimentation. As a result, analysis focused on the national level pays insufficient attention to the influence of sub-national government upon the national agenda. This premise seems, initially, to be of more limited validity in the UK as local government has relatively limited autonomy in comparison to state government in the USA.

However, Sabatier's call to bring multi-level governance back in to the analysis should not be dismissed, for three reasons. First, local government has some autonomy, derived from its policy formulation and implementation role (see Chapter 7, and also Atkinson and Coleman, 1989, p. 51). Second, as decision making has become more complex it creates 'enormous pressures for specialisation' in sub-national units of policy experts (Sabatier, 1993, p. 23). Finally, at a supra-national level, Sabatier's call to incorporate multi-level governance is irresistible as the growth of EU legislative competence in many areas of domestic policy making has produced the 'Europeification' of a number of policy areas (Andersen and Eliassen, 1993, pp. 10-14).

In suggesting that the evolution of public policies will reflect the belief systems of those charged with their development, Sabatier argues that the 'ability to map beliefs and policies on the same "canvas" provides a vehicle for assessing the influence of various actors over time, particularly the role of technical information (beliefs) on policy change' (1993, p. 17) – it is this aspect of Sabatier's analysis which has been most widely commented upon and adopted by political scientists (See for example Grant, 1995 and Dudley and Richardson, 1998. See Sabatier, 1998, pp. 100-1 for a survey of work adopting this approach).

Within the policy subsystem itself, actors are 'aggregated into a number of advocacy coalitions composed of people from various governmental and private organisations who share a set of normative and causal beliefs and who often act in concert' (Sabatier, 1993, p. 18). A number of advocacy coalitions may form within a policy subsystem, espousing contradictory proposals which are mediated by a group of '"policy brokers" whose principal concern is to find some reasonable compromise that will reduce intense conflict' (Sabatier, 1993, pp. 18-19). According to Sabatier advocacy coalitions revise their proposals in response to changes in knowledge through a process of policy orientated learning over a considerable time period, which affects the policy agenda.

Underlying Sabatier's framework are two types of exogenous variables – one relatively stable and the other more dynamic – which provide both constraints on and resources for subsystem actors. As Sabatier argues, policy orientated learning provides 'only one of the forces affecting policy change over time. In addition to this cognitive activity, there is the real world that changes'. Socio-economic conditions (such as the 1973

OPEC oil price shock) or the systemic governing coalition can change (e.g. the election of Thatcher in 1979); such changes 'can dramatically alter the composition and the resources of various coalitions and, in turn, public policy within the subsystem' (p. 19). Furthermore, advocacy coalitions can be strengthened or weakened by turnover in personnel resulting from uncontrollable phenomena such as death or retirement.

This focus on external systems events is extremely important to Sabatier's framework, providing the primary explanation for changes in core aspects of policy: 'The basic argument of this framework is that, although policy-oriented learning is an important aspect of policy change and can often alter the secondary aspects of a coalition's belief system, changes in the core aspects of a policy are usually the results of perturbations in noncognitive factors external to the subsystem, such as macroeconomic conditions or the rise of a new systemic governing coalition' (pp. 19-20).

In his framework the external environment is divided into 'parameters that are relatively stable over several decades and those aspects of the system that are susceptible to significant fluctuations over the course of a few years and thus serve as a major stimuli to policy change' (p. 20). Relatively stable factors surround and permeate the subsystem. They are extremely difficult to change, which discourages actors from serious consideration of their reform. In addition they limit the range of alternatives which can be feasibly adopted and have profound implications for the balance of resources and power which actors command within the subsystem. Sabatier identifies four sources of external stability: the basic attributes of the problem area; the distribution of natural resources; the fundamental cultural values and social structure, and the essence of the legal structure. Overall these relatively stable parameters reinforce the status quo in policy making and severely constrain the options open to policy makers. It is extremely difficult for opponents of that status quo to affect these parameters, with any change requiring at least a decade of concerted effort with often minimal results.

In contrast, dynamic systems events can have substantial impact over a relatively short time frame, fundamentally destabilising policy subsystems over a few years. 'Because such changes alter the constraints and opportunities confronting subsystem actors, they constitute the principal dynamic elements affecting policy change. They also present a serious challenge to subsystem actors, who must learn how to anticipate them and respond to them in a manner consistent with their basic beliefs and interests' (p. 22). Sabatier suggests that dynamic events can affect the stability of the subsystem in three ways: through changes in socio-economic or technological conditions; through changes in the systemic governing coalition, and through policy inputs from other subsystems. The following chapters will make clear how such dynamic systems events have worked in the UK transport sphere.

Overall, Sabatier's framework is important because it emphasises the fact that in a union state system, such as the UK, policy networks are particularly vulnerable to systemic changes, resulting from changes in governing priorities at the centre. Overcoming the limitations of models which focus exclusively on networks, he provides a framework which is capable of incorporating multi-level governance, policy networks and dynamic systemic events, while explaining factors which mitigate against change and secure the autonomy of the network. As such it is worthy of more detailed incorporation into sub-sectoral analysis of policy making and change.

Exogenous Political Change: The Impact of Government on Agenda Setting

> Of course, there is nothing innovative about pointing to broad social changes or to ideological shifts in government when seeking to explain policy innovation and program changes. But at the moment the study of policy networks includes very little reflection on the impact of these variables. [This is despite the fact that] ... studies of major policy changes show that environmental disturbances [of which changes of government or policy emphasis can often be the most significant] are quite capable of crushing networks and dispersing communities. (Atkinson and Coleman, 1992, p. 175)

It is clear from the discussion of the advocacy coalition framework that dynamic exogenous changes can have a significant impact on the processing of issues in sub-governments. In this section of this review of the agenda setting literature I will focus on the activity of government which is arguably the most important source of exogenous change. Such a focus is justified by the Thatcher decade which changed perceptions of the capacity of the British government to intervene in the policy process (Richardson, 1993b, pp. 95-98).

According to Holliday, the 1980s witnessed a period of conviction government in which, contrary to the views expressed in the policy networks literature, government was not constrained by groups operating within networks. In fact the opposite was true: 'In the Thatcher years, even interests which had hitherto enjoyed insider status were forced by government refusal to negotiate and bargain to adopt the tactics of outsiders' (1993, p. 311). No amount of pressure or lobbying can lead to effective representation of interests under these circumstances: even organisations such as the BMA (British Medical Association) and the teaching unions were forced into 'outsider' status in conflicts with the government.

However, the process did not stop there: the Thatcher government was actually ideologically opposed to any dealings with organised interests. 'Its key argument was that a mature political society with a long history of peaceful, incremental change will gradually become infested, and eventually overrun, by distributional coalitions which pursue not the general good, but merely their own sectional interests' (Holliday, 1993, p. 310). For Thatcher, groups were synonymous with government stagnation, the fall of the Heath government, the Winter of Discontent and Britain in decline.

The aim of the Thatcher administration, therefore, was to destabilise the existing policy sectors in order to change relationships between the government and the sector as a whole and between the actors within the sector (see Richardson, 1993a, pp. 9-12 for a summary of some of the changes instigated by the government in fields such as education, health and employment law). This is not to say that under Thatcher, no interest groups or policy networks had 'a rather good 1980s' (Holliday, 1993, p. 312). But, contrary to network theory, this was not due to pressure from such networks forcing concessions from the government, or even due to their ability to resist the reformist aspirations of government; success was simply due to the fact that government policy happened to be evolving in the direction of the group's interest.

In his article, 'Doing Less by Doing More', Richardson challenges the view that government has extensive capacity to exercise control over policy agendas in the long term. He asks whether or not increased governmental intervention in the policy sectors may be a temporary phenomenon, 'the governmental equivalent of forcing people to be free' (1993a, p. 1). However, this conclusion brings with it the problem that the state was able to pursue this 'forcing' at all. For network approaches, in which the government is seen as having a limited capacity for top-down leadership, the 1980s pose a fundamental challenge. Even if 'forcing to be free' is a temporary phenomenon, who is to say that the government will retire into the background after it has finished? It may well reassert itself if it does not like the sort of freedom it has forced.

Overall, the government's actions during the Thatcher era (and its capacity to dismantle a number of established policy communities and develop policy initiatives against the will of a number of pressure groups) are an excellent example of the capacity of government to act as an agent of exogenous change, and hence of the limitations of models which focus exclusively on group conflict in order to explain agenda setting.

Putting Policy Networks and Autonomy into Perspective: The Case of Systematic Luck

> Some groups are lucky: they get what they want from society without having to act. Some groups are systematically lucky: they get what they want without having to act because of the way in which society is structured. (Dowding, 1991, pp. 152-53)

Dowding argues that on many occasions when groups appear to be powerful, because their objectives are being served by government programmes, in fact they are simply benefiting from systematic luck. 'Systematic luck is not the same as power for, though it attaches to individuals in certain positions in society and it attaches to them *because* they hold those positions in society, they individually have no control over those outcomes' (1991, pp. 137-38). 'The crucial point here is that if the dominant ideology legitimises a particular group's interests as the "national interest", then that group's interests are likely to be served regardless of any representation it makes to government' (Marsh, 1983, p. 11).

According to Dowding, capitalists are particularly well positioned to benefit from systematic luck: 'Capitalists may be just lucky that what is in the interests of the government is also, by and large, in their interests too. They have no need to intervene.' (1991, p. 137). The principal reason for this, according to Dowding, is that government depends on high levels of economic activity for both its revenue and as an important source of electoral legitimacy.

Capitalists also derive systematic luck as a result of the 'law of anticipated reactions', which argues that government will not develop which are 'too contrary to their [the capitalists] interests in case they may be provoked to intervene' (p. 137). However, this view of the relationship between capital and government does not suggest that the state is captured by capital; instead Dowding argues that the state can still act with high levels of autonomy:

This can still imply an autonomous state in the sense that the state actors do not act as they do because it is in the interests of capitalists but because it is in their own interests. However, as it happens, it is in their interests to do what is in the interests of capitalists, although capitalists have no control over this fact. It is an empirical fact beyond their control. This argument does not demonstrate that the state always acts in the interests of capitalists, but that, even if it does, it does not follow that the state is not autonomous nor that the capitalists have any great power. They may be merely lucky. (p. 137)

Benson's model of a policy sector can be used to provide a diagrammatic representation of the operation of systematic luck (1982, see Figure 2.1. Benson's model is summarised in Parsons, 1995, pp. 148-50). The policy making process, according to Benson, takes place within three interlinked levels: rules of structure formation, interest structure and the administrative surface level, with the rules of structure formation providing a baseline which constrains the operation of the higher levels (1982, p. 160).

Figure 2.1 Benson's model of a policy sector

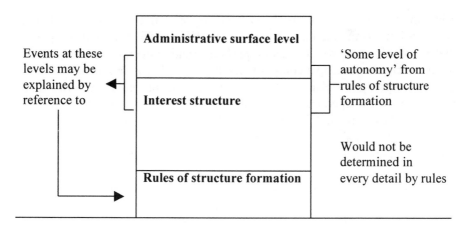

Source: Parsons, 1995, p. 149

Parsons argues that the rules of structure formation level 'shapes the way in which issues are brought into the realm of decision-making and others are kept outside the decisional processes ... In terms of agenda setting, Benson's framework stresses how the analysis of administrative and interest structures in given policy sectors are shaped by "deep rules" which operate to ensure that some demands are excluded from the decision making process, and which limit the choices and behaviour of policy makers' (1995, p. 149). Thus, interest groups and policy proposals which are in step with the rules of structure formation[5] are likely to be served by government policy regardless of the exercise of power, while those interests and policy proposals which are out of step with the rules of structure formation are likely to be ignored (Benson, 1982, pp. 162-65).

These ideas are extremely important within this book, where I argue that the 'rules of structure formation' and the related concept of 'systematic luck' have both played an important role in explaining the development of transport policy in the UK since 1945. In the transport case, it is the bias of doctrine, not overt lobbying, which has generated the pattern of power relations between the pro-roads groups and their opponents (Hillman, 1992, p. 226. See also Dowding, 1991, pp. 154-57 for the importance of 'systematic luck' in the case of agricultural policy making in the UK).

A Synthesis of Problem Centred, Actor Centred and Exogenous Models: Kingdon's Agenda Setting Model

Kingdon's work has rightly been seen as one of the most significant contributions to the agenda setting debate. His model is almost unique in that it combines the role of actors, problems and exogenous developments in an attempt to develop a comprehensive model of agenda setting.[6]

According to Kingdon three streams of problems, politics and policies flow independently through the political system (1984, p. 20). 'Each [of these streams] develops according to its own dynamics and rules. But at some critical junctures the three streams are joined, and the greatest policy changes grow out of that coupling of problems, policy proposals and politics' (p. 20).

The dynamics which affect the *problem stream* have considerable similarities with the problem centred models of agenda setting which I have already outlined. 'Problems are brought to the attention of people in and around government by systematic indicators, by focusing events like crises and disasters, or by feedback from the operation of current programs. People define conditions as problems by comparing current conditions with their values concerning more ideal states of affairs, by comparing their own performance with that of other countries, or by putting the subject into one category rather than another' (pp. 20-21).

According to Kingdon, problem recognition is critical to agenda setting. When a condition is accepted as a problem, if a solution can be found which will solve it, it is much more likely to rise on the agenda. 'Some problems are seen as so pressing that they set agendas all by themselves. Once a particular problem is defined as pressing, whole classes of approaches are favoured over others, and some alternatives are highlighted while others fall from view' (p. 207).

Strong parallels can also be drawn between Kingdon's *political stream* and accounts which focus on the exogenous impact of government on the policy agenda. The political stream, he argues, is responsive to factors such as changes in national mood, changes in the composition of the government, and campaigning by pressure groups, all of which effect the external environment in which policy makers operate. Thus, 'potential agenda items that are congruent with the current national mood, that enjoy interest group support or lack organised opposition, and that fit the orientations of the prevailing legislative coalitions or current administrations are more likely to rise to agenda prominence than items that do not meet such conditions' (p. 21).

When a conflict develops within the political stream, say between the priorities of an organised interest and the prevailing national mood, the latter is likely to prevail, at least as far as setting the agenda is concerned. 'Interests are often able to block consideration of proposals they do not prefer, or to adapt to an item already high on a governmental agenda by adding bits a bit more to their liking. They less often initiate considerations or set agendas on their own' (p. 208).

Overall, Kingdon's focus on political streams overcomes the narrow focus of a number of models of agenda setting which attribute control over agenda setting role to a restricted group of policy insiders. The focus on the political stream is able to incorporate outsiders and account for the potential of public pressure to affect policy change, through, for example violence, strikes or the rise of social movements.

Finally, the *policy stream* is closely related to work by other theorists on the role of actors in agenda setting. In his treatment of actors Kingdon distinguishes between visible and hidden participants. Visible actors are all those who receive a high profile in the news media which, in the American case studied by Kingdon, include the President and his high-level appointees, key actors in political parties and prominent members of congress. Hidden participants include think tanks and academics, bureaucrats and staff in Congress who form loosely knit networks of specialists around a policy issue (p. 206).

The distinctiveness of Kingdon's account lies in his view that agenda setting and alternative specification are carried out by different types of actors, with agendas set by visible actors and alternatives set by hidden ones. 'So the chances of a subject rising on a governmental agenda are enhanced if that subject is pushed by participants in the visible cluster, and dampened if it is neglected by those participants' (p. 208). The more visible an actor the more powerful he or she is, and so the President, above all others, is pre-eminent in the process of agenda setting:

> At least as far as agenda setting is concerned, elected officials and their appointees turn out to be more important than civil servants or participants outside of government. To those who look for evidence of democracy at work, this is an encouraging result. [So, in the operation of the agenda process, at least, a top-down model] ... comes surprisingly close to the truth. (pp. 208-09)

In contrast, 'alternatives, proposals and solutions are generated in communities of specialists ... Each community is composed of people located throughout the system and potentially of very diverse orientations and interests, but they all share one thing: their specialisation and acquaintance with the issues in the particular policy area' (1984, p. 209). Ideas are bounced around in these communities; working papers are put forward; speeches are given; committees issue reports; and conversations are held. The result, is a vast array of ideas which float around in a 'policy primeval soup' some of which are plausible, some are unrealistic, some are costable and some are not (1984, Ch. 6). A great number are both feasible and well supported and attainable, and it is these which come to the fore when the agenda dynamic changes in ways which open up opportunities for them.

The ideas which are generated in the policy community float around in the *policy stream*, 'bumping into one another, encountering new ideas, and forming combinations and recombinations' (p. 209), resulting in the origins of policies being difficult to trace: 'While the origins are somewhat haphazard, the selection is not. Through the imposition of criteria by which some ideas are selected out for survival while others are discarded, order is developed from chaos, pattern from randomness. These criteria include technical feasibility, congruence with the values of community members, and the anticipation of future constraints, including a budget constraint, public acceptability, and political receptivity' (p. 210).

According to Kingdon, if a policy is seen as unfeasible it is much less likely to survive. The feasibility of an issue is conditioned by its definition and so policy entrepreneurs devote considerable energy to ensuring that their 'pet proposals' are acceptable to the widest possible audience. 'In the process of policy development, recombination (the coupling of already-familiar elements) is more important than mutation (the appearance of wholly new forms). Thus entrepreneurs, who broker people and ideas, are more important than inventors. Because recombination is more important than invention there may be "no new thing under the sun" at the same time there may be dramatic change and innovation. There is change, but it involves the recombination of already-familiar elements' (p. 210).

The three streams of policies, problems and politics all act independently. There are times, however, when they all become joined 'into a single package. [At such times] ... advocates of a new policy initiative not only take advantage of politically propitious moments but also claim that their proposal is a solution to a pressing problem' (p. 211). Entrepreneurs search for solutions which they can couple with a particular problem. When they have achieved this they seek an opportunity to join the three streams. 'At points along the way, there are partial couplings: solutions to problems, but without a receptive political climate; politics to proposals, but without a sense that a compelling problem is being solved; politics and problems both calling for action, but without an available alternative to advocate. But the complete joining of all three streams dramatically enhances the odds that a subject will become firmly fixed on a decision agenda' (p. 211).

The linkage of these streams occurs when a policy window is opened. Windows, which are opened by events in either the political or problem stream, serve as a period of opportunity for entrepreneurs to push their pet solutions to the fore. A new problem may arise, providing the opportunity to attach a solution to it, or political events such as a change in administration, in national mood or a media campaign, may highlight or suppress problems or proposals. 'Predictable or unpredictable, open windows are small and scarce. Opportunities come, but they also pass. Windows do not stay open long. If a chance is missed, another must be awaited' (p. 213). The result of this is that open windows act as a magnet to entrepreneurs aiming to create a complete linkage from a partial coupling.

In evaluating Kingdon's work, there can be little doubt that it is an important addition to the literature on agenda setting. However, there are a number of limitations to his model which particularly affect its application to agenda setting in the case of UK transport policy, with which this book is concerned.

The first criticism is aimed at Kingdon's desire to distinguish between hidden and visible actors in his model. The problem is that his model makes no distinction between high and low politics and appears to assume that the central executive has the time, energy and level of interest to involve itself in conflict over all aspects of agenda setting. This seems particularly unlikely in the transport sector in which highly specialist, technical issues predominate.

Secondly, Kingdon's discussion of the generation of alternatives seems to imply that all of the interests operating within a sub-government have an equal capacity to suggest alternatives, place them on the agenda for consideration and have them adopted. This fails to account for the fact that in many sub-governments there is considerable imbalance between different groups' access to political power. According to Marsh's research on the interaction between groups operating within sub-governments, 'there are a limited number of powerful economic groups which enjoy a privileged position in the [pre-]decision-making process'. In contrast, he found that ideological groups were largely ineffective unless they were involved with issues which involved limited public expenditure or which did not concern powerful economic interests. As a result, 'in disputes which involve conflict between economic and ideological groups, the ideological group can only hope to exert any influence if it can generate enough public support to make the single issue with which it is concerned a significant electoral issue ... The conflict is unequal because the economic groups do not have to fight for recognition or support, but rather enjoy it because of their structural position in the economy' (1983, p. 15).

Thirdly, Kingdon argues that the processes of agenda setting and alternative specification operate independently. However, in many cases agendas are set with specific alternatives in mind. When governments change, the range of options which are realistically considered often also changes. Thus the actors which determine the agenda are also likely to have a significant role on the selection of policy alternatives.

Finally, Kingdon's model only allows for a limited discussion of non-agenda setting. It implies that the process of agenda setting is extremely open and that almost any issue can acquire systemic agenda status if it can find a sufficiently motivated policy entrepreneur to promote it. However, as I have argued earlier, on the one hand a number of issues do not gain agenda status even with extensive sponsorship by interested parties, while on the other, many issues gain representation even without the backing of an entrepreneur.

Agenda Setting in Three Dimensions: An Examination of Luke's Typology

On a number of occasions in this chapter I have identified the potential importance of ideas such as structural power, non-decision making and ideological hegemony in the discussion of models of agenda setting, but thus far I have not discussed them in any systematic way. Therefore the aim of this, the last section of this review, is to outline the importance of these ideas for studies of agenda setting.

The history of the scholarship focusing on non-decisions is rooted in the work of four key authors: Peter Bachrach and Morton Baratz; Stephen Lukes, and Matthew Crenson. They all started with the same premise: that a pluralist methodology which, in Merelman's words, 'studied actual behaviour, stressed operational definitions, and turned up evidence' and that 'seemed to produce reliable conclusions which met the cannons of science' (cited in Lukes, 1974, p. 12), in fact produced exactly the opposite results:

> The pluralists concentrate their attention, not upon the sources of power, but its exercise. Power to them means 'participation in decision-making' and can be analysed only after 'careful examination of concrete decisions'. As a result, the pluralist researcher is uninterested in the reputedly powerful. His concerns instead are (a) to select for study a number of 'key' as opposed to 'routine' political decisions, (b) identify the people who took an active part in the decision process, (c) obtain a full account of their actual behaviour while the policy conflict was being resolved, and (d) determine and analyse the specific outcome of the conflict. (Bachrach and Baratz, 1970, p. 6)

A pluralist methodology thus has two key defects: a failure to differentiate between important and unimportant issues, and a failure to recognise the importance of an exercise of power which confines agenda conflict to comparatively 'safe' issues (Bachrach and Baratz, 1970, p. 6).

Bachrach and Baratz do not deny the pluralist's assertion that power is exercised when A makes decisions which affect B. But they argue that the pluralists do not go far enough, not being alive to the fact that, 'power is also exercised when A devotes his energies to creating or reinforcing social and political values and institutional practices that limit the scope of the political process to public consideration of only those issues which are comparatively innocuous to A. To the extent that A succeeds in doing this, B is prevented, for all practical purposes, from bringing to the fore any issues that might in their resolution be seriously detrimental to A's set of preferences' (p. 7).

In this sense, issues which do not arise on the political agenda can be just as important as those which do. Non-issues are therefore important to the study of political power in any society as they conceal demands for changes in the social balance of resources: either by suffocating them before they are voiced; by keeping them covert; by preventing them from gaining access to the decision making system, or, at the final stage, by ensuring that they are not implemented (p. 44). The key distinction between the pluralists and these alternative theorists, therefore, is in their definition of what constitutes an issue. To the pluralists, as Dahl argues, 'a political issue can hardly be said to exist unless and until it commands the attention of a significant segment of the political stratum' (Dahl, 1961, p. 92). In contrast, Bachrach and Baratz argue that issues are defined by their potential to become issues. It is the operation of the process of non-decision making which prevents their realisation.

Lukes takes the process of non-decision making a stage further, arguing that Bachrach and Baratz are themselves guilty of adopting an overly limited frame of reference. He argues that their conceptualisation of non-issues within a conflict focus misses the potential power of actors, in particular the state, to shape people's wants in the first place, through the operation of an ideological hegemony (1974, pp. 18-20). Pertinently, he poses the question, 'is it not the supreme and most insidious use of power to prevent people, to whatever degree, from having grievances by shaping their perceptions, cognitions, and preferences in such a way that they accept their role in the existing order of things, either because they can see or imagine no alternative to it, or because they see it as natural and unchangeable, or because they value it as divinely ordained and beneficial?' (p. 24).

Regardless of what critics may have to say about the conclusions advanced by this body of knowledge it has, at the very least, injected some lively ideas into the debate on agenda setting. At best, it has fundamentally challenged the conventional wisdom. The result has been to generate an extensive academic debate on the issue of non-decision making, which I will now review.

The first criticism that the pluralists advance is a methodological one. How, they argue, can one study, let alone explain, what does not occur?

Polsby has captured the feeling well: 'It has been suggested that non-events make more significant policy than do policy making events. This is the kind of statement that has a certain plausibility and attractiveness but that presents truly insuperable obstacles to research'. How, he argues, is the researcher to chose which non-issues to study? 'One satisfactory answer might be: those outcomes desired by a significant number of actors in the community but not achieved ... A wholly unsatisfactory answer would be: certain non-events stipulated by outside observers without reference to the desires or activities of community residents. The answer is unsatisfactory because it is obviously inappropriate for outsiders to pick among all the possible outcomes that did not take place a set which they regard as important but which community citizens do not. This approach is likely to prejudice the outcome of research' (1963, pp. 96-97, repr. 1980).

Polsby poses other fundamental questions. What right, he asks, has the researcher to select a non-issue above another in the first place? What right has a researcher to judge an issue as a non-issue when the community itself does not regard it as important? Is the researcher not guilty of greater methodological bias than the methodology he or she is criticising? Finally, what right has any researcher to assign a 'real' class or social interest to any social grouping when the class or social interest in question disagrees with the analyst? Why should a researcher be better equipped to evaluate the interests of these groups than they are themselves? (pp. 95-97).

There is little point in denying either that these questions are fundamental or that they aim at the heart of Luke's methodology. Lukes himself responds to the first criticism, that non-agenda setting is methodologically unmeasurable: 'It does not follow that, just because it is difficult or even impossible to show that power has been exercised in a given situation, we can conclude that it has not. But, more importantly, I do not believe that it is impossible to identify an exercise of power of this type' (1974, p. 39).

Lukes then proceeds to outline the way in which he can identify that an exercise of power has taken place in his approach. An exercise of power, he argues, requires the existence of two related conditions. Firstly that A can affect, either on its own or with other sufficient conditions, B so that B does what it would otherwise not do. In this case, without the presence of A, we can assume that B would otherwise have done b. This provides Lukes with what he refers to as a relevant counterfactual, which if it can be empirically identified, proves that a successful exercise of power has occurred (pp. 40-41).

In cases of open political conflict between *A* and *B* the existence of a relevant counterfactual is fairly obvious. It is in situations in which no political conflict is obvious that a more subtle process is required to reveal the relevant counterfactual. 'That is, we must provide other, indirect, grounds for asserting that if *A* had not acted (or failed to act) in a certain way – and, in the case of operative power, if other sufficient conditions had not been operative – then *B* would have thought and acted differently from the way he did actually think and act. In brief, we need to justify our expectation that *B* would have thought or acted differently; and we also need to specify the means or mechanisms by which *A* has prevented or else acted (or abstained from acting) in a manner sufficient to prevent, *B* from doing so' (pp. 41-42). This task has tackled by, in particular, Matthew Crenson (1971) who attempts to explain why certain things do not happen.[7]

In the book, *The Un-Politics of Air Pollution*, Crenson inquires why it was that some American cities took action on the issue of air pollution while others, which were equally polluted, did not. In order to investigate this question he undertakes a number of case studies of neighbouring cities with similar pollution levels and socio-economic characteristics, asking why the city of Gary, Indiana, took thirteen extra years to enact anti-pollution legislation (1971, p. 36). His case is that U.S. Steel, because of its dominance of the industrial complex in Gary, was clearly identified with the town's prosperity. Due to power based on its anticipated reactions to any proposed legislation, it managed to limit any attempts to raise the pollution issue. 'Moreover, it did all this without acting or entering into the political arena' (pp. 77-78).

Non-action, according to Gary's environmental activists, was a crucial factor in the non-implementation of early anti-pollution legislation. As one of Crenson's respondents recalled: 'The company executives would just nod sympathetically "and agree that air pollution was terrible, and pat you on the head. But they never *did* anything one way or the other. If only there had been a fight, then something might have been accomplished!" What U.S. Steel did not do was probably more important to the career of Gary's air pollution issue than what it did do' (pp. 76-7).

Not only is the structural position of interests important in determining how effectively issues are treated but so are the political priorities of those interests. This notion of agenda displacement, where one issue can be excluded by the prioritisation of others, is inextricably linked with notions of structural power. Crenson once more provides evidence of the concept, as his research leads him to refute agenda models taking a pluralist frame of reference and arguing that issues are free to rise independently of one another regardless of any inherent contradictions which may exist between them. In truth, issues are not mutually independent and action in one area almost inevitably has an impact on another (p. 169). 'Civic leaders who promote the economic development issue, for example, may thereby discourage the promotion of the dirty air issue. The influence of these political activists extends beyond the field of their visible actions to other issues and would-be issues' (p. 170).

In consequence the political system is considerably less fragmented than a narrow focus on political action indicates. 'Several issue-areas may, in effect, be subject to the influence of local leaders who are visibly active in only a single field of public concern, and this influence may operate to reduce the penetrability of community political systems. By promoting one political agenda item, civic actors may succeed in driving others away'. These findings can not be incorporated in any framework which argues that ideas can come from anywhere (p. 170).

The arguments of Lukes and Crenson have done much to refute the criticisms raised by Polsby and his colleagues. In particular, Crenson's work satisfies Lukes' two criteria of a relevant counterfactual and the identification of a power mechanism particularly well. As he argues, there is good reason to suspect that most members of the public would prefer not to be poisoned, especially if pollution control did not lead to unemployment. In addition, Crenson offers a plausible explanation of the power of U.S. Steel to prevent the rise of the pollution issue through inaction. However, as Lukes himself points out, many other issues are not as clear cut. In these cases it is extremely difficult to justify the relevant counterfactual (1974, p. 46).

However, this still does not address Polsby's central question: how do Lukes and his colleagues know which issues to study as non-issues? The answer, in short, is that they have considerable difficulty. As I have already argued, a number of issues are not as clear cut as the pollution issue described by Crenson. As the other models of agenda theory have argued, other factors could explain the failure of an issue to rise on the policy agenda: an item may not be fashionable; it may be crowded out; it may not have an attractive solution attached to it; it may not have an efficient entrepreneur or a sufficiently motivated public, or it may simply not have luck on its side. Thus, an issue may gain a place on the agenda for any one of a number of reasons which the other models outline, and this powerful criticism is difficult to challenge in many cases.

Conclusion

This chapter has presented a review of a number of models of the process of agenda setting and alternative selection. It has focused on the roles of problems, actors, exogenous factors and non-decision making, and posed a series of questions which are designed to structure the remainder of this book. In particular, in explaining the increasing salience of the transport issue the following questions will prove centrally important. To what extent has the transport issue occupied a significant place on the agenda of central government and how has central government responded? Which, if any, of the models of agenda setting are best able to explain the rise of the transport issue in the Major and Blair periods? Historically, how much autonomy have the core insiders had? How dependent have they been on the support of central government and has this changed in any way? And, if so, how can such changes be explained?

Notes

1   Cobb and Elder (1972, pp. 160-61) also utilise the concept of governmental agenda in a very similar way to Kingdon. They further add a useful distinction between items up for active consideration by a decision making unit (the formal or governmental agenda) and the systemic agenda of controversy which 'consists of the full range of issues or problem areas that are both salient to a political community and commonly perceived as legitimate subjects of governmental concern' (p. 160).

2   Peters and Hogwood (1985) argue that the issue attention cycle can be used to model a broader range of issues than were originally considered by Downs, and reflects the pattern of agenda setting in areas such as transport policy, economic policy and energy policy. They also emphasise that issue attention cycles have a significant impact on the levels of organisational activity undertaken by government, with peaks in the cycle corresponding to peaks in the development of new organisations and the reform of existing ones (pp. 246-50), and troughs in the cycle coinciding with the succession or closing of organisations (p. 248).

3   Stringer and Richardson (1980) argue that insiders have a greater capacity to manage the agenda setting process, by for example, developing placebo policies, manipulating statistical data and controlling the policy image of issues.

4   Outsider groups have a number of resources open to them which they can use to influence the agenda. For example they can use direct action or influence the outcome of elections, both of which are discussed in more detail below (pp. 27-28 and pp. 30-32).

5   I refer to the base line rules of structure formation within this book as the structural imperatives of the state.

6   Kingdon's model draws on the work of Cohen *et al* who in their article, 'A Garbage Can Model of Organisational Choice' (1972), argue that 'a decision is an outcome or interpretation of several relatively independent streams within an organisation'

(pp. 2-3). Furthermore, choices can be 'made only when the shifting combinations of problems, solutions and decision makers happen to make action possible' (p. 16). For an application of this model to the EU policy process, see Richardson, 1996c, pp. 3-23.

7   Dearlove (1973, pp. 169-73) and Gaventa (1980, pp. 192-99) have also undertaken detailed case studies in which the application of ideas connected with Lukes' model of three dimensional power has enabled them to find evidence of a relevant counter factual.

3 History: From the Un-Politics to the New Politics of Transport

Introduction

> Good roads, canals and navigable rivers, by diminishing the expense of carriage, put the remote parts of the country more nearly upon a level with those in the neighbourhood of the town. They are upon that account the greatest of all improvements. They encourage the cultivation of the remote, which must always be the most extensive circle of the country. They are advantageous to the town, by breaking down the monopoly of the country in its neighbourhood. They are advantageous even to that part of the country. Though they introduce some rival commodities into the old market, they open many new markets to its produce. Monopoly, besides, is a great enemy to good management, which can never be universally established but in consequence of that free and universal competition which forces everybody to have recourse to it for the sake of self-defence. (Smith, 1776, p. 251)

Although over two hundred years old, the writings of Neo-Classical economists such as Adam Smith effectively summarise the historical rationale of transport policy in the UK. This rationale is based on the premise that government policy fosters economic growth through the extension of the size of markets and responds to the demands of transport consumers in a market-based system of transport provision. This chapter argues that this *predict and provide* rationale explains the focus of government policy in the post-war period, in which the priority has been to expand the road network in response to increasing congestion and the rapid growth of road transport (Barker and Gerhold, 1993).

The central aim of this chapter is to examine the impact of such a policy rationale upon the historical development of transport policy in the post-war period, and I argue that policy in the post-war era is most accurately evaluated if it is divided into four time periods. The first, until the early 1980s, provides evidence of the importance of the predict and provide orthodoxy to central government policy makers, and demonstrates an apparent structural domination of the policy process by the road lobby at this time; the second, from the early until the mid-1980s, reflects a period in which the rise, and decline, in public concern over the impact of the motor car on the environment and public health had a significant impact on the policy process for the first time; the third, from the mid-1980s until 1989, corresponds to a re-emphasis by central government of the importance of the predict and provide orthodoxy. The dominance of this orthodoxy culminated in 1989 with the publication of national traffic forecasts which predicted a rise of road traffic levels of between 83% and 142% (DTp, 1989a) and the government's announcement of a 'more than doubling [of] the size' of the road programme in response (Cm 693, para. 1). The final period, from the early 1990s to date, corresponds to an unprecedented challenge to the hitherto dominant policy orthodoxy. Faced by this challenge, the pro-roads groups are attempting to undermine this challenge by advocating an extension of the technical solutions which were first used in the early 1980s. In consequence, on the surface, the dynamics of transport policy face an uncertain future: an uncertainty which is driven by the conflict between the anti-roads groups' utilisation of the language of sustainable development and the pro-roads groups' attempts to mitigate against change through the use of technical solutions to manage the political agenda.

It is important to emphasise that the separation of the history of transport policy into the four periods which I have adopted is unorthodox. In particular, a number of authors have focused on the 1970s as a period in which an organised campaign was conducted by the anti-roads groups to disrupt the highway inquiry process. This, they argue, was the first time that the pro-roads groups and national transport policy were subjected to sustained political pressure (see for example Dudley, 1983, Dudley and Richardson, 1995 and 1996a, Tyme, 1978 and Levin, 1979). However, I will show that the impact of these protests was, with hindsight, limited. The protests had little lasting impact either on the balance of power between the insider and outsider groups (because the pro-roads groups maintained control within the arenas in which conflict took place) or on the ideas orthodoxy which had dominated the politics of transport from the inter-war period. Consequently, it was only after the rise in knowledge which linked motor transport more explicitly to the degradation of the environment and to issues of public health in the early 1980s that the opponents of roads were, for the first time, able to challenge the rationale of policy.

Transport Policy Making: Towards a Multi-level Model of the Agenda Setting Process

I argue in this chapter that the development of transport policy in the post-war period reflects insights from a number of the models of agenda setting which were discussed in the previous chapter. In particular, Benson's model of multi-level policy making (1982) and Dowding's work on systematic luck (1991, pp. 152-57) can be used to provide a framework which accounts for the development of transport policy during this period.

First, Benson's model of a multi-level policy sector is utilised in support of the argument that the agenda setting process is constrained by the structural imperatives of the state which operate to exclude some issues from the agenda, thus limiting the choices open to policy makers.

Second, insights from Dowding's work on systematic luck are utilised in order to explain the formation of the policy networks which have developed around the transport issue. This chapter argues that the road lobby has been able to maintain its status as an insider group during this period simply because the structural imperatives of the state and the policy objectives of all governments in the post-war era have *happened to* reflect the objectives of the pro-roads groups. Thus, for much of the post-war period the nature of the institutional relationship between the government and the road lobby has inevitably favoured the road lobby, regardless of the effectiveness of its lobbying activity.

Consideration of Benson's model suggests that throughout this period the transport agenda has operated on three levels: issues located within the upper level of the policy sector have been able to operate with a relatively high level of agenda dynamism; issues located within the middle level of the policy sector have been able to operate with relatively limited dynamism, only affecting the agenda in the Major era; and issues within the bottom level have had no dynamism, being unable to overcome the structural imperatives of the state throughout the post-war period (see Figure 3.1).

Figure 3.1   Application of Benson's model to the transport policy sector

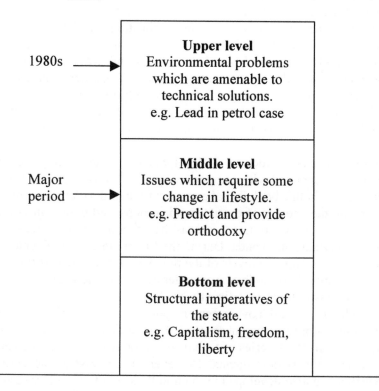

1980s ⟶

Upper level
Environmental problems
which are amenable to
technical solutions.
e.g. Lead in petrol case

Major
period ⟶

Middle level
Issues which require some
change in lifestyle.
e.g. Predict and provide
orthodoxy

Bottom level
Structural imperatives of
the state.
e.g. Capitalism, freedom,
liberty

Benson's model can also be used to illuminate the periodization of policy which is set out within this chapter. The first period, until the early 1980s, provides evidence of a time during which the structural imperatives of the state (operating within the lower level of the policy sector) exerted almost total control over both the medium and upper levels of the policy sector. Thus, as I shall argue later in this chapter, the agenda remained tightly controlled throughout this period, with the anti-roads groups unable to affect the agenda setting process.

However, by the mid-1980s, the agenda setting process began to be affected by an increase in public concern over the environmental impact of road vehicles. I argue in this chapter that, at this time, conflict first developed in the upper level of the policy sector as the anti-roads groups attempted to undermine the positive policy image of road transport. However, central government responded by developing a series of technical solutions which managed the policy agenda, reduced the level of conflict within the upper level, and maintained the dominance of the structural imperatives of the state over the agenda setting process.

The third period centres on the publication of the *Roads for Prosperity* White Paper in 1989 (Cm 693). At this time the Thatcher government forcefully re-emphasised the predict and provide orthodoxy, regaining control over the agenda setting process. Thus, developments in the agenda setting process during this time strongly resemble those in the first period, with the structural imperatives of the state exerting considerable control over both the medium and upper levels of the policy sector.

Finally, this chapter focuses on developments in the Major period, in which the agenda operated with comparatively high levels of dynamism. A key argument within this book is that a combination of developments in the problem stream, the activity of the anti-roads groups, and policy initiatives in the EU and local government arenas has facilitated unprecedented conflict over the transport agenda. During the Major era conflict developed in both the upper *and* middle levels of the policy sector for the first time, as the predict and provide orthodoxy was undermined and the positive policy image of road transport was significantly eroded.

As with the central government response to the problems of the mid-1980s, the Major government responded to the challenges of the 1990s by attempting to invoke a series of technical solutions which would enable them to manage the policy agenda. However, in contrast to the earlier period, conflict had also developed in the middle level of the policy sector, and in response the government moved the rationale of policy away from the predict and provide orthodoxy, altering a central element of the historical orthodoxy which had underpinned transport policy for the whole of the post-war period (see Chapter 4). But in spite of the changes to the nature of the predict and provide orthodoxy, the capacity of the anti-roads groups to push issues which challenge the structural imperatives of the state onto the agenda has been negligible: issues which challenge the structural imperatives of the state still remain excluded from the agenda setting process (Chapter 5).

Transport Policy before 1983: Predict and Provide

The Ideas Paradigm: The Domination of Market Orthodoxy

> A generation hence, people won't ask what the Government is doing to meet increased demand for transport, any more than they now ask what the Government is doing to meet the increased demand for chocolate. (Paul Channon, then Secretary of State for Transport, cited in Roberts et al, 1992, p. 102)

The words of the then Minister for Transport in April 1989 capture the essence of the ideas orthodoxy which has dominated transport policy throughout the post-war period, without coherent institutional or political opposition until the mid-1980s. This paradigm operated consistently across changes of government and had three bases: that roads were essential for economic prosperity as they enabled the free movement of produce and the expansion of the macro-economy; that transport policy ought to be market based and respond to the demands of transport consumers, and that transport policy should not aim to incorporate the impact of external costs such as congestion, accidents or environmental effects (externalities).

Government documents published in the 1960s and 1970s demonstrate the key aspects of this policy orthodoxy. Firstly, they demonstrate that government had a very positive policy image of the motor car at that time. The 1966 White Paper, *Transport Policy*, produced by the Labour government, provides one such example of this governmental view:

> The rapid development and mass production of the motor vehicle over the past 20 years has brought immense benefits to millions of people: increased mobility, a fuller social life, family employment, new experiences. (Cmnd 3057, para. 1)

For the first time, the 1966 White Paper also identified environmental concerns related to the impact of road vehicles and outlined the importance of a multi-modal transport strategy, which included diverting freight from road to rail, encouraging public transport in urban areas and subsidising socially necessary railway lines (Cmnd 3057, paras 55-62 and 25-28). However, as Barbara Castle has acknowledged in her memoirs, the thinking behind the White Paper did not signify any change to the policy image of the motor car. It was designed to 'come to terms with the motor car while not allowing it to ruin our environment. This meant an expanded road programme to relieve the growing congestion' (Castle, 1984, p. 154).

Of the aims in the White Paper, only the proposed expansion of the road programme was successfully implemented. The policies designed to encourage mode switching, such as the creation of the Passenger Transport Authorities in the metropolitan boroughs and the promotion of rail freight, failed to slow the growth of road traffic. Thus, policy remained motivated by the predict and provide orthodoxy, with the government unwilling to advance proposals to restrict road use or the growth of road vehicle ownership. Government policy thus reflected the sentiments of the Buchanan report, published in 1963, which argued that:

> before very long the majority of the electors in the country will be car owners. What is more, it is reasonable to suppose that they will be very conscious of their interests as car owners. It does not need any gift of prophecy to foresee that the governments of the future will be increasingly preoccupied with the wishes of car owners. (Steering Group of the Buchanan Committee, 1963, para. 9)[1]

The view that government ought to accommodate the projected rise in traffic levels on the basis of predict and provide orthodoxy was also expressed within the Buchanan report itself:

> The choice is society's. But it will not be sensible, nor indeed for long be possible, for society to go on investing apparently unlimited sums in the purchase and running of motor vehicles without investing equivalent sums in the proper accommodation of the traffic that results. It is true to say that there are many other claims on material resources, but it is a weak argument to say that the needs of traffic cannot be met, seeing that it is a problem that we are creating by our extreme readiness to invest in motor vehicles. (Buchanan Committee, 1963, para. 444)

The 1966 White Paper was strongly influenced by the sentiments of the Buchanan report and acknowledged that government investment in the post-war period had been inadequate to cope with the rise in traffic levels. 'The crucial questions therefore are how much of our national resources can be devoted to roads in the 1970s, having regard to all the other demands on public investment, and how to get full value for the money spent' (Cmnd 3057, para. 35).

Not only was government committed to the ideals of road building; it also believed that the congestion problem could be ended by 'one last push' to the roads programme. In 1970, following the election of a Conservative government, the White Paper, *Roads for the Future*, emphasised the continuity of central government policy and the importance of the predict and provide orthodoxy:

> With the Government's new target we can look forward by the end of the 1980s to an inter-urban trunk road system where capacity has doubled (compared with a 70 per cent increase in traffic) and on which traffic can travel freely, safely and without frustration and congestion. (Cmnd 4369, para. 29)

Thus the interests of both existing and future transport users were to be served by an unparalleled expansion of the infrastructure network. The concerns which were later to emerge about the environmental impact of road transport were simply not an issue at that time; the contrast with the policy image of roads in the Major era could not be more stark. In the 1970 White Paper, road building was seen as an environmental enhancement:

> New roads do improve the total environment although, inevitably, amenity is reduced in some areas and for some people. The aim will be to safeguard and, indeed, to enhance both amenity and the environment to the maximum possible extent. (Cmnd 4369, para. 22)

In this climate the structural interests of the road lobby were assured because the market orientation of government policy coincided with the demands of those groups' interests. Therefore, at this time, the road lobby was the beneficiary of systematic luck and its interests were served by the priorities of central government and not as a result of its lobbying activity.

The Unchanging Nature of the Transport Policy Network: 1945-1989

> When I took over at the Ministry of Transport the most vociferous lobby in this country was that represented by the road interests. The propaganda and pressure groups led by the British Roads Federation said we must concentrate all our resources on building the first 1,000 miles of motorway. The environment lobby had barely been born, and when I tried to suggest that there were other considerations that we should bear in mind I had an uphill task because the whole of public opinion and the then opposition were against me. (Castle in *Hansard*, 4th July 1973 col. 556)

Studies of the road lobby, such as those by Finer (1958), Dudley (1983) and Plowden (1971), have all illustrated that historically the Department of Transport (DTp) and the pro-roads interests have formed a structurally quiescent policy network which did not 'have to fight for recognition or support, but rather enjoyed it because of its structural position in the economy' (Marsh, 1983, p. 15).[2]

Until the Major era the pattern of transport policy making accorded with these studies and the dynamics of the conflict over policy is well described by a network metaphor.[3] Figure 3.2 provides a diagrammatic representation of the transport policy network in this period. It illustrates that the pro-roads groups were well organised and formed 'an integral part of the "policy community"', enjoying frequent contact with ministers and having representatives serving on a number of Department of Transport advisory committees (Dudley, 1983, p. 109).

Figure 3.2   Location of actors on a policy network continuum (pre-Major period)

Insiders   Outsiders

←——→

core insiders/ specialist insiders	peripheral insiders	outsider by goal	outsider by choice
British Roads Federation			
AA/RAC (users)		Transport 2000	Friends of the Earth ALARM UK
Construction interests			
Society of Motor Manufacturers and Traders			

In this time period, the road lobby derived insider status from its structural linkage to economically powerful interests and industrial competitiveness:

> If the companies who support you represent something in the region of two point five million, three million working individuals then that gives you, clearly is going to give you, more leverage than if you represent, you know, how many – four hundred and fifty [thousand], I can't remember how many members Friends of the Earth has got. But clearly, if you are talking about issues related to industrial competitiveness then you are going to talk to people who represent industry. (Interview, Paul Everitt, BRF, 21st August 1996. See also interview, John Dawson, AA, 4th July 1996)

At this time the interests of the road lobby and those of central government were virtually indistinguishable, with the predict and provide philosophy dominating the thinking of both.

Outside the core policy community were the anti-roads groups which had relatively limited access to government (Figure 3.2). Dudley and Richardson (1996a) argue that by the 1980s the opposition to the road programme had become increasingly sophisticated and campaigners had moved 'attention away from the highways themselves to the polluting effects of vehicles' in response to increased knowledge regarding the impact of vehicles on public health (p. 76). 'Notwithstanding this lobbying, however, the environmentalists had seemed to be unable to penetrate the core policy community which still had a momentum of its own' (p. 77).

In the pre-Major period the scope of the actors which had mobilised themselves to oppose policy was relatively limited and the breadth of the opposition to the roads programme was relatively narrow. As Figure 3.2 illustrates, the anti-roads groups were restricted to those representing the 'traditional' arm of the movement: groups such as Transport 2000 and ALARM UK had not been joined by either 'quasi-insiders', such as the RSPB or the National Trust, or 'radical' outsiders in the form of the direct action movement, neither of which had a significant impact on the transport agenda until the Major era.

Figure 3.2 illustrates that in the pre-Major period the predominance of the road programme in national transport policy meant that, in practical terms, no distinction existed between core and specialist insiders: governments treated the British Roads Federation (BRF) and its constituent actors both as policy experts, with specialist knowledge, and as generalists, qualified to advise on policy at a strategic level.

The strength of central government commitment to the objectives of the road lobby meant that it was very difficult for any anti-roads groups to gain even peripheral insider status. At this time, Transport 2000, in particular, was trying to pursue an insider strategy with little success. The principal reason for this, as Maloney *et al* explain, is because its goals were seen as completely incompatible with the goals of government (1994, p. 32). Thus, Transport 2000 is best seen as a group with peripheral insider tactics and outsider goals (in the eyes of government civil servants), and is consequently located on Figure 3.2 accordingly.

At the other end of the spectrum were groups which were operating as outsiders by choice. These groups, such as ALARM UK, undertook a series of campaigns, designed in particular to disrupt the highway inquiry process:

> [In the 1970s and early 1980s] they made a lot of noise but they made a lot
> of noise fundamentally working within the accepted structures. I think this
> was the key difference, because what the actual roads protesters did was
> they accepted that they would campaign against a road through the given
> channels; public consultation, public enquiry. They made elegant, and in
> their case, noisy arguments at public enquires and they all lost. Now and
> that's because they were campaigning on the territory set out by the
> Department of Transport, by officialdom. (Interview, John Stewart,
> ALARM UK, 23rd November 1995)

Overall, the campaigns of outsiders by choice, working through
official channels, had a limited impact: it was not until the development of
new, and more radical, forms of protest in the 1990s that the anti-roads
groups achieved a significant effect. These campaigns, by operating outside
official channels, were able to command and sustain the attention of the
media and overcome the institutional biases of the road lobby which
dominated those channels.[4]

According to the insider-outsider model, the limited scope and
breadth of the opposition to the roads programme in the pre-Major era was
crucial. Thus, it was not until both the scope and breadth of the opposition
to roads increased in the Major period that the anti-roads groups were able
to mount a sustained challenge to the stability of the road lobby.

The Road Lobby and Institutional Autonomy

Mick Hamer (1987) has argued that the road lobby has an almost unique
capacity to control decision making in the transport field. Throughout the
twentieth century, according to Hamer, the development of national
transport policy has reflected the demands of the pro-roads groups: 'The
road lobby calls for a new road; the environmentalists protest (don't they
always); the department decides; and a road is built. The sequence of events
is clear, and the inference is obvious' (p. 6).

However, my analysis, while acknowledging that the road lobby is
comparatively well organised and supported, argues that we cannot say that
that lobby has in a causal sense determined government policy. In fact, the
reason for the success of the road lobby is simply that the priorities of
central government have happened to favour its interests over and above
those of its opponents. Consequently, on occasions in which the interests of
the road lobby and government have not coincided the road lobby has had
to engage in lobbying activities in a manner more commonly associated
with an outsider pressure group (Finer, 1958, pp. 54-56).

The explanation for this apparent paradox of sectoral domination juxtaposed with the need for traditional lobbying is explained by the constraints which have been placed on the policy objectives of the road lobby by exogenous factors, of which the role of the Treasury and the low political salience of the transport issue are particularly important (Finer, 1958, pp. 56-57).

The Treasury and the Roads Interests

The role of the Treasury as a constraint on the operational autonomy of the road lobby centres on the creation, and subsequent abolition, of the road fund in the early twentieth century (see Plowden, 1971, especially Chapter 3 and Chapter 9).

The origins of the road fund can be traced back to 1905, when a Royal Commission was established to examine the full scope of the problems of motoring: the damage which motor vehicles caused to roads; the question of whether or not motorists ought to be expected to pay for this, and how, if so, such a scheme should be administered. The Royal Commission recommended that a national road fund should be established, with the money paid to a central department which would channel the money through local authorities not for 'ordinary and customary repairs, but in works which have for their object the creation of more durable and less dusty road surfaces' (Cd 3081, para. 74).

The Liberal government was strongly influenced by the findings of the Royal Commission, and legislation for the creation of a national road fund to be funded from a petrol tax and vehicle excise duty was enacted in 1909. Following several years of protracted bargaining between central government and the road user groups, an agreement was reached that, providing that the revenues which were collected, less administrative costs, were spent exclusively on the road system, then the road lobby would support the introduction of these new taxes, against considerable opposition from the Treasury.

At the time of the introduction of the road fund in the 1909 budget, the then Chancellor, Lloyd George, gave such an assurance to the road lobby. 'I want to make it clear,' he said, 'that expenditure undertaken out of the fund must be directly referable to work done in connection with the exigencies of the motor traffic of the country' (HCD, 29/4/09, col. 469-7 cited in Plowden, 1971, p. 90). Thus, at this time, following the creation of the road fund in 1909, the road lobby had secured a high level of operational autonomy from the Treasury.

The Treasury strongly opposed the principle of revenue hypothecation which was enshrined in the road fund, and waged an ongoing campaign throughout the inter-war years to overturn the principle on which the tax had been founded. In an informal protest to the then Prime Minister, Asquith, the then Permanent Secretary to the Treasury, Sir George Murray, stated:

> Why take all the trouble in a year of great stress to collect a new tax, not a 1/2d of which is to find its way into the Exchequer? Petrol is defined in the Budget as any liquid containing hydro-carbon which is calculated to propel a motor vehicle with reasonable efficiency – or something like that. I have not got the exact words. You might as well define *wine* as any liquid containing alcohol, which if taken in unreasonable quantities is calculated to make a man intoxicated. (Asquith papers cited in Plowden, 1971, p. 89)

The Treasury campaign against the principles on which the road fund had been founded successfully reduced the operational autonomy of the road user groups from the early 1920s. In particular, by 1921, with the road fund showing a surplus, the Treasury argued that the proceeds could be used to offset the financial difficulties which were being experienced by the Exchequer:

> The great change in the financial position since last year will involve the reconsideration of many pledges, and the question may well arise not whether the state is entitled to raise eight or nine millions per annum by taxation on motors, but whether, if it does so, it must spend that sum on roads. (Otto Niemeyer, Treasury Official in Communication, to the then Chancellor, Sir Robert Horne, 1921, cited in Plowden, 1971, p. 187)

By the 1930s, growing economic difficulties resulting from the depression had further reduced the autonomy of the roads groups and Treasury raids on the road fund had become common practice. Thus the decision in 1937 to end the financial independence of the road fund (and the principle of hypothecated revenues from motor vehicle taxation) was almost inevitable. After this, the road fund 'would submit annual estimates, like any department, and would receive its income from annual votes' (Plowden, 1971, p. 295), with the financial and operational autonomy of the Ministry of Transport and the road lobby reduced as a result.

Public Opinion and the Road Lobby: There May be No Votes in Roads but Congestion Provides its Own Pressures

The second constraint on the autonomy of the road lobby has resulted from the relatively low support which the Department of Transport has enjoyed within Cabinet and with the electorate (Finer, 1958, p. 54). Consequently, following the decision to end the financial independence of the road fund, investment in road construction declined, and it was not until congestion began to emerge as a political issue in the 1950s that sufficient exogenous pressure developed to push transport up the agenda (Painter, 1980, p. 167).

In the post-1945 period total motor vehicles in use grew threefold in less than fifteen years, from 3.1 million in 1946 to 9.4 million by 1960. Car ownership showed an even more rapid rise, with growth from 1.8 million to 5.5 million over the same period (SMMT, 1964, Table 53). In addition, official traffic forecasts had constantly underestimated predicted traffic growth, particularly with reference to private cars. Tetlow and Goss, writing towards the end of the 1960s, summarise the problem:

> In 1945 the Ministry [of Transport] estimated that traffic increases by 1965 would be 75 per cent over 1933 figures in urban areas and 45 per cent more in rural areas; but by 1950 – five years later – the number of vehicles had already nearly doubled compared with 1933. In 1954 the Ministry told highway authorities to plan for a 75 per cent increase in traffic by 1974. But by 1962 the number of vehicles was already 75 per cent above the 1954 figure. In 1957, the Ministry forecast there would be eight million vehicles by 1960; but there were nine million. In 1959, the Ministry of Transport forecast that there would be twelve and a half million vehicles by 1969; but this figure was passed before the end of 1964. (cited in Plowden, 1971, p. 326)

It was thus developments in the exogenous sphere in the form of rising demands on the road network, and the underestimation of this demand by government, which enabled transport civil servants and the road lobby to regain influence over the agenda setting process and begin the process of developing a network of trunk roads for the first time.

Rising congestion coincided with an expansion of investment in the trunk road sector which rose from £4.5m in 1954/5 (MoT, 1962, p. 10) to £77.2m in 1962 (MoT, 1962, p. 9). By 1970 expenditure on trunk road construction and improvements had trebled in real terms (Cm 7132, p. 31, Table 1). The result of this was an extension of the motorway network from 130 miles in 1961 in England and Wales (MoT, 1962, p. 19) to 676 miles by 1971 (MoT, 1971, p. 20), with the network having expanded to 1185 miles by 1976 (Cm 7132, p. 34, Table 4).

Therefore, at this time, the activities of the road lobby did not directly influence the process of agenda setting and policy formulation, but rather the agenda was changed because rising congestion levels were undermining a central element of the ideas orthodoxy which had dominated government thinking: namely that freedom and liberty should be promoted by the usage of the motor car.

This discussion of the impact of both the Treasury and of congestion as exogenous variables has thus served to qualify the extent to which the road lobby can be seen historically to have retained control over the development of transport policy. The lobby has in fact relied upon exogenous developments before being able to instigate changes in the political agenda. Some of these developments have been beneficial to the road lobby (in particular the rising levels of congestion), while some have hindered its objectives (in particular the role of the Treasury).

Transport History, 1983-1989: Exogenous Pressure on the Road Lobby

The second stage of the history of transport policy corresponds to the period between 1983 and 1989 when, for the first time, the car became linked to public and environmental health problems, damaging its hitherto positive policy image. The groups which had been engaged in disrupting the highway inquiry process were joined by a number of environmental groups, such as the 'Campaign for Lead Free Air' (CLEAR) and Friends of the Earth. In addition, the new information which had become available concerning the environmental impact of the motor car on issues such as global warming and ozone depletion attracted the attention of 'institutional' environmental interests, such as the statutory standing Royal Commission on Environmental Pollution (RCEP) (see Figure 3.3). These developments combined to pose an unprecedented challenge to the road lobby.

The effect of this challenge was to subject the road lobby to political pressure in multiple policy arenas. For the first time, pressure extended beyond the confines of the highway enquiry process as conflict developed over the environmental impact of the predict and provide orthodoxy and its emphasis on a demand led justification for the expansion of the trunk road network.

In response to this growing pressure the government promoted a number of technical solutions to these 'problems', enabling them to manage the issue through an issue attention cycle. This, as I shall argue throughout the remainder of this book, has been a strategy adopted by government on a number of occasions when the predict and provide orthodoxy has been challenged (see, in particular, Chapter 4 and Chapter 7). As an example of this management strategy, the next section examines the way in which one particular problem associated with the car in this period, that of lead pollution, was dealt with by government. Technical solutions have generally enabled such challenges to be managed by the government, while the central question of the relationship between the car and the lifestyle choices of society remains unanswered.

Figure 3.3   Location of actors on a policy network continuum (1983-89)

Insiders			Outsiders
core insiders/ specialist insiders	peripheral insiders	outsider by goal	outsider by choice
British Roads Federation			
AA/RAC (users)		Transport 2000	
			Friends of the Earth
Construction interests			ALARM UK
	Royal Commission on Environmental Pollution	Campaign for Lead Free Air	
Society of Motor Manufacturers and Traders			

The Issue Attention Cycle and Transport Policy: The Lead in Petrol Case[5]

As outlined in Chapter 1, the issue attention cycle is made up of five clearly separable stages, which the transport issue followed in the early 1980s in relation to lead pollution: the *pre problem stage*; *alarmed discovery and euphoric optimism*; *realising the cost of significant progress*; *gradual decline of intense public interest*; and the *post problem stage*.

In the transport case the first stage corresponded to the period from the late 1970s until the early 1980s, before road vehicles were identified as 'a major source of the lead pollution implicated in the damage to human health' (McCormick, 1991, p. 136). Lead in petrol first emerged as a specialist issue in 1971 when the Chief Medical Officer to the UK government recommended that atmospheric lead levels should not be allowed to increase any further and the British government agreed to a phased reduction of lead in petrol from 0.84 grams per litre to 0.4 g/l over a 10 year period (McCormick, 1991, pp. 136-37). At this time the lead issue remained under the control of a core policy community and public interest was limited.

The second stage focused on the publication of the 9th Report of the statutory Royal Commission on Environmental Pollution in April 1983 (Cmnd 8852), entitled *Lead in the Environment*. This report had two primary functions: a comprehensive study of the effect of lead in the environment, covering the effect on human health and the natural environment; and an evaluation of the methods which could be adopted in order to reduce lead emissions. The Royal Commission identified the road transport sector as the most significant source of lead in the environment at that time, and so it concluded that any policy designed to reduce lead in the environment should focus on removing lead from petrol. The Royal Commission's strategy to offer a technical solution as its principle policy recommendation was based on the view that 'if you take the lead out of petrol then you arrive at 100 per cent of the solution. In such a climate there is no need to offer a lifestyle solution' (Interview, Sir John Houghton, Chair of the RCEP, 6th August 1997).

The Royal Commission's report marked a watershed as, for the first time, the policy image of road transport was subjected to exogenous pressure and *alarmed discovery* by the public. Within half an hour of the publication of the Royal Commission's report the government had announced that it would begin negotiations with the European Commission to remove the minimum permitted levels of lead in petrol, and ultimately to lobby for the introduction of cars which would run on unleaded petrol. Pressure groups such as Transport 2000 and CLEAR used scientific reports in order to foster a new, negative policy image for the car.[6]

The satisfaction of the immediate demands of the anti-roads groups contributed to the decline of public interest in the issue of lead in petrol. With the government agreeing to phase out the use of lead in petrol by the end of the decade, and with the cost to the average motorist only £10 per year, the impetus for further change evaporated (Vogel, 1986, p. 68. See Cm 552, pp. 2-3 for details of the government's initiatives).

During stage three, *realising the cost of significant progress*, the government ensured that the problem remained defined in such a way that it only required a 'quick fix' technical solution. Consequently, the government were able to instigate the fourth stage, the *gradual decline of public interest*, and thus contain the demands of those elements of the environmental movement which saw the removal of lead in petrol as only the first step in a process which should result in fundamental changes to the lifestyles of road transport users. Thus, no actors were able to provoke a strategic rethink of the future of transport policy or to capture the public's imagination and the issue rapidly progressed through stages three and four of the cycle.[7]

Finally, the issue attention cycle was completed and the transport issue entered the *post problem stage*. Downs argues that during an issue attention cycle a number of policies, institutions or programmes may have been created which aimed to solve the problem; thus once a problem has completed an issue attention cycle it is likely to sporadically reoccur, either attached to another problem or propelled there by one of the vested interests which were created when the problem previously enjoyed issue salience (1973. pp. 65-66). This pattern of events indeed developed in the Major era, although not until after the implementation of the initial stages of a significantly expanded roads programme which the Thatcher government announced in 1989, through the *Roads for Prosperity* White Paper (Cm 693).

Transport Policy in 1989: The Roads For Prosperity Programme

Following the conflict over the environmental implications of road transport in the mid-1980s, a period of apparent stability developed at the end of the decade with central government reasserting a strong commitment to the predict and provide orthodoxy and to the strategic importance of road building:

> Effective transport is a vital element of economic growth and prosperity. The continuing advance of our economy requires progressive development of the motorway and trunk road network. Now is the time for a large step forward. A major extension of the Government's programme for building and improving inter-urban roads is being put in hand to meet the forecast

needs of traffic into the next century. The Government is committed to taking the programme forward as a matter of urgency. (Cm 693, para. 52)

This programme was developed in response to the *National Road Traffic Forecasts* of 1989, which predicted that traffic levels would grow by between 83% and 142% by the year 2025 (DTp 1989a). Thus, government itself was instrumental in outlining the nature of the problem of congestion. In response to these figures the government launched an expanded roads programme, *Roads for Prosperity* (Cm 693), presenting itself as the catalyst for the development of the solution designed to overcome the problem. Once more the pro-roads groups regained a central role in policy making as the priorities of central government and the road lobby coincided:

> Clearly that [*Roads for Prosperity*] was a watershed for this organisation because it was a lot of what had been asked for. And it was an acceptance of many of the things that the organisation had been saying throughout the late 1980s and was, at the time, a significant change. (Interview, Paul Everitt, BRF, 21st August 1996)

A number of explanations for the *Roads for Prosperity* initiative have been identified by the interviewees during this research. Paul Everitt of the BRF identified a combination of factors which exerted pressure on central government, including the growth in car ownership, industry lobbying and the impact of the media:

> I guess, one because of the late 1980s boom: the growth in car ownership, or certainly in car registrations, in road traffic generally, grew at phenomenal rates. They were growing at more than five and ten per cent per annum during a three to four year period. At the same time many of the messages that were being put across by the British Road Federation were being recognised and echoed by large numbers of organisations across the business [community]: through the CBI, engineering employers, a whole range of organisations who were into growth expansion. We have to have the capacity, we have to have the new infrastructure down. I think at the same time that we got good press. The press was full of stories about how congested the road network was; how little had been done to improve it; you know, why schemes had been languishing in the planning process for twenty years ... So the BRF was, during a period in the late 1980s, in direct opposition to government because it was saying, 'spend, spend more money' and they were saying, 'we don't want to spend any more money'. So, in terms of the media resonance it was much more interesting because

there you have a pillar of business establishment criticising government: it is a much more interesting story. (Interview, 21st August 1996)

A senior transport consultant interviewed for this book also identified a number of factors, sharing the BRF's emphasis on the importance of growing car ownership. However, in contrast to the focus of the BRF on the importance of lobbying and the media, he argued that the priorities of the Thatcher government, especially in reducing levels of bureaucracy, had an important spillover effect for the road programme:

> Part of the dynamics of the late eighties was that there shouldn't be congestion of any sort, whether it was bureaucratic, paper congestion or road congestion. It should all be efficient and free flowing: you should be able to get from A to B with the minimum of cost and inconvenience. (Interview information, February 1996)

Following the publication of *Roads for Prosperity*, the policy process appeared once more to re-establish clear demarcation lines between insider and outsider groups and to conform to the model in Figure 3.2 (see above). But the apparent stability of the policy sector at this time was misleading. The road lobby had been subjected to sustained exogenous pressure and differing conceptions of the future had, for the first time, evolved as a source of conflict in the transport sector:

> There surely must come a point, however, when the environmental problems associated with high levels of car ownership – an increase in greenhouse gases, physical congestion, destruction of habitat for road building, the finite nature of oil resources for running and producing cars, etc. – increase to a point where ideology must give way to the demands of the environment movement. (Robinson, 1992, p. 191)

Also, it became clear almost immediately that the scale of the congestion problem outlined by the government's traffic projections could not be solved by the proposed *Roads for Prosperity* programme. In particular, studies by Friends of the Earth and the BRF both aimed to evaluate the extent to which future road provision would accommodate the projected growth in road traffic: both studies reached very similar conclusions.

The Friends of the Earth study examined the effect of the projected rise in UK traffic levels on the motorway network (McLaren and Higman, 1993 cited in Cm 2674, paras 6.26-6.27). The FoE survey focused on 'the situation at the automated national traffic census points ... which are selected to represent free-flowing traffic conditions and do not therefore include the most congested sections of the motorway' (Cm 2674, para. 6.26). According to the FoE survey, even at these points there was considerable congestion at 14 of the 29 census points in 1989. Furthermore, by 2025, even assuming that all of the extensions to the road network envisaged in *Roads for Prosperity* were fully implemented, 'there would be chronic congestion at all but one of the 29 points' (Cm 2674, para. 6.26). Finally, the FoE study calculated the scale of extensions to the road network which would be necessary in order to accommodate the projected traffic increases and ensure that chronic congestion was prevented. Its conclusions were that on the M1 between Luton and the M25, to take the most extreme example, the road would need to be widened to ten lanes in each direction (CM 2674, para. 6.27). Overall, the conclusion of the FoE study was that the programme of road building which the government had outlined in *Roads for Prosperity* was insufficient to sustain the predict and provide orthodoxy, and that very real doubts must exist of the capacity of central government to sustain the orthodoxy at all in the long term.

The British Road Federation was also concerned with the capacity of the trunk road network to accommodate future traffic growth (Centre for Economics and Business Research, 1994). 'The conclusion reached was that, if expenditure on the trunk road programme continues at the present level, congestion will increase by 14% between 1993 and 2010 and the average speed of traffic will fall by 5%. Even with a 50% increase in expenditure on the trunk road programme, it was calculated that congestion would increase by 7% and speeds fall by 3%' (Cm 2674, para. 6.28). Thus, both studies illustrated that the expansion of the road programme envisaged in *Roads for Prosperity* would not be sufficient to accommodate predicted traffic growth, and both posed a serious challenge to the long term stability of the predict and provide orthodoxy.

In a theoretical sense the *Roads for Prosperity* initiative can thus be described as, what Dunleavy has termed a 'policy disaster' (see Dunleavy, 1995 and Grant, 1997). According to Dunleavy, a policy disaster can be identified as 'a large scale, avoidable policy mistake' which is 'eminently foreseeable – but decision-makers systematically choose to ignore an abundance of critical or warning voices in order to persevere with their chosen policy' (Dunleavy, 1995, p. 52).

The simultaneous publication of the *National Road Traffic Forecasts* and the government's *Roads for Prosperity* initiative conform to the criteria which Dunleavy has outlined. Firstly, it is reasonable to assume that policy makers should have been aware that the proposed road programme would not be able to ameliorate the anticipated growth in road traffic. Thus, it was clear that the proposal was inadequate to solve the problem:

> 'Roads for Prosperity' was the last symbol of the old orthodoxy. It appeared to be justified by the 1989 road traffic forecasts which preceded it, but actually the 1989 forecasts, having as it were launched roads for prosperity, then immediately undermined it. (Interview, Phil Goodwin, SACTRA, 20th June 1997)

Secondly, it should have been clear to policy makers that the extent of the imbalance was such that the anti-roads groups would almost inevitably derive great benefit politically. Thus, government decision makers should have foreseen that *Roads for Prosperity* would strengthen the campaigns of the anti-roads groups and enable them to argue that it was not possible to accommodate the government's own projections within a sustainable expansion of the road network:

> I think the government at that particular moment saw there to be votes in roads, so they had the biggest programmes that they'd ever had, but the reality was that they'd already had a fairly substantial road programme, they always knew those things were going to require attention, they just hadn't ever, perhaps, published them in quite the same way with quite so much attention. So, yes, I think the government's own pride in it made it a very tempting target. (Interview, Paul Everitt, BRF, 21st August 1996)

Thus, the government's own forecasts, and its proposed solution, unwittingly aided the opposition of the anti-roads groups. The anti-roads groups were further aided by the publication of the BRF report mentioned above, which compounded the sense that *Roads for Prosperity* was a government instigated policy disaster. According to Phil Goodwin of the SACTRA committee, the conclusions of the BRF report:

> [were] interpreted by the BRF at the time as being a very powerful argument in favour of additional road building because if one didn't have a very big, much expanded road programme, congestion [would get worse which would] effect economic growth and so on. What actually the report demonstrated though, was under the *Roads to Prosperity* roads programme, still extant at the time, congestion would actually get a bit worse every year. And even if the roads programme were increased by 50% ... congestion would still get a bit worse every year; though not so quickly on their calculations. ... Now, the fact that it was the British Roads Federation demonstrating that the largest conceivable roads programme wasn't actually going to make congestion better (was only going to slow down the pace at

which it got worse) was an absolutely decisive part of the argument in then casting doubt on the whole strategy of which capacity construction was a core. (Interview, 20th June 1997)

In spite of the appearance of a return to the pattern of policy making which had predominated the post-war period, the events in 1989 were thus important in providing the basis for the conflict which would develop in the Major era. 'The scene was set, therefore, for another series of set piece battles between the two adversarial communities, and it could be argued that the rivalry between the two communities took on increasingly the characteristics of a "dialogue of the deaf"' (Dudley and Richardson, 1995, p. 27).

Transport Policy in the 1990s: Towards a 'New Politics' of Transport?[8]

The Major era saw a number of developments which had an important impact on the agenda setting process. A key development was the emergence of a coherent challenge to the hitherto dominant transport orthodoxy, centred around a debate over the obligation which society ought to have to future generations. Transport policy, it was argued, should follow the broader aim of government policy, which is to focus on 'development that meets the needs of the present without compromising the ability of future generations to meet their own needs' (Cm 2426, para. 26.18). This marked a significant change from the earlier periods of transport history in which, as I have argued, obligations to future generations were conceived of only on the basis of the provision of demand based services. This change coincided with a number of other changes in the Major era which I outline here before evaluating them in greater detail in the remainder of the book.

Firstly, the number of actors actively involved in the conflict over roads policy increased considerably during the 1990s. This growth in the numbers of groups opposing the road programme increased the political pressure on decision makers, while the increase in the scope of the opposition to the road programme changed the nature of that opposition. Groups such as Council for the Protection of the Rural Environment (CPRE) or the National Trust are quasi-insider groups (representing a 'twinset and pearls' membership, and thus taking the roads issue to a much more important political strata electorally) which have historically had good access to policy makers. At the other end of the spectrum, the direct action movements enabled the anti-roads groups to exploit the opportunities presented by actors which resort to extra-legal activity (see Figure 3.4. I explore the impact of these changes fully in Chapter 5).

Secondly, in the Major era the anti-roads groups were increasingly successful at infiltrating a number of institutional venues such as the media, and the construction sites, thus enabling them to operate in forums in which the insider groups were not dominant.[9] This marked an important contrast with the past, when the only institutional arena which was open to the anti-roads groups was the highway inquiry process, itself closely controlled by the pro-roads groups (Dudley and Richardson have written a number of extremely valuable contributions from this perspective, for example (1996) and (1998). See also Chapter 5).

Figure 3.4   Location of actors on policy network continuum (Major period)

Insiders   **Outsiders**

◄──►

| core insiders | specialist insiders | peripheral insiders | outsider by goal | outsider by choice |

Pro-roads groups   *Anti-roads groups*

British Roads Federation   CPRE   ALARM UK   Dongas

AA/RAC   Construction   Friends of
(car users)   interests   the Earth

road haulage
  sector

Transport 2000
National Trust

Society of Motor
Manufacturers and Traders

Thirdly, the direct action movements engaged in a new form of transport protest which resulted in the act of protest becoming news in, and of, itself. These campaigns changed the profile of the transport issue in the eyes of editors: transport became interesting, and was no longer seen as a dull, routine or technical issue. This was extremely important for the 'moderate' groups, such as Transport 2000, who were able to gain unprecedented access via the media to the general public to inform them of their proposals.

The impact of the direct action campaigns illustrates that effective opposition by outsider groups needs the support of groups which are willing to resort to extra-legal means (see discussion of Cobb and Elder, 1972, in Chapter 2). Communicating through the media, the direct action groups were able to challenge both the need for a road in the first place *and* its proposed route in a way which had not been open to objectors operating through the highway inquiry process (Levin, 1979. See also Chapter 5).

Overall then, a number of changes occurred in the nature of the conflict between the insider and outsider groups. In addition, a number of fortuitous parallel developments, independent of the activity of the anti-roads groups but acting to their benefit, increased the impact of the opposition to roads in this period.

Firstly, the pattern of Parliamentary politics was particularly important in the Major era. Major's small majority following the general election in 1992, combined with the vulnerability of a number of Conservative seats in the south-east of England, in particular, resulted in a series of 'Not In My Constituency' campaigns by MPs attempting to secure local support in the face of the parliamentary party. Such actions were an important factor in the cancellation of the proposed M25 widening and of a number of bypass schemes. However, as I argue in Chapter 5, the actions of these MPs were not indicative of any sea-change in government policy but were based on short term perceptions of personal electoral gain. Thus, the actions of these MPs merely responded to a need to secure the support of middle class voters and did not indicate more broad support for the objectives of the protests.

Secondly, transport increasingly came to be seen as a policy problem. In the last ten to fifteen years the problems associated with transport such as congestion and vehicle related air pollution have become more serious. In addition, both expert and public knowledge about the environmental effects of transport increased immeasurably: this has in part identified a series of new policy problems, such as global warming. These new policy problems have created an impetus for new solutions which the anti-roads groups have exploited. As Kingdon (1995) argues, problems tend to develop as a result of events which are independent of the actions of groups. This has proven to be true in the transport case (see Chapter 4 for an examination of these developments).

Thirdly, the anti-roads groups also benefited from a significant policy disaster by central government. In 1989, as we have seen, the government produced both the *National Road Traffic Forecasts* (DTp 1989a) and an expanded roads programme, *Roads for Prosperity* (Cm 693). The legacy of these initiatives was to make it clear that the scale of the problem which the government identified in its traffic projections could not in anyway be solved by the proposed programme, a fact of great benefit to the campaigns of the anti-roads groups.

These anti-roads groups gained a further boost following the publication of the SACTRA report, *Trunk Roads and the Generation of Traffic*, in 1994, which argued that new roads could induce extra traffic journeys (SACTRA, 1994). Their opposition thereby gained the tacit support of a quasi-governmental actor, further challenging the credibility of the predict and provide model.

Finally, the anti-roads groups benefited from a number of systemic developments (Sabatier and Jenkins-Smith, 1993a) which reduced the control of the Department of Transport over policy. These overspill pressures resulted from three main sources: the Department of Environment, global environmental forums (in particular those surrounding the Climate Change Convention), and the Treasury. In the five to ten years culminating in the Major period the Department of the Environment and the Department of Transport became increasingly divided, as the Department of the Environment became progressively concerned with the impact of deregulated transport policy on the issues such as land-use planning, deteriorating ambient air quality and sustainable development (see Chapter 4).

The internationalisation of environmental policy following the climate change conference at Rio also put pressure on the UK government to provide a series of policy initiatives to reduce transport's contribution to global warming. This escalated the division and conflict between the the Department of the Environment and the Department of Transport and prevented the Department of Transport from maintaining autonomy over transport policy making.

The Treasury, too, continued to have a considerable systemic impact (Dudley and Richardson, 1996a). Since the election of Thatcher in 1979 a key objective of all governments has been to reduce state spending (Thain and Wright, 1995, p. 439). In the Major era the cuts to the roads programme were rationalised by an impending general election and the growth of a pan-European consensus on the need to control government spending in order to meet the convergence criteria for monetary union (Chapter 6).

Overall, the transport agenda, on the surface, became increasingly volatile in the Major era. A number of developments occurred which may explain this increasing instability, and examination of these developments has enabled me to provide a series of working hypotheses which I will investigate in the remainder of the book:

- Firstly, that the increasing diversity and scope of the opposition to the road programme has led to the increasing salience of the transport issue.
- Secondly, that the anti-roads groups have used and exploited a number of alternative arenas in order to pressure government and promote their objectives.

However, although both of these developments are significant, they do not alone provide a sufficiently comprehensive explanation. A genuinely comprehensive account of political change in the Major and Blair eras must also acknowledge that changes to the political landscape have been instrumental in enabling the anti-roads groups to become more effective. These have occurred on a number of levels:

- Firstly, the problems – or the perception of the problems – associated with transport have got worse: congestion is rising; ambient air quality is deteriorating; global warming has been 'discovered'.
- Secondly, the government has itself acted as an 'unwitting policy entrepreneur'. The government's 1989 traffic forecasts and the accompanying road programme provided an implicit acknowledgement that government policy could not solve the transport problem.
- Finally, a series of overspill pressures have reduced the operational autonomy of the pro-roads groups.

All of these explanations assume that change to the policy agenda has been extensive in the Major and Blair eras and so I will also explore this view.

Conclusion

This chapter has reflected on the dynamics of transport policy making in the twentieth century. I have argued that for much of the period until the early 1980s policy was dominated by a strong government orthodoxy based on the predict and provide model. The road lobby has gained considerable legitimacy in the eyes of government from its association with this orthodoxy. However, in spite of it being a beneficiary of systematic luck in this way, I have argued that the capacity of the road lobby to secure favourable policy outcomes has in fact been generally conditional on favourable exogenous developments, as transport policy as a whole has been of low political salience in comparison to other issues such as health or education. In particular, following the loss of control of the road fund to the Treasury the road lobby has had to rely on increasing congestion in order to rationalise investment in the road programme, resulting in relatively low levels of state spending on roads until the 1960s.

Since the mid-1980s, the opposition to the road programme has become more coherent. Initially, this opposition was unable to challenge the dominant orthodoxy of central government, which continued to manage the agenda through issue attention cycles by the promotion of a series of technical fixes designed to support the predict and provide model. However, from the beginning of the Major era, the challenges to such a model have become more focused, and an alternative discourse has developed on the basis of sustainable development which has posed a fundamental challenge to the dominance of the predict and provide orthodoxy.

Notes

1   The Buchanan report, *Traffic in Towns*, was published in 1963 (Buchanan Committee, 1963) and was, at that time, 'the most far-reaching and influential survey yet published of the impact of the motor vehicle on its environment and the way it might be controlled' (Plowden, 1971, p. 353). The report aimed to suggest ways of balancing the door-to-door flexibility offered by motor vehicles and the environmental costs which they were imposing on urban life (Buchanan Committee, 1963, para. 42). 'This was far from an anti-motorist tract; on the contrary, it aimed at maximising the pleasures both of a civilised urban environment and of motor vehicles (and has been criticised for assuming that private transport was inevitable)' (Plowden, 1971, pp. 354-55).

2   For discussion of the network approach see, for example, Marsh and Rhodes, 1992a, Rhodes and Marsh, 1992, Jordan, 1990, Döhler, 1991, and Dowding, 1994 and 1995.

3   Although conflict did occur during the 1970s and 1980s between the road lobby and
         the anti-roads groups this did not destabilise the cohesion of the core policy network
         surrounding roads, and the interests of the road lobby were protected. I argue below
         that it was not until the Major era that the anti-roads groups were able to mount a
         sustained challenge to either the ideas orthodoxy which had dominated policy or to
         the institutional relationship between the road lobby and central government.

4   I explore the impact of the direct action movement in Chapter 5.

5   For a detailed summary of the controversy surrounding the role of different actors in
         this case refer to McCormick, 1991, Chapter 7.

6   There is considerable dispute within the literature concerning how the agenda was
         set in this case. Des Wilson (1984) identifies the role of the single issue campaigning
         group CLEAR. Richard Southwood, Chairman of the RCEP, claims that the RCEP's
         report was the key (cited in McCormick, 1991, p. 138). Other scholars identify the
         crucial role of the EU at a systemic level and of developments in the German
         political system (see McCormick, 1991, pp. 136-40 for a summary of this
         discussion).

7   Strong parallels exist between the issue of lead in petrol and the issue of dust on the
         roads in the early 1900s. At this time, as with the lead in petrol issue, the road lobby
         was able to suggest a quick-fix solution which ameliorated against any serious
         challenge to the lifestyle implications of growing car dependency.

8   The analysis in the remainder of this chapter is necessarily brief because the aim of
         this book is to examine this period of the history of transport policy in detail.

9   The conceptualisation of institutional venues is drawn from the work of
         Baumgartner and Jones, who argue that policy makers will aim to 'seek out new
         venues that they hope will be more favourable to their views'. These venues can be
         both physical, such as the construction sites, or more ethereal, such as the mass
         media (see Baumgartner and Jones, 1991, pp. 1052-55).

4 Problem Centred Models of Agenda Setting

We're a five car family
We got what it takes
Eight thousand cc
Four different makes

One each for the kids
I run two
One for the missus
When there's shopping to do

Cars are Japanese of course
Subaru and Mazda
And the Nissan that the missus takes
Nippin down to Asda

We're a load of noisy parkers
We never do it neat
Drive the neighbours crazy
When we take up half the street

Unleaded petrol?
That's gotta be a joke
Stepping on the gas we like
The smoke to make you choke

Carbon monoxide
Take a deep breath
Benzine dioxide
Automanic death

'Cos it's all about noise
And it's all about speed
And it's all about power
And it's all about greed

And it's all about fantasy
And it's all about dash
And it's all about machismo
And it's all about cash

And it's all about blood
And it's all about gore
And it's all about oil
And it's all about war

And it's all about money
And it's all about spend
And it's all about time
That it came to an end.
(McGough, 1993, pp. 40-42)

Introduction

In the Major era, transport increasingly came to be seen as a policy problem on three key levels: public health; congestion, and lifestyle, marking a significant change from the Thatcher period. Problem centred models of agenda setting argue that changes such as these are likely to have a negative effect on the policy image of an issue, and thus form an important element of any explanation of policy change. This chapter explores this hypothesis and evaluates the impact of each of these changes in the transport case.

Firstly, knowledge increased of the effects of transport on public health. In particular, transport became linked with increases in respiratory diseases, such as childhood asthma, thus eroding the positive policy image of motor vehicles as they became associated with damage to public health in a highly emotive manner.

In response to this increasing knowledge of the effects of transport on public health the government developed a twin track strategy in order to manage the policy agenda. First, it introduced a number of 'technical fixes', designed to manage the problem through an issue attention cycle. The government introduced a legislative framework for the reduction of emissions from the road transport sector which improved air quality, protected the policy image of road transport and mitigated against demands for widespread changes to transport behaviour.[1] Second, central government attempted to devolve responsibility for reducing traffic levels and the health related problems of road transport to local authorities. The rationale for this, according to central government, was that in spite of the national framework which it had introduced to reduce vehicle emissions, local 'hotspots' were likely to persist which would be best dealt with at a local level (Cm 3587, p. 58, para. 2). However, my analysis challenges the explanation offered by central government, arguing that its primary motive was to manage the policy agenda, in this case by attempting to displace it to local government.[2]

Secondly, a fundamental change also occurred in the Major era as transport came to be seen as a problem on the grounds of congestion, which affected both economic development and the quality of urban and rural life. This perception became more acute following government forecasts which predicted traffic growth of between 83% and 142% between 1989 and 2025 (DTp, 1989a). Following publication of these figures, policy makers became concerned that the scale of the projected increases in traffic levels could not be accommodated in the long term through the provision of sufficient infrastructure. This enabled the anti-roads groups to challenge the whole rationale of the road programme and, more broadly, of the predict and provide model: both of which, according to the protesters, were unable to accommodate projected future traffic growth (Chapter 3).

The credibility of the predict and provide model was further damaged by the publication of a report by the quasi-governmental Standing Advisory Committee on Trunk Roads Assessment (SACTRA) in 1994. This report investigated the impact of new road building on traffic generation and concluded that new roads would generate at least some additional journeys. However, the political impact of this report was arguably considerably more significant than its findings justified. Critics of the predict and provide model were able to argue that it was internally flawed and thus the model was heavily discredited, especially in media discussion of transport policy. Overall, the effect of the SACTRA report was to compound the policy disaster which central government had committed with the publication of the *National Road Traffic Forecasts* and the *Roads for Prosperity* programme in 1989, discussed in Chapter 3.

Finally, in the Major era, conflict also developed in relation to lifestyle, especially around the question of whether the transport system *ought* to encourage increases in future levels of mobility or not. On the one hand, concerns about the capacity of the predict and provide model to accommodate future traffic growth were joined by an increased knowledge of environmental problems, such as global warming, both serving to increase the pressure on national governments to reduce mobility. On the other hand, structural changes to the economy reduced the capacity of policy makers to restrain mobility: distances between home and work have increased; out of town retail and leisure developments have become widespread; and 'just in time delivery' has become common place – all of which have required increased mobility.

In contrast to their management of the effects of transport on public health, the Major government had considerable difficulties in responding to the problems associated with congestion and lifestyle. In the short term, they followed a policy of political inertia, launching a policy review which culminated in the transport Green Paper, *Transport: the Way Forward* (Cm 3234), and implementing annual cuts to the road budget which significantly reduced the scale of the roads for prosperity programme. These actions indicate that government was unable or unwilling to deal with the problems of congestion or lifestyle in the short term. The explanation for this apparent policy inertia is provided by the analysis in Chapter 3, which argues that, historically, policy in the UK has been based on the structural imperatives of the state which have emphasised a strong link between transport, mobility, economic development and lifestyle through the operation of the predict and provide orthodoxy.

However, in analysis of the Major era the focus of policy has become much more difficult to rationalise as a result of the challenge to the predict and provide model which stemmed from a combination of the policy disaster by central government in 1989 and the findings of the SACTRA report in 1994. These developments closed off the option of widespread strategic road building which had, up until this point, served as a 'technical fix' designed to retain control over the policy agenda.

In the Major era, conflict over the predict and provide orthodoxy created considerable instability in the agenda setting process as actors fought over the development of a new policy orthodoxy designed to replace the old one. The anti-roads groups attempted to undermine the historic link between mobility and economic development and to gain acceptance for an alternative discourse based on sustainable development and low mobility. In contrast, the Major government attempted to develop a new orthodoxy which was still compatible with the old one, focusing on a change from a predict and provide orthodoxy to one based on *restrict and provide*. This aimed to maintain the emphasis on mobility and economic development, while building a consensus on the need to restrict access to the transport network to *essential users* – thus still protecting the policy imperatives of government.

However, despite these changes, for electoral reasons the Major government lacked the political will to implement measures designed to restrict mobility, such as road pricing, which would manage levels of demand on the road network. Consequently, during the Major era access to the road network was simply rationed by congestion in the short term and no long term solution was tabled which could both maintain the policy imperatives of government and gain the support of the electorate.

Overall, therefore, these focal problems of health, congestion and lifestyle enable an examination of the full scope of the agenda dynamics which operated in the Major era with regard to problem centred accounts of policy change. They provide examples of agenda management and highlight the importance both of Downs' work on issue attention cycles and of government intervention designed to protect the link between economic development and mobility and the positive image of road transport. These considerations enable us to recognise that the government has structural imperatives which it will attempt to vigorously defend.

Road Transport, Air Pollution and Public Health

> We [the Royal Commission on Environmental Pollution] are concerned that the present use of road vehicles may be causing serious damage to human health by triggering or exacerbating respiratory symptoms and by exposing people to carcinogens from vehicle emissions. The situation should therefore be regarded as unsustainable. Despite the many uncertainties about the effects of transport pollutants on human health and the environment, there is a clear case, on the basis of what is already known, for increasing the precautionary action taken to improve air quality. (Cm 2674, para. 3.43)

In the Major era transport became identified as a significant contributor to deteriorating public health. Transport has replaced industrial activity and domestic coal burning as the predominant source of many pollutants: 'In many areas, particularly urban, they have become the dominant source of air pollution emissions' (Cm 3587, p. 43). This rise in the contribution of the road transport sector to air pollution is explained by increases in levels of vehicle ownership and usage up until the late 1980s. In the Major era, however, a significant paradox developed, in which public concern with the effects of transport on public health grew at a time when, according to government statistics, the emissions of many vehicle-related pollutants had actually fallen (Cm 3587, p. 45).

This paradox may be resolved by the fact that, in the same period, knowledge of the effect of these pollutants on public health increased significantly. In an interview Tony Bosworth, air quality campaigner for Friends of the Earth, outlined the nature of this change:

> We are developing a lot of knowledge about health impacts. It's a very, very rapidly moving field. If you just take particulates – in 1992 the Chairman of one of the Department of Health's leading committees, to the press, Steven Holdgate, was saying 'particle levels are low and not thought to pose a significant danger to health'. In 1994, he is saying, 'there is convincing evidence for a link between particle levels and mortality rates'. In 1995, the government is saying 'we accept that there are very close statistical links between particle levels and death rates' and particulates are now the number one air pollution problem from transport. That is an indication of the speed at which knowledge is moving. It's not that three or four years ago, five years ago, whatever, that everything was being swept under the carpet – to some extent it might have been – but it's just moving so quickly that we are only now discovering what the real problems are. (Interview, 12th December 1995)

In the Major era, a number of studies by scientific experts emphasised the significance of road transport as a source of emissions (see for example, DoH, 1995a, 1995b). As Table 4.1 (on the following page) indicates, the significance of transport emissions varies between different types of chemicals and depends on the 'level of other sources, the amount and type of traffic and the degree of congestion. Moreover, the source of pollution can vary considerably from these figures during a smog episode. For example, during winter episodes in most major UK cities the dominant contribution to PM10 levels comes from road traffic (notably from diesel powered vehicles), increasing from about a quarter to in excess of 70%' (Cm 3587, p. 44). Thus, the following figures are indicative of the typical contribution of road transport to national emissions, with peak levels being much higher.

These figures clearly establish the importance of transport as a source of emissions, particularly in urban areas in which transport, for many of the pollutants identified, exceeds 75% of all emissions. In the Major era the knowledge concerning the effects of these transport related emissions on public health also increased significantly, with the recognition that they could damage the respiratory system, hinder the functioning of the brain and cause the development of leukaemias and cancers (see Table 4.1 overleaf). Of all of these, arguably the most significant factor affecting the agenda setting process has been the impact of vehicle emissions on the respiratory system.

Transport and Asthma: Public Concern Without Scientific Evidence

> One of the things which has really started changing is the link being drawn
> between transport emissions and health. That is starting to really get to
> people. We are now talking about one in seven children in the country
> suffering from asthma. And asthma is costing the country a billion pounds a
> year. We're estimating that particulate pollution might be leading to the
> aggregate premature deaths of 10,000 people a year in England and Wales.
> When you start talking to people about health impacts of vehicles and
> transport you're really starting to hit home, very, very, very hard. It's
> something which concerns people. Everybody knows, or has in the family,
> or knows a kid with asthma. When you can start making those very personal
> links, family links, that really does start changing things. I think that is
> probably the one thing, more than anything else, which has happened over
> the last few years which has really started to change. (Interview, Tony
> Bosworth, FoE, 12th December 1995)

A common trend throughout the developed world has been an
increase in the *prevalence* of asthma (i.e. the number of registered
asthmatics), particularly amongst children. These trends have been
reflected in the UK. A 1994 report by the Joseph Rowntree Foundation,
Trends in Applications to the Family Fund, showed that since 1983 there
had been a fivefold increase in the number of families applying for
disability grants for children with severe asthma (cited in Cm 2674, para.
3.23).

The *incidence* of asthma (i.e. the number of recorded asthma attacks)
has also shown a considerable increase since the 1970s. The 18th report of
the RCEP, *Transport and the Environment*, published in 1994, and a
Department of Health report, *Asthma: An Epidemiological Overview*,
provided data which indicated the scope of the problem: between 1976 and
1993, acute asthma attacks rose more than fivefold in England and Wales,
rising from 10.7 per to 50.32 per 100,000 patients a week (Cm 2674,
para 3.24 and DoH, 1995a, p. 2). 'The greatest increase [during the period
1976 to 1987] was in children (from 13.5 to 74.4 per 100,000 in the 0-4 age
group and from 17.4 to 58.9 in the 5-14 age group)' (Cm 2674, para. 3.24).
These increases in both the prevalence and incidence of asthma have
created pressures from a problem centred perspective as public alarm has
grown (Grant, 1995, p. 172):

> There is this sort of tick list of items that are likely to push a policy issue up
> the agenda and in the public consciousness. One is illness to children;
> another is for example cancer. Illness to children obviously is highly

Table 4.1   Contribution of road transport to UK emissions and their effect on public health

	Contribution from road transport			Suspected health effect
	1995 National emissions (k tonnes)	% of national emissions	% of emissions in London	
Benzene	39	67%	not available	Carcinogen, causing for example leukaemia (Cm 2674, para. 3.21-3.22)
1,3-Butadiene	10	77%	not available	Carcinogen, causing cancers and leukaemia (Cm 2674, para. 3.21-3.22)
CO	5478	75%	99%	Reduces oxygen supply, causing angina attacks, reducing mental activity and hand-eye co-ordination (Cm 3587, p. 100)
Lead	1.47	78%	not available	Damage to nervous system, kidneys, reproductive system. Effects pronounced in children. (Cm 3587, p. 107)
Nox	2295	46%	76%	Respiratory diseases: especially rising *prevalence* and *incidence* of asthma (Cm 2674, para. 3.23-3.24; Cm 3587, p. 114)

	Contribution from road transport			Suspected health effect
	1995 National emissions (k tonnes)	**% of national emissions**	**% of emissions in London**	
PM10	232	26%	not available	Respiratory diseases: especially rising *prevalence* and *incidence* of asthma and mortality (Cm 2674, para. 3.23-3.30; Cm 3587, pp. 152, 154-55). Total health costs estimated at between £10.53bn and £26.11bn per annum, 1995 prices (Cm 3587, p. 186).
Black smoke	356	50%	94%	
SO₂	2365	2%	22%	Acid rain and rising incidence of asthma. N.B. transport is of relatively low significance in this area (Cm 3587, p. 161)
VOC	2337	29%	97%	Involved in chemical reaction which causes rise in ground level ozone (see below)
Ozone	Caused from chemical reaction between other substances, especially NOx and VOC			Inflammation of airway; breathing difficulties following exercise (Cm 2674, para. 3.20; Cm 3587, p. 128). Total estimated cost of damage £4.34bn-£4.52bn 1995 prices (Cm 3587, p. 185)

(see Cm 3587, p. 44 for data)

> emotive, it's an easy symbol of environmental damage or public health damage, and it's one that politicians obviously like to use, as well as other people. The picture of children in smog masks is more striking than an adult in a smog mask, obviously. (Interview information, senior civil servant, DoETR, Air Quality Division, September 1997)

The increase in both the prevalence and incidence of asthma has been an important factor in explaining the rise of transport on the policy agenda, with both public and media being strongly convinced that these increases can be explained by rising vehicle emissions. This has helped to erode the positive policy image of road transport, as the sector is blamed for deteriorating public health. According to Jeremy Vanke of the RAC, the public reaction has been understandable as there is strong evidence that poor air quality may be linked to the rise in the number of asthma attacks:

> If someone is prone to asthma or has asthma the effects will be worse because of poorer air quality. And there again there is a caveat because poor air quality isn't purely the result of car use. There are all sorts of other factors in play. (Interview, 29th May 1996)

Developments in Greenwich, London, in August 1995 provide a good illustration of the interaction between emotion and public health in the transport case. In this case the parents of seven children were granted legal aid to challenge the 'council's decision not to halt traffic when health guide-lines are breached' in spite of the powers granted to them by the 1984 Road Traffic Regulations Act, which enable local councils to close roads when air quality breaches World Health Organisation minimum standards (*Guardian*, 2nd August 1995, p. 4). The aim of the parents' legal challenge was to force councils to close local roads if they believed the health of residents to be at risk. The solicitor for the children made the case's importance clear:

> The council decided the motorist deserved its support more than the local children whose health was being put at risk. We believe they have the power to close roads but the council has closed their minds to the possibility despite the fact that the Government is clearly moving in that direction. (*Guardian*, 2nd August 1995, p. 4)

Although the parents ultimately lost this case it is indicative of the changing nature of, and the conflict over, the future orientation of transport policy and the importance to both the media and the public of the perceived link between transport emissions and public health. However, as Jeremy

Vanke of the RAC has argued, this perception is based largely on emotion and not scientific evidence: 'in terms of public perception there is a mismatch in that the public thinks that pollution from cars is going up and is a serious problem. I don't deny the latter but it is going down quite fast' (Interview, 29th May 1996).

Data contained in the Major government's *National Air Quality Strategy* indicates that since the mid to late 1980s the levels of all of the major pollutants from vehicle emissions have been in absolute decline, following improvements in vehicle and fuel technology (see Cm 3587, especially Chapter 6). Thus, the perception of both the public and the media that emissions from road vehicles are increasing is not in fact borne out by the data.

Further, the public and media perception that such rising emissions are responsible for the increasing prevalence of asthma is not reflected in the findings of a number of scientific studies (see in particular, DoH, 1995b. See Cm 2674, paras 3.23-3.30 for an overview). In fact these investigations have refuted the link between vehicle emissions and rising numbers of asthmatics, suggesting that factors such as deteriorating indoor air quality and increases in the numbers of household dust mites are a more likely explanation:

> If you look at New Zealand, which has some of the best air quality in the world, it also has the highest rate of asthma in the world. Now there are lots and lots of factors at play here. Not least of which is indoor air pollution which is completely excluded from all of this, most of the air we breathe is indoor air, we've seen a tenfold increase in the number of house dust mites over the past decade which is the direct cause of asthma. We see high levels of oxides of nitrogen because of gas cookers and there are all sorts of other factors at play – and just to pin it down, as some people have, to cars, is wrong. There are lots and lots of other potential causes out there. (Interview, Jeremy Vanke, RAC, 29th May 1996)

The scientific community has been almost unanimous in acknowledging that a number of different factors could be responsible for the increasing numbers of asthmatics, leading one expert to describe asthma as a disease caused by 'late twentieth century lifestyles':

> There are lots of different theories about the increasing incidence of asthma, I mean the dust mites, allergens in general is one of them ... Diet is another big favourite. It is absolutely clear that it is a developed world disease. It's to do with something about late twentieth century lifestyles, but it's not pollution. When I mean things to do with late twentieth century lifestyles, if

it was dust mites it would be the increase in wall-to-wall carpeting and central heating. Asthma is going up at the same rate in unpolluted rural areas of Scotland as it is in central London. Also the incidence of asthma in East Germany is far lower than in West Germany, but East Germany is far more polluted. That kind of evidence is coming out, and you know stress is another, or certain types of stress. (Interview information, senior civil servant, DoETR, Air Quality Division, September 1997)

Thus a significant imbalance has developed between the public perception of the impact of vehicle emissions and the conclusions of the scientific community, with the public making a strong link between emissions and rising asthma while the scientific community suggests that the link is weak. The explanation for this imbalance is, according to a number of respondents, explained by a reluctance by the public to admit that personal lifestyle choices are responsible for increasing levels of asthma. Increases in the numbers of dust mites, for example, may suggest that hygiene within the household is inadequate and thus that the public themselves may be responsible for the problem:

People always latch on to things that they don't have to do something about. One of the other frustrating things that we have to deal with, when we are under constant pressure to improve air quality, is that people think that it's the government's responsibility to improve air quality. Now most people spend at least 50, 60, 70 per cent of their time indoors, and mothers or fathers with young children spend up to 90 per cent of their time indoors. Indoor air quality is another issue altogether. And the factors affecting indoor air quality are actually quite different from outdoor air quality, but they're much more difficult to control. But people focus on the outdoor air quality because it's something that someone else is responsible for. (Interview information, senior civil servant, DoETR, Air Quality Division, September 1997)

Overall, in the Major era transport was identified as a significant contributor to deteriorating public health, particularly in media and public opinion. In spite of the scientific knowledge to the contrary, the media and the public remained convinced that vehicle emissions were causing a rise in the number of asthmatics and that the problem would become worse in the future. I will now explore the response by the Major government to these developments.

Transport and Public Health: Agenda Management by the use of Technical Fixes

The response by the Major government to the development of transport as a policy problem on the basis of public health focused on work towards the implementation of the *National Air Quality Strategy* (published in 1997 as Cm 3587 – hereafter NAQS) which contained the following key measures: the use of an EU regulatory framework; devolution of responsibility to local authorities where national measures failed to reduce emissions sufficiently, and the implementation of 'technical fixes'. These measures, according to one senior civil servant, reflected the consensus of the scientific experts and did not result from pressure from the media or public opinion:

> One of the reasons why air pollution has come up the agenda as far as we are concerned is less the public perception – it's more the perception amongst medical experts that there is a health effect of pollution at the levels we're talking about. There's evidence emerging all the time of what those effects are. And it's not just asthma in children, it's the whole range – the carcinogenic pollutants like benzene, there's heart and lung problems, a whole range of things. That we just didn't know about, 10 years ago. (Interview information, senior civil servant, DoETR, Air Quality Division, September 1997)

A primary objective of the NAQS was the setting of air quality targets for 8 primary pollutants, such as benzene, carbon monoxide, nitrogen dioxide and particulates. These targets reflected the conclusions of the Expert Panel on Air Quality Standards, which the government had earlier formed in 1991 in order to advise it on specific figures for air quality standards (Cm 3587, p. 17, para. 13. See p. 20, Table 3.1 of that report for the targets for each pollutant). The aim of the strategy was to achieve the targets by 2005, which the Panel argued was the earliest date by which they could be implemented:

> If many of the objectives are to reflect health-based standards, substantial improvements in vehicle emissions will be required which can only be agreed in the European Community, and on which formal negotiations are not yet concluded. Technology and industrial lead times mean that the improvements the Government supports could not now be implemented and have much effect before the 2005 deadline. (Cm 3587, p. 18, para. 17)

This focus of the NAQS on the setting of targets for emission levels provides evidence to support the view that the strategy of central government was designed to resist solutions which would significantly reduce mobility. The strategy itself acknowledged that transport has become the most significant source of most of the pollutants which it aims to reduce (Cm 3587, 1997, p. 44) yet the Major government rejected the idea of setting specific targets for the transport sector. Targets, according to the strategy, 'could inhibit flexibility and conflict with the aim that reductions in emissions should be achieved by the most cost effective route across the sectors. In addition, sectoral targets ignore the variation in emissions profiles of different regions and locations. Therefore, there will be no separate target for the transport sector' (Cm 3587, p. 46, para. 13).

The NAQS also recognised that many of the effects of air quality were transboundary in nature (Cm 3587, p. 9, paras 1-5). Thus, the development of EU legislation was integral to the development of the strategy and without it there would have been considerable difficulty with achieving the government's objectives for air quality (Cm 3587, p. 9, para. 5):

> We knew that there was going to be European legislation setting air quality targets coming along, so that whatever we had to do, it would be silly to create something that wasn't compatible with that. The second thing, for transboundary pollution, like ozone, you can't solve it at a national level. To solve ozone in the South East of England in particular, you need to reduce emissions in Germany, in Denmark, and the Low Countries. So that's why we say in here [i.e. the NAQS], we want to get to certain levels of ozone but we can't promise to do it because it depends on us persuading everyone else to do it as well. (Interview information, senior civil servant, DoETR, Air Quality Division, September 1997. I explore the impact of EU regulatory policy in more detail in Chapter 6)

The focus within the strategy on developing a legislative framework to reduce emissions also provides evidence that central government intentionally resisted solutions based on lifestyle, which would have challenged the structural imperatives of the state. The primary focus of regulation, as I will discuss in detail in Chapter 6, has been to reduce the impact of road vehicles through improvements in engine technology and fuel quality. The development of a European regulatory framework was supported by the Major government because it helped it to retain control over the policy image of the road transport issue. This solution demonstrates strong parallels between the rise of the vehicle-related asthma concerns in the 1990s and the lead in petrol controversy in the mid-1980s. In both cases a technical solution was evoked to mitigate against widespread policy change affecting lifestyle, the problem was managed through an issue attention cycle and the pro-roads groups were thus able to retain the positive policy image associated with motoring.

The NAQS also identified a key role for local authorities in the development of government policy on air quality. In particular, local authorities were to be responsible for cleaning up 'local hotspots' in areas in which national policy was insufficient:

> What the strategy says is [that], on the whole, air pollution problems will be solved at the national level. That's what it says. And what it also says is that there will remain a few areas which will be local hotspots, and local authorities should be in a position to see what they can do to mop those problems up. If there aren't any ways in which local authorities can deal with it then the government will have to think again about national changes in policy. That's what the strategy says. Whether that's a viable approach remains to be seen. And whether we have underestimated the extent to which national policies won't solve the problem remains to be seen. (Interview information, senior civil servant, DoETR, Air Quality Division, September 1997. I explore the relationship between central government and local government in more detail in Chapter 7)

But, in fact, the Major government's principal aim was to to manage the agenda through the operation of central-local relations. According to the NAQS, local air pollution hotspots are to be tackled by initiatives devised at the local level. However, as I argue in Chapter 7, in order to reduce emissions in these areas local authorities would have to take decisions which reduce the levels of road transport and force people to use alternative modes of transport. Such decisions are likely to prove very unpopular electorally – hence central government's strategy of displacing them to local government.

Overall, the primary focus of the NAQS was to reduce emissions from road vehicles through the implementation of 'technical fixes' (Cm 3587, p. 47, para. 18). According to a number of interviewees, such a focus will actually 'solve the problem' of poor ambient air quality in the short to medium term:

> There will be very soon technical fixes in Britain to deal with local pollutants (and local pollutants are going down from cars), and new technology, that is not far away, will deal with the remaining problems of

cold starts. I am absolutely confident that further advances will reduce that to a minimum. (Interview, Jeremy Vanke, RAC, 29th May 1996)

Thus the successful implementation of the strategy will mean, according to government opinion, that by 2005 all of the major pollutants, apart from in some localised hotspots, would reach emission standards consummate with both the government's Expert Panel on Air Quality Standards and World Health Organisation standards. However, further reflection from the lead in petrol case has led many commentators to challenge this view.

The fuel for motor vehicles requires aromatic components to aid the combustion process and, historically, lead had been used for this. When the use of lead was phased out benzene was deemed to be the most suitable alternative and was therefore added to unleaded petrol. This solution, however, itself caused a number of serious problems which are now manifesting themselves. Button describes this as the inevitable implication of a policy trade-off:

> The removal of lead from petrol to prevent potential brain damage to children, for example, may reduce the harm done by that pollutant but only at the expense of increasing other local atmospheric pollutants, such as benzene (a carcinogen), or at the cost of higher fuel consumption with consequences for carbon dioxide emissions and the depletion of a non-renewable resource. (1995, p. 177)

In the 1990s, a number of reports attempted to respond to the problem of rising benzene and particulate levels from transport related air pollution: in common with developments in the lead in petrol case these tended to emphasise technical solutions. For example, the conclusions of the 1994 House of Commons Transport Select Committee report on *Transport Related Air Pollution in London* (HC 506-I) were dominated by a number of technical solutions. In particular the report called for the phasing out of super-unleaded petrol and improvements to the numbers, efficiency and reliability of catalytic converters, arguing that both these measures would reduce the effects of road transport on public health. These solutions, as with those in the lead in petrol case, aimed to facilitate the completion of another issue attention cycle, protect the interests of the pro-roads groups and mitigate against any coherent challenge to the lifestyle implications of growing traffic levels.

In the same period, however, a number of scientific studies were published which expressed concern that technical fixes might not have the desired effect. In particular, there are doubts that catalytic converters can deliver the health benefits which are predicted. Firstly, although catalytic converters hinder the dispersal of 90% of the benzene levels otherwise released into the atmosphere, as at 1994 only 13% of petrol-engined cars were equipped with this technology (HC 506-I, para. 34). Secondly, according to the 18th report of the Royal Commission on Environmental Pollution, *Transport and the Environment*, catalytic converters may also cause a policy trade-off resulting in increases in low lying ozone:

> Experience in the USA, where three-way catalytic converters have been fitted to cars for some years, shows that reducing emissions of primary pollutants does not always lead to a corresponding reduction in the concentrations of secondary pollutants. There could even be some local increases in urban ozone levels in the UK in future, as the increased use of catalytic converters reduces emissions of substances which scavenge ozone. (Cm 2674, para. 3.17)

Aside from this ambiguity over the impact of catalytic converters on air pollution, there is also considerable concern that the current systems suffer from poor reliability with inadequate operation at cold engine temperatures. The RCEP assumed that technology devised to overcome the latter problem will 'generally be available within the next few years' (Cm 2674, para. 8.5). However, they were much more concerned about the ongoing poor reliability of catalytic converters and their vulnerability to damage:

> An issue which has attracted increasing attention is the extent to which vehicles which comply with a given standard at the time of manufacture continue to perform at the same level when in service ... UK experience shows that catalysts are being damaged or failing at a higher rate than had been foreseen. They are vulnerable to grounding, drowning, bump starts, running out of petrol and overheating; one manufacturer [not specified] has suggested that a car will, on average, need a new catalyst every three years. (para. 8.69)

A further limitation with the use of technical fixes, which the NAQS itself acknowledges, is that they will only provide a solution until 2005, after which the growth of traffic levels will begin to offset the technical benefits (Cm 3587, p. 45):

> We have got nowhere near sussing out a solution to the carbon dioxide problem, and when it comes down to it there is no solution to the problem

of sheer numbers: of congestion. And even if every single car were perfectly clean there would still be a need to limit traffic growth because of congestion. (Interview, Jeremy Vanke, RAC, 29th May 1996)

Overall then, in response to the increasing impact of transport as a policy problem in connection to public health, we have seen that the Major government attempted to protect the policy image of the road transport sector, manage the issue through an issue attention cycle and reduce the capacity of the opponents of roads to suggest solutions designed to lower vehicle mobility. However, in the longer term arguably the most pressing of all problems, namely congestion, would seem unsolvable by such a strategy. Therefore, an important element of the remainder of this analysis is to evaluate the impact of congestion and rising mobility on the agenda setting process and the Major government's response to it.

The End of the Road for Roads: SACTRA's Challenge to the Roads Orthodoxy

The public outcry after the great gridlock had been horrendous. Hundreds of thousands of Londoners had been left stranded in their cars for up to three days while the jam was cleared from the outside in. The knock-on effect had shot up the motorways and down to the Channel Tunnel, causing more horrendous delays. The complete shut-down of the capital for over half a week had affected business and commerce all over the country and into Europe. Countless deals had been lost, food had rotted, looting had occurred. The whole country had been absolutely astonished to discover what Chief Superintendent Ross had known for years, which was: that we are completely and utterly hopeless in the face of motor cars, they can cripple us, any day, any time. They are a monster that we have created, we worship them, sacrifice the riches of the Earth to them and will die for them, the moment it is demanded of us. (Elton, 1991, pp. 433-34)

In the Major era transport came to be identified as a significant problem in relation to rising traffic levels and increasing congestion on four key levels: as a policy disaster; as affecting quality of life; as affecting economic development, and in relation to the capacity of the predict and provide model to cater for future traffic growth.

Firstly, as I have argued in Chapter 3, the legacy of the government's proposed expansion of the road network outlined in the *Roads for Prosperity* White Paper (Cm 693) inadvertently eroded the predict and provide orthodoxy. *Roads for Prosperity* was developed in response to the government's own confirmation of the rising problems of congestion, the *National Road Traffic Forecasts* of 1989 which predicted that traffic levels would grow by between 83% and 142% by the year 2025 (DTp 1989a). In response to these figures the government launched *Roads for Prosperity* as an expanded roads programme, presenting it as the solution to the congestion problem. However, as Chapter 3 argued, it quickly became clear that this solution was wholly inadequate. Thus, the government itself was responsible for unwittingly contributing to the perception of transport as a policy problem through the initiation of a policy disaster (Dunleavy, 1995).

Secondly, the projected rise in traffic levels led to concern over their impact on quality of life. Tony Bosworth, of Friends of the Earth, has captured the concern well:

> If you look at how much traffic levels have grown since the '70s and then you say to people 'Well, what we are talking about now, if the government's forecasts come true, is an effective doubling of current traffic levels within 30 years', they just say, 'No way! You can't ...' People cannot comprehend that that is actually possible. It is drivers who can't see that that is possible, they say, 'The amount of congestion we have at the moment. What? There are going to be twice as many vehicle kilometres?' They just can't accept that. (Interview, 12th December 1995)

This linkage of rising traffic levels and quality of life issues was also demonstrated through opposition to the government's road programme. As Lily Matson of CPRE has emphasised, road building is a highly visual manifestation both of the impact of congestion and of the solutions which are prescribed by the predict and provide orthodoxy:

> I think it has just become painfully obvious that the car option won't work because the evidence of pollution, and congestion, and frustration of people trying to get around is so much in peoples face, and road building was just a very helpful, visual, trigger which happened to spur people into action. (Interview, 20th August 1996)

Thirdly, increasing traffic congestion led to concerns over its effect on economic development. In a survey by the British Road Federation in 1988 the costs of congestion in urban conurbations were estimated to be £3 billion per annum alone. A similar survey by the CBI in 1989 produced an estimate of £15 billion for the UK as a whole (cited in CBI, 1995b, para. 38). Following the discrediting of the predict and provide orthodoxy in the Major era, the CBI has been particularly concerned with the economic costs of congestion. In a series of documents released in the 1990s, it made its position clear:

> Demand on parts of the network is effectively being rationed by the economically and environmentally inefficient tool of congestion. The Government's wish to see a shift in traffic from road to rail is one way of relieving pressure on the road network, for environmental reasons, is welcome and well documented; but neither the size of shift which government believes feasible is clear, nor the mix of policies needed to achieve it. (CBI, 1995, para. 80)

Finally, in the Major era transport was identified as a significant problem as a result of the publication of the report by the Standing Advisory Committee on Trunk Roads Assessment (SACTRA) in 1994.

In their report, *Trunk Roads and the Generation of Traffic*, SACTRA aimed to undertake two key tasks: to evaluate the efficiency and accuracy of the traffic forecasting models used by the DTp and to examine the impact of infrastructure developments on traffic generation. These tasks reflected the terms of reference set by the Secretary of State for Transport, which were:

> To advise the Department [of Transport] on the evidence of the circumstances, nature and magnitude of traffic redistribution, mode choice and generation [resulting from new road schemes], especially on inter-urban roads and trunk roads close to conurbations; and to recommend whether and how the Department's methods should be amended, and what if any research or studies could be undertaken. (SACTRA, 1994, para. 4, p. i)

Given the long term strategic nature of transport infrastructure planning the role of forecasting is clearly significant. As the SACTRA report argued: 'at the heart of the planning process is traffic forecasting – that is, the estimating of future levels of traffic on the relevant part of the highway network ... Much therefore turns on the forecasts of future traffic' (SACTRA, 1994, paras 2.06-07). In the light of this, the SACTRA report was concerned to note that the existing forecasting system did not consider that expansion in capacity could generate additional traffic, a fact which was surprising given the scale of public investment involved in the road programme and its environmental impact:

> Every scheme involves the investment of a large sum of public money, and can also imply large private sector investment. Highway development can have a profound and long-term effect not only on the fabric of the nation,

but also upon regional and local land-use patterns, the environment and the way in which people conduct their business and personal lives. (para. 2.02)

According to the Department of Transport this omission could be justified 'on the grounds that any estimates of generated traffic would be very uncertain and (for the most part) would have a very small effect on traffic flows' (para. 2.11). Whilst SACTRA acknowledged that research into induced traffic was complex, it argued that this potential effect should not be overlooked as it could have an important impact on the evaluation of proposed road schemes:

> These studies demonstrate convincingly that the economic value of a scheme can be overestimated by the omission of even a small amount of induced traffic. We consider that this matter is of a profound importance to the value for money assessment of the Road Programme. (p. iii, para. 12)

Furthermore, the conclusions of the SACTRA report found that this factor was indeed extremely important: new, or improved, trunk roads actually contribute significantly to the generation of traffic. This was unsurprising to the SACTRA members who in posing the question, 'is induced traffic a real phenomena?', argued:

> The layman's response to this question is that it is obvious that the answer is yes. The M25 has entered folklore as a road which is a victim of its own success, and must have induced significant amounts of new traffic ... We do not feel able to endorse the Department's conclusion that the balance of this evidence is against the existence of induced traffic. (p. ii, paras 7 and 9)

The impact of this report on the agenda setting process was considerable. In a political climate in which the roads programme was under sustained pressure generally, the SACTRA report further discredited the roads for prosperity orthodoxy. By citing the example of the M25 as a 'victim of its own success,' the conclusions of SACTRA were clear: due to the phenomena of induced traffic, new or improved roads were not only unlikely to generate prosperity but they were also unlikely to end congestion and enhance freedom. In fact, the opposite was true:

> The importance of research like SACTRA's on induced traffic generation can't really be underestimated because it shows in a very strong and sedate way that building more roads isn't going to tackle the problem of congestion, or future traffic growth, that is driving everybody mad at the moment. (Interview, Lily Matson, CPRE, 20th August 1996)

The legacy of this report was considerable: it undermined the coherence of the predict and provide orthodoxy and the rationale of the historical mechanisms which had been used for planning roads. As a result:

> We are seeing the end of the theory, the myth, that simply by building roads that we can accommodate everybody's need to travel. I think that argument has been fairly well debunked now and we are now getting to the stage of okay, the transition from that, to how are we going to accommodate people's requirements to travel in the future. And that is painful because it is meaning lots of people's long held, firmly held beliefs, which they have spent all their life following, and believing in, are now having to have said to them, 'Look, great, thanks for all your work but what you believed, we don't believe it anymore'. The government is coming round to those sort of opinions, slowly. There is sort of a consensus developing. (Interview, Tony Bosworth, FoE, 12th December 1995)

Following the publication of the SACTRA report it became increasingly clear that government does not have the capacity to provide sufficient infrastructure to accommodate predicted traffic growth, and the predict and provide orthodoxy has thus been modified accordingly. Lily Matson of the CPRE reflected the opinions of a number of interviewees when she argued that:

> It's changed. No, it has changed. It's hard to think that the government could have really retained such a dogmatic stance in favour of roads and motor cars for as long as it did, which shows just how much it has changed: they really don't/aren't putting that same view out. They are much more cautious about bowing down to the needs of traffic. There has been fundamental shifts in what they actually say about, you know, 'We will now manage traffic demand. We will not provide capacity for all the traffic'. That is a huge shift in philosophy. (Interview, 20th August 1996)

However, the erosion of the predict and provide model has not resulted in a significant change to the structural imperatives of the state, which still support the need to facilitate mobility in order to promote economic development and personal liberty (Chapter 3). In the Major era, the end of the predict and provide orthodoxy combined with the need to retain an efficient transport network simply led to a change in the nature of the transport orthodoxy on which policy was based from predict and provide to *restrict and provide*. This restrict and provide orthodoxy is based on an acknowledgement by government that its capacity to provide sufficient infrastructure to accommodate the predicted growth in traffic is limited. Hence, a mechanism, such as road pricing, must be introduced which manages demand on the road network, so maintaining network efficiency.[3]

This change of approach in the Major period is evidenced by two factors: a shift away from a focus on strategic road building towards the completion of 'missing links' within the road network, focusing in particular on bypasses; and an acknowledgement by government of the need for road pricing on both motorways and urban roads (see Chapter 7). However, in the short term the change in orthodoxy was slow to filter through to concrete changes in policy, with a continuing reluctance to provide financial support for investment in public transport alternatives, and delay, in the short term, in implementing measures to restrict access to the road network:

> There are things happening but what is deeply, deeply frustrating, and it is shown by the green paper, is that (and I guess it is the atmosphere of an election) but there is very little that is radical or new that is actually going to shift direction from the course we are already set on. Yeah we are going to be building a few less roads but we are still investing £1.6 billion in the national roads programme: largely existing commitments. There is little real new money for any alternatives. There is absolutely no political will to tackle traffic in the form of charging more for it or introducing any form of fiscal policy. (Interview, Lily Matson, CPRE, 20th August 1996)

The implications of this change in orthodoxy should, however, prove to be significant in the medium term. In particular, some form of pricing reform must inevitably be introduced as it is the only way that government could successfully continue to achieve its structural imperatives following the end of the predict and provide orthodoxy.

This change in approach also illustrates that the apparent division between road user groups and construction interests in the Major era has been overstated. I argue in Chapter 5 that although the road user groups accepted this change of government orthodoxy, and the reductions to the scale of strategic investment which it implies, they have not changed their core view that the road network ought to provide free mobility for those with the capacity to access it. Thus, the conflict between the construction and user groups is based only on a difference of perception as to whether the state has the capacity to provide further infrastructure and maintain the predict and provide orthodoxy (favoured by the construction interests) or whether some form of restriction should be imposed, signifying a change of orthodoxy (favoured by the user groups).[4]

To sum up, in the Major era transport became a policy problem on the basis of congestion due to a combination of factors: the legacy of the policy disaster which resulted from the *Roads for Prosperity* programme in 1989; growing opposition both to the effects of congestion on quality of life and on economic development, and the legacy of the SACTRA report. Together these developments forced a change of ethos from the predict and provide orthodoxy to a restrict and provide orthodoxy.

These developments, as I shall argue in Chapter 5, were very significant for the growth of the anti-roads movement in the Major era. In particular, the critique which these groups have historically mounted of the capacity of the predict and provide orthodoxy to accommodate increases in traffic in the long term was legitimated by the 1994 SACTRA report. Following these changes to the basis of government policy, the anti-roads groups have tried to introduce a new policy discourse on the basis of reduced mobility and sustainable development which implies significant changes to the pattern of lifestyle which has historically operated in the UK. However, the next section argues that they have been largely unsuccessful in their efforts to change either the agenda in this area or the discourse on which transport policy is based.

Ideology, Sustainability and Lifestyle: The Un-politics of Political Change

In the Major era, a combination of increased scientific knowledge and the end of the predict and provide orthodoxy led to transport becoming identified as a problem on the basis of lifestyle. Initially, concern with issues such as damage to the ozone layer and global warming came to the fore in the late 1980s, becoming directly linked both to the development of the discourse on sustainable development generally, and later, specifically to the transport issue (Naess, 1997, p. 68):

> Although transport in the UK is not the major contributor to carbon dioxide emissions it is the fastest growing sector ... If UK transport was the only source of the increased carbon dioxide pollution then the problem would be minimal, but in fact a similar pattern of carbon dioxide increase is being observed across Europe and elsewhere. (Button, 1995, p. 176)

The identification of transport as a primary contributor to greenhouse gas emissions and global warming occurred simultaneously across much of the developed world during this period, and became a prominent concern in many government documents. For example, in the review of the road programme, published in 1994, the UK government argued that:

> The Government's policy for sustainable development is to strike the right balance between securing economic development, protecting the environment and sustaining the future quality of life. We cannot deal with the problems of increasing traffic simply by road building though we must improve our roads where it makes good sense to do so. (DTp, 1994, para. 2.2)

As sustainable development covers issues such as climate change, the depletion of mineral resources and the destruction of natural habitats it potentially poses a far greater challenge to the pro-roads lobby than do concerns with either congestion or declining public health (Button, 1995, pp. 176-77). As Krause *et al* have argued:

> Much of the current climate warming debate still proceeds along the narrow lines of conventional air pollution abatement policy. But climate stabilisation is an entirely different challenge. The greenhouse effect is driven by a confluence of environmental impacts that have their source not only in the nature of human resource use, but also in the nature of the current international economic order. Climate stabilisation therefore requires a comprehensive turn around towards environmentally sound and socially equitable development – in short, an unprecedented North-South compact on sustainable development. (Kraus, Bach and Kooney, 1990, para. 1.7 cited in Redclift, 1995, p. 288)

Thus, the discourse of sustainable development has widespread implications for the basis of many government policies, posing a significant challenge to the structural imperatives on which transport policy has historically been based in the UK (see Baker *et al*, 1997, for an overview of sustainable development philosophy and Richardson, 1997, for a critique of the concept as it has been interpreted by policy makers). However, as the remainder of this chapter will show, the solutions which are suggested by sustainable development discourse, such as fundamental reform of the planning process, had only a limited impact in the Major period. The reason for this is that they were (and remain in the Blair era) incompatible with the structural imperatives of the state, which reject many of the elements of the sustainable development model.

*Illustrating the Limitations of the Problem Centred Approach: Policy
Problems, Sustainability and Land-Use Planning*

> The number of new developments each year is relatively small but the
> development patterns we set today will endure into the next century. If land-
> use policies permit continued dispersal of development and a high reliance
> on the car, other policies to reduce the environmental impact of the
> transport may be less effective or come at a higher cost. (DoE and DTp,
> 1994, para. 1.10)

As with the other problems which have been discussed in this
chapter, in the 1990s a number of reports were published which identified
problems caused as a result of market-led planning policy. In particular, a
number of documents published by the DoE outlined its concerns over the
effect that unregulated car usage will have on the future of urban centres.
This concern is well illustrated by the DoE report, *Vital and Viable Town
Centres*, which reflected a growing concern with the predict and provide
ethos of transport and with the impact of the car on traditional town centres
(DoE, 1994, para. 2.19):

> While increased car ownership has expanded mobility for many, it has not
> helped the accessibility of town centres. Town centres were generally not
> built with cars in mind, and capacity will always be less than potential
> demand. (para. 2.20)

According to the DoE report, inaccessible town centres coupled with
the growth of car ownership and a deregulated, market-driven planning
process have caused a retail revolution resulting in greater numbers of
out-of-town shopping and leisure facilities:

> Until about a decade ago, the private sector was broadly content to support
> town centres as the principal places in which to invest and trade ... There
> was widespread agreement that the town centre was the right place to locate
> most forms of offices, commercial services and shopping, together with the
> employment and the development that went with it. (para. 2.25)

But in the mid-1980s, even though the majority of retailers were still
focusing their attention on town centre development, they were becoming
increasingly aware of the impact of the motor car. The Chairman of Marks
and Spencer, in his organisation's annual report in 1984, emphasised the
problem:

The use of family cars for shopping has increasing importance to our customers. Where local authorities have recognised this need and worked with retailers to improve parking facilities and good access roads, the public continue to prefer to shop in the High Street. Unfortunately, the response by some local authorities to the requirement of the car-shopping public is inadequate. Unless there is a change of attitude by some local authorities, the importance of the High Street will continue to decline. (cited in DoE, 1994, para. 2.34)

According to the DoE report, a combination of market-led demands for greater access and liberal planning policy have resulted in three clear waves of out-of-town development since the 1970s. The first wave, which began in the mid-1970s, concerned the growth of out-of-town food retailers and had a minimal impact on the viability of town centres (paras 2.38-2.40). The second wave involved the rapid rise of retail parks involving bulky, space intensive, typically low value goods, such as DIY products: here the impact upon town centres was also limited (para. 2.41). It is the most recent, third wave, according to the DoE's report, that poses a real danger to the future viability of town centres. It has coincided with the expansion of out-of-town retail into the sale of high-value, low-bulk durable goods such as clothing, toys and hi-fi equipment, seriously threatening the long-term viability of the high street. It is the onset of this third phase of the 'retail revolution' which forms the focus of the DoE's concern (para. 2.42). Tony Bosworth of pressure group Friends of the Earth reflected these concerns when he argued:

What we have had up until now is a planning system which has really reflected people's desire for access – for mobility – and not people's need for access. So we make it easy for people to travel around ... Maybe we don't need to make it easy for them to drive around and spend N hours doing that. Put the facilities nearer where they're at and you can achieve the same ends but in a much less environmentally damaging way. Obviously you are talking about major changes in urban infrastructure there, and that is going to take years, decades, but its something we need to be moving towards now. PPG 13 is starting that [but] we need a much more vigorous push. (Interview, 12th December 1995)

The response of the Major government to the development of transport as a policy problem on the basis of lifestyle focused on the development of a number of policy documents designed to change the planning process. In particular, the Major government published a number of planning policy guidance notes designed to 'set out Government policy on planning issues and provide guidance to local authorities and others on the operation of the planning system' (DoE and DTp 1994, p. 1). These covered a number of subjects such as housing (PPG 3), industrial and commercial development (PPG 4), town centres and retail development (PPG 6), transport (PPG 13), sport and recreation (PPG 17) and tourism (PPG 21). The guidance notes on retail development (PPG 6) and transport (PPG 13) have particular significance for this analysis.

The guidance note for transport (PPG 13), in particular, has been cited as evidence that the Major government acknowledged the impact which land planning decisions have on transport demand in the long term. PPG 13 offered the following advice to local authorities of how best to develop a strategy to integrate transport and land-use planning:

- promote development within urban areas, at locations highly accessible by means other than the private car;
- locate major generators of travel demand in existing centres which are highly accessible by means other than the private car;
- strengthen existing local centres – in both urban and rural areas – which offer a range of everyday community, shopping and employment opportunities, and aim to protect and enhance their viability and vitality;
- maintain and improve choice for people to walk, cycle or catch public transport rather than drive between homes and facilities which they need to visit regularly; and
- limit parking provision for developments and other on or off-street parking provision to discourage reliance on the car for work and other journeys where there are effective alternatives. (DoE and DTp, 1994, para. 1.8)

In order to secure these objectives, PPG 13 offered guidance to local authorities in a number of areas such as housing, employment, leisure and retail, emphasising in each case that new developments should offer a choice of different transport modes (see for example paras 3.4 and 3.11). Furthermore, developments should be integrated, reducing the distances between home, work and shopping facilities and thereby minimising the need to travel (see for example paras 3.2 and 3.10).

The impact of PPG 13 on the perception of the link between transport and land-use planning was considerable, and a number of actors have argued that it was indicative of a significant shift in the policy objectives of the Major government:

The shift to integrating road planning with land-use planning is hugely significant because it should mean, if done properly, that you are putting the houses and the developments where they should go and transport planning follows in those footsteps, rather than the other way around, which it has been for a number of years. So I think on the land-use planning front we have seen probably the most changes. (Interview, Lily Matson, CPRE, 20th August 1996)

This perception was shared by the Royal Commission on Environmental Pollution, which argued in *Transport and the Environment* that PPG 13 'emphasises the need to reduce growth in the number and length of motorised journeys, encourage more environmentally friendly means of travel and reduce reliance on the private car' (Cm 2674, para. 9.41). In addition, commentators have argued that the publication of PPG 13 was indicative of the development of conflict between the DoE and the DTp in the Major era, which also led to a greater emphasis on sustainable mobility:

I think it is fair to say that the main driving force behind PPG 13 was DoE and [Department of] Transport was, in some cases, probably rather reluctantly carried along behind. For at least 10 years beforehand, transport policy people had been going along to conferences to be berated by transport professionals and academics and the rest for the fact that they were too roads orientated: their policy was decades behind the times – 'Isn't it about time you got over to Ministers that there is more to transport policy than allowing the car to have a free rein in everything?' I think the main thrust for that policy change certainly came from John Gummer and from the DoE policy side generally, and particularly from the planners, who were seeing this very much as a way of giving a stronger environmental emphasis to planning policy. They recognised that transport policy and planning policy were symbiotically related and [shouldn't] be treated as separate departments, and they felt, I think rightly, that now was the time to emphasise the need for a change. (Interview information, senior civil servant, Government Office for the West Midlands, DoETR, August 1997)

However, in spite of the publication of PPG 13, and the policy pronouncements which it contained, there are a number of reasons to argue that its actual impact on the planning process was limited.

Firstly, the guidance which government offered to local authorities in other planning policy guidance documents often contradicted the emphasis within PPG 13. A particularly clear example of this was provided in the advice offered to local authorities with regard to planning for retail developments. In PPG 13 the government argued that:

Structure plan policies for retailing should seek to promote the vitality and viability of existing urban and surburban and rural centres. Shopping should be promoted in existing centres which are more likely to offer a choice of access, particularly those without the use of a private car. (DoE and DTp, 1994, para. 3.9)

PPG 13 offered a number of specific principles which local authorities 'should' follow in order to achieve the objectives of protecting the vitality and viability of shopping centres, such as: prioritising development within existing centres of retail activity; encouraging retail development close to residential housing developments, and prioritising edge-of-town rather than out-of-town developments (para. 3.10). The section ôn retail development concluded with advice for local authority policy makers to seek more detailed guidance from PPG 6, which offered specific advice on planning for the retail sector. However, the advice within PPG 6 contained a number of elements which contradicted the sentiments of PPG 13 and consequently reduced the impact of the government's measures.

PPG 6 also offered specific principles which local authorities should follow when taking decisions regarding proposed retail developments. In particular, two key objectives which the government was committed to realising were outlined. The first of these was:

- to sustain or enhance the vitality and viability of town centres which serve the whole community and in particular provide a focus for retail development where the proximity of competing businesses facilitates competition from which consumers benefit. (DoE, 1993, para. 1)

This objective is clearly very closely related to those within PPG 13. However, the government's second key objective in PPG 6 appears both to contradict the first objective and to illustrate that there were significant ambiguities within the philosophy driving government policy. According to PPG 6, the second objective of planning policy for the retail sector was:

- to ensure the availability of a wide range of shopping opportunities to which people have every access (from the largest superstore to the smallest village shop), and the maintenance of an efficient and innovative retail sector. (para. 1)

A more detailed examination of the contents of PPG 6 reveals that the guidance given to local authorities on decision making with regard to retail planning was in fact consistently influenced by the second of the government's key objectives for planning policy, rather than the first. For example, the government argued that retail planning ought to respond to consumer demands:

> It is not the function of the planning system to preserve existing commercial interests or to inhibit competition between retailers or between methods of retailing. Nor is it the function of the local planning authority to regulate changes in the supply of retail services, unless interests of acknowledged importance would be adversely affected. Retailing must generally be able to respond to consumer needs and demands; the public can then enjoy the benefits of improved choice and lower prices that may flow from the competition that may be provided by new retail developments. (DoE, 1993, para. 32)

Thus the view within PPG 13 that local authorities '*should* seek to promote the vitality and viability of existing urban and surburban and rural centres' (DoE and DTp, 1994, para. 3.9. Emphasis added) was considerably downgraded in PPG 6, which stated that the planning process should in fact 'facilitate innovations in the retail sector, *preferably* in locations accessible to all sectors of society, and providing a choice of transport mode' (DoE, 1993, para. 32. Emphasis added).

The result of this difference of emphasis between the two documents was that the presumption within PPG 13 that planning permission ought to be refused for out-of-town or edge-of-town developments in favour of those within existing retail centres was rejected. According to PPG 6:

> Local planning authorities should not refuse permission for development on the grounds of the effect on a town centre, *unless there is clear evidence* to suggest that the results would be to undermine the vitality and viability of that centre which would otherwise continue to serve that community well. (DoE, 1993, para. 37. Emphasis added)

The second reason for the limited impact of PPG 13 is that this ambiguity within government policy created a considerable implementation gap between the aims of PPG 13 and the policies undertaken in a number of local authorities which continued to grant planning permission to projects which were seemingly against the spirit of PPG 13. In particular, a number of local authorities proposed extensive housing developments in green field sites. To the suggestion that the trend towards out-of-town developments was being reversed in the Major era Peter Bottomley, MP and member of the Transport Select Committee, responded:

> How is that reconciled with the two and a half thousand extra homes being built outside Basingstoke and the four and a half thousand homes being built outside Andover ... I could go around the whole country. Where is the change? (Interview, 26th February 1996)

Lily Matson of the pressure group CPRE agreed with Peter Bottomley, arguing that a significant implementation gap still remained in the planning of new housing:

> The housing thing is really, really interesting because ... yeah, I don't think the transport land-use agenda has really hit the housing debate at all. The DoE, again at national level, says, 'Yes. We agree with you, we think as many houses should go in urban areas, where there is public transport, as possible' ... I guess what I am trying to express is that in many ways I think the DoE is quite clever in being able to talk the language of integrating transport with land-use, and all those sorts of things, and be quite convincing in a sort of broad-brush way, but they are still giving these massive housing allocations which local authorities are now struggling with, and saying, 'Well we will have to put it on this green field site somewhere'. So I think the implementation, yeah, we've still got a long way to go. (Interview, 20th August 1996)

The significance of this implementation gap also manifested itself in other areas such as out-of-town retail developments, questioning fundamentally the hypothesis that the DoE had changed its emphasis with regard to planning policy. The impact of this was very important, as it undermined many of the other objectives concerning planning such as the focus on integrating housing with work, leisure and retail facilities. This demonstrates the difficulties which the DoE had in pursuing policy objectives which contradicted the predominant emphasis of the Major government on liberal planning and transport policy:

> I suspect they are being corporatised by the rest of the government. They can't be seen to be standing too far out of the government kilter. Effectively the DoE, the DTi and DTp have to be singing from the same song sheet and so the DoE can't go out on too much of a limb, if the other two departments are lobbying in step. (Interview, Tony Bosworth, FoE, 12th December 1995)

The implementation gap also resulted from the internal competition which exists between local authorities for new investment. This led to many cases where there was little incentive for a local authority to pursue the emphasis within PPG 13 on reducing out-of-town development. For example, if a local authority followed the guidance within PPG 13 and rejected a planning submission for an out-of-town retail development, a neighbouring authority would often step in and accept the planning application:

> Government policy under PPG 13 is that they [out-of-town developments] should be curbed. The reality is rather different, if one local authority is presented with an application for, say a hypermarket out of town, and they think, 'Oh PPG 13 says we shouldn't have these therefore we will say no' they lose the opportunity to create jobs in their district, their borough, what-have-you. There is nothing to stop the neighbouring borough, just over the border, saying 'Yeah we'll have you. We'll have the jobs'. As a result, the borough that said 'No' still gets all the traffic impact, it still gets the land use distortions but doesn't get the jobs. And that is the reality of the current system. When it comes down to it each bit of local government is going to want the development and guidance is not enough to stop that sort of development, you need strict development control: very strict rules about it. You also need things like the Dutch system whereby companies locating within walking distance of public transport provision get tax breaks. So as well as the stick you've got a carrot there. (Interview, Jeremy Vanke, RAC, 29th May 1996)

Overall, the planning policy of the Major era provides a further indication of the lasting resonance of the structural imperatives of the state, in which pressures caused by increases in mobility were to be accommodated, and the emphasis on the need for behavioural changes placed on transport consumers rather than on central government:

> The actual switch you need is for more people to think before they change their job or change their home. Up to now, every time there has been a transport improvement, people have used the same amount of time to get to work. So instead of going forty minutes from Hayes to Heathrow they now go from Godstone. So instead of 4 miles they go 40 miles. Because you can go a mile a minute you have got so much time ... If you want to make the biggest change either to congestion or to fuss and rush, what I have said is the one that does it. But no one ever talks about it. When was the last time in an integrated transport policy article or editorial did you see anyone talk about the distance between home and work? It doesn't happen. The 'Great Debate' hasn't started. (Interview, Peter Bottomley MP, 26th February 1996)

Thus, as Peter Bottomley has argued, historically an important element of government policy has been to emphasise the role which individuals ought to play within the decision making process. The reason for this is that government policy in the Major period was based on a sense that the government should not force changes in people's behaviour, or force policy makers to approve developments which emphasised sustainable patterns of living and working. Such forced changes would contradict the liberal emphasis of government policy:

> The future is in providing shopping facilities, leisure facilities, where people live. Work is different. The ideal of the new town doesn't work (the idea that people will live near where they work) simply because work changes. And particularly with increasing female participation in the workforce it's much much easier for someone to change jobs, stay in the same place where they live, drive further to get to the new job and substitute transport for moving. And that is one of the reasons that the new towns didn't work. There is also a psychological desire to separate oneself from work. A lot of people genuinely don't like living where they work. So there's lots of ideals in planning but lots of nitty gritty realities that mess up the ideal. But come what may, even if we were to implement PPG 13 on a statutory basis now, it doesn't deal with the problems that already exist, and in many ways they are far greater. We have already got dispersed development. What do you do about changing that? Can you change that? I don't know the answer to that. (Interview, Jeremy Vanke, RAC, 29th May 1996)

Overall, therefore, the problem for the promoters of vital and viable town centres in the Major period was that the impact of deregulated land-use planning remained inextricably linked to the demands for access and freedom which were bound up in the transport policy emphasis of the UK government. And as the experience of the USA has illustrated, this is likely to lead to only one outcome:

> It has taken less than three decades to destroy the heartbeat of many American cities. It will take a century to repair the damage and return those cities to a semblance of health. (Robert Carey, President of Urban Centre Development in Oakland California, cited in DoE, 1994, para. 3.12)

Conclusion

This chapter has sought to evaluate the ability of problem centred models of agenda setting to account for political change in the Major era. I have argued that transport policy was affected by three different agenda setting processes, each triggered by different perceptions of transport as a policy problem on the basis of public health, congestion and lifestyle respectively. The different outcomes of these processes can, I suggest, be explained by the importance of the structural imperatives of the state. In cases in which a solution to a transport problem is compatible with, or does not challenge, the structural imperatives of the state the agenda setting process operates with relative dynamism. However, in cases in which a problem or its solution challenges the structural imperatives of the state, the agenda setting process is tightly controlled by the government and agenda management is common place, greatly restricting the potential for change.

We have seen that transport first came to be seen as a policy problem on the ground of increasing scientific knowledge of the effects of vehicle emissions on public health. In this case the transport agenda was able to operate with relatively high dynamism, as the government instigated a solution which did not challenge the structural imperatives of the state. During this period, the perceived effect of vehicle emissions on public health damaged the policy image of road vehicles as the public and media became concerned with the effects of vehicle emissions on deteriorating public health; the Major government's response centred on the publication of the *National Air Quality Strategy* (Cm 3587), primarily aimed at the implementation of a legislative framework to improve fuel and vehicle technology and significantly reduce the impact of vehicle emissions on ambient air quality. The NAQS was, of course, entirely compatible with the government's broader policy objectives: to manage policy problems with technical solutions; protect the policy image of road transport, and maintain the historical focus of public policy which has been to promote freedom and mobility, albeit with 'greener and cleaner' credentials.

Congestion on the road network was the second policy problem to confront government in this period. In this case the agenda setting process operated with only medium level dynamism, as the Major government was able to re-orientate its priorities without challenging the structural imperatives of the state. I have argued that congestion manifested itself as a policy problem on four distinct bases: as a policy disaster; as affecting quality of life; as restricting economic development, and as exposing the limitations of the predict and provide model. Together these perceived problems had a significant cumulative effect on the agenda setting process.

In the short term, increasing congestion began to impose significant costs on the economy, leading to increased opposition from road user groups such as the CBI. In the longer term, the predict and provide orthodoxy was undermined as it became increasingly clear that central government did not have the capacity to provide sufficient infrastructure to accommodate the projected increases in road traffic. The cumulative effect of these developments was to significantly weaken the coherence of the predict and provide orthodoxy, putting considerable pressure on central government to introduce a new policy orthodoxy which restricts access to the road network while at the same time enabling the state to maintain its commitment to high levels of freedom, mobility and economic activity (i.e. the restrict and provide orthodoxy). Thus, although the restrict and provide orthodoxy places significant restrictions on marginal road users, these are restrictions imposed in order to maintain macro-level mobility in the long term. Thus the apparent change in orthodoxy still works to protect the structural imperatives of the state.

Finally, transport also came to be seen as a policy problem on the basis of lifestyle. In this case the transport agenda operated with low levels of dynamism, being tightly managed by the Major government. During the late 1980s, a new policy discourse on the basis of sustainable development challenged the capitalist development model, suggesting an alternative pattern of economic development based on low levels of transport mobility. However, this chapter has argued that the lifestyle implications of such sustainable development discourse have had only limited impact on the agenda setting process, because they are incompatible with the structural imperatives of the state.

In the Major period this sustainable development discourse had, on the surface, a significant impact on the process of transport planning, with detailed planning policy guidance produced to restrict developments on greenfield or out-of-town sites (see especially PPG 13). However, I have argued in this chapter that the commitment to reform the planning process was largely rhetorical; planning permissions for housing and retail developments on green field and out of town sites continued, even though this contradicted the government's own guidance. This apparent imbalance between the stated objectives of central government and their manifestation through the policy process can also be explained by the importance of the structural imperatives of the state.

Sustainable development implies an economic system which prioritises low mobility and tightly regulated, localised planning. However, as I argue in the next chapter, such objectives are incompatible with the structural imperatives of the state in the UK. Thus, the Major government maintained close control over the policy agenda in this area and rejected the model for transport planning outlined within the discourse of sustainable development.

Notes

1   Most of the legislation which has been enacted in order to reduce the emissions from road vehicles has been developed within the framework of the European Union. I will consider it in full in Chapter 6, which considers the impact of the European arena on the development of national transport policy.

2   I discuss the nature of central-local relations in the transport field in detail in Chapter 7.

3   I discuss the politics of road pricing in detail in both the Major and Blair eras in Chapter 7 and Chapter 9 (Postscript) respectively.

4   The nature of this change and its effect on the cohesion of the road lobby will be explored in more detail in Chapter 5.

5 Actor Centred Models of Agenda Setting

Introduction

> It must be considered that there is nothing more difficult to carry out, nor more doubtful of success, nor more dangerous to handle, than to initiate a new order of things. For the reformer has enemies in all those who profit by the old order, and only lukewarm defenders in all those who would profit by the new order, this lukewarmness arising partly from fear of their adversaries, who have the laws in their favour; and partly from the incredulity of mankind, who do not truly believe in anything new until they have had actual experience of it. (Machiavelli, 1513, p. 21)

The explosion in the number and diversity of actors involved in the conflict over the transport issue was one of the most significant changes between the Thatcher and Major eras. It is a common hypothesis within the political science literature that changes to the nature of the opposition to a policy are often an instrumental precondition for changes to the agenda (see in particular Dudley and Richardson, 1995, 1996a and 1998 for analysis with reference to the roads issue). This chapter aims to explore this view in relation to the transport issue in the Major era.

This chapter argues that during the Major period both the *scope* and *breadth* of the opposition to the roads programme increased significantly. In this context, *scope* refers both to the number of actors which mobilise to oppose policy, and to the level of public opposition which they represent. For example, in the transport case, the involvement of the Royal Society for the Protection of Birds (RSPB) represents both an additional actor and, in the shape of the RSPB's membership, the *de facto* involvement of 850,000 members of the public (figures from CBD Research, 1996, p. 402).

The *breadth*, or diversity, of the opposition to transport policy also underwent significant change. At one extreme the 'traditional' transport groups with a long history of transport campaigning, such as Transport

2000 and ALARM UK, were joined by the direct action movement, which operated outside the established policy making arenas through their occupation of the road construction sites. In addition, the 'traditional' groups were joined by a number of 'moderate', mass membership, campaigning organisations such as the RSPB and the National Trust, which due to the nature of their membership enjoy quasi-insider status (Young, 1993, pp. 20-21).

This chapter explores these changes in a number of different ways: it provides an overview of the changing nature of the policy network centred around the transport issue in the Major period; describes the increasing scope and breadth of the opposition to the roads programme; puts forward the view that the road lobby became increasingly fragmented in response to this conflict; and finally evaluates the impact of these changes on the agenda setting process.

One possible contention is that the increasing scope and breadth of the opposition to the road programme, combined with the rising internal division within the road lobby, *could* have resulted in changes to the pattern of alliances between actors, with a new core policy community forming based on reductions in future road building. Such a view would imply significant changes to the cohesion of the road lobby, together with the formation of new alliances between hitherto 'moderate' anti-roads groups, such as Transport 2000, and the road user groups, such as the AA and RAC. This chapter argues that this first hypothesis fails to offer a convincing explanation of developments in the Major period.

One reason for this is that that the apparent division within the road lobby has been overstated. Sabatier's work on advocacy coalitions (see in particular Sabatier, 1993, pp. 23-34 and Sabatier and Jenkins-Smith, 1993b, pp. 218-27) is used to argue that apparent divisions within the road lobby have only occurred in terms of secondary and near core beliefs: the road lobby remains united on fundamental, core beliefs.

This observation is linked to the second reason for the failure of this hypothesis, which is that the apparent coherence of the opposition to the road programme has been overstated. In particular, the 'moderate' anti-roads groups do not share common core beliefs with the more 'radical' elements of the anti-road coalition. Thus the anti-roads coalition is not as stable as that involving the pro-roads groups. The instability within this alliance therefore posed both practical and operational problems for the anti-roads groups during this period, and indicates that the durability of such an alliance is limited in the long term.

The second way in which opponents of roads *could* have fostered change relates to their capacity to open up new institutional venues which are not dominated by the priorities of the road lobby. Dudley and Richardson's view that the changes in the scope and breadth of the opposition to the roads programme opened up a number of new arenas to the opponents of roads provides a useful working hypothesis. Firstly, the direct action movement opened up new institutional venues (the media and the construction sites) which were not dominated by the institutional bias of the road lobby (Dudley and Richardson, 1996a, 1998). The act of protest became news in, and of, itself (Anderson, 1997, p. 122). The impact of the direct action campaigns in the Major period illustrates that effective opposition by outsider groups needs the support of groups which are willing to resort to extra-legal means – without this support, outsider groups have much less impact on the agenda. Secondly, the increasing activism of quasi-insider groups such as the Council for the Protection of Rural England (CPRE), the National Trust and the RSPB facilitated greater access to the channels of formal consultation for the opponents of roads.

However, the arenas which are now available to the opponents of roads have in fact offered only limited opportunities for them to gain control of the agenda setting process. I argue in this chapter that conflict at the construction sites and within the media and parliamentary arenas had only a limited impact on the agenda in the Major period as the anti-roads groups retained only an arm's length relationship to policy makers, thus reducing their influence. The key decision making arenas (i.e. the European Union (see Chapter 6), local government (see Chapter 7) and national government) remained dominated by significant institutional biases which favoured the pro-roads groups.

The Changing Nature of the Transport Policy Network

The changes to the nature of the roads policy network between the end of the Thatcher government and that of the Major period were extensive. Chapter 3 has argued that in the pre-Major period the nature of policy making is aptly described by a network metaphor. The pro-roads groups were well organised, integrated within a core policy community which enjoyed frequent contact with Ministers, and their interests were served well by the predict and provide orthodoxy which then dominated government policy.

The anti-roads groups, in contrast, had relatively limited access to government, and the scope of the opposition to government policy was limited. Outsider groups mounted a number of campaigns through the highway inquiry process but failed to overcome the institutional bias of the road lobby, which continued to assert itself within this arena. The pattern of policy making at this time is represented by Figure 3.2 (reproduced below).

Figure 3.2   Location of actors on a policy network continuum (pre-Major period)

Insiders   **Outsiders**

◄──►

core insiders/ specialist insiders	peripheral insiders	outsider by goal	outsider by choice
British Roads Federation		Transport 2000	ALARM UK
AA/RAC (users)		Friends of the Earth	
Construction interests			
Society of Motor Manufacturers and Traders			

The Major Era

In the Major era, in contrast, it is suggested that a number of significant movements occurred to the position of different interests on the policy continuum (see Figure 3.4 which is reproduced on the following page). According to this view, such changes involved parallel developments: the road lobby became increasingly fragmented and at the same time the anti-roads groups moved towards insider status. This is potentially extremely important to an exploration of actor centred models of agenda setting, because those models would suggest that such changes will explain, in a causal sense, changes to the transport agenda.

Figure 3.4   Location of actors on policy network continuum (Major period)

Insiders   **Outsiders**

◄──►

core insiders	specialist insiders	peripheral insiders	outsider by goal	outsider by choice

Pro-roads groups   *Anti-roads groups*

British Roads   CPRE   ALARM UK   Dongas
Federation

AA/RAC   Construction   Friends of
(car users)   interests   the Earth

road haulage
sector
                            Transport 2000
                            National Trust

Society of Motor
Manufacturers and Traders

The changes in the Major era do provide some evidence that the road lobby became increasingly fragmented. A senior member of a motoring organisation has suggested that two principal fault lines began to emerge within the road lobby:

> The first is between the users and the constructors: the aggregate industry still yearns after lots of concrete, lots of aggregates, and they should be modernising their business and realising that that isn't the way forward. There should be lots of small scale projects out there for the same industry: things like traffic calming, local road safety schemes, local junction improvements and bypasses. But they are not seeing things that way, they are still dreaming of the eight lane motorways that they once dreamed of. (Interview, June 1996)

According to this interviewee, the division between road users and construction interests is the most fundamental. During the Major era, the predict and provide orthodoxy which had dominated policy was increasingly called into question, and road user groups acknowledged that it would not be possible to provide sufficient infrastructure to accommodate the projected increases in traffic levels. In response, they pragmatically re-oriented their objectives towards ensuring that the existing network operated more efficiently, arguing for a change of focus for policy from the predict and provide orthodoxy to a restrict and provide orthodoxy (see Chapter 4).

In contrast, the construction interests failed to adjust to the change in government orthodoxy which followed the publication of the SACTRA report, continuing to emphasise the link between extensions to the road network and economic growth: a link which, they argued, would be threatened if congestion continued to increase:

> It is still difficult to see that a policy that stops people using their cars, or motor vehicles in general ... would work, given the reasons people are using those vehicles don't change: the place where they live; the place where they work; the goods and services that they want to receive. Unless, those things change the demands aren't going to change. Consequently, this year it is perhaps out of fashion but in five years or ten years time, when people are, 'Well yes we have got more people cycling, yes more people are taking the bus, more people are using the rail service but the level of congestion is still worse, traffic conditions are still poor, despite the fact that more people are walking': this particular town still has heavy traffic going through it, is not going to change. They still want a bypass. The fundamentals are the same today as they were five, ten, fifteen, twenty, twenty five years ago, and one suspects, certainly for the next five, ten, fifteen, twenty years, they are still going to be the same and so, therefore, there will still be the demand to improve the road network. (Interview, Paul Everitt, British Road Federation, 21st August 1996)

According to the view that change was indeed significant in the Major era, the construction interests became increasingly marginalised as the focus of government policy changed. Steven Norris, former Minister for Public Transport, captured the essence of this view well:

> [The] basic environment which I have outlined: one of trying to balance the paradox of increasing car ownership with concern about the environment and congestion and the limitations of a predict and provide model, are absolutely common ground from the Road Haulage Association to ALARM UK. Very few people, as I say, who are prepared to take part in a sensible democratic debate seriously think otherwise. (Interview, 29th May 1996)

The second fault line which emerged within the road lobby in the Major era was founded on the environmental impact of road transport. A senior member of a motoring organisation provided a concise summary of this division:

> The second potential split is between the two lots of user groups: essentially road freight and car users. [... Our] members, motorists generally, hate lorries, no two ways about it. The car user is being faced, at the moment, with a lot of the costs of road freight. So for example, if we talk about pollution, cars are a declining source of local pollutants, lorries aren't. Look at recent publicity on particulate matter – a lot of it talks about car restrictions – the single biggest source of particulate matter is the road freight sector. So, there is a potential split building there. (Interview, June 1996)

Sydney Balgarnie of the Road Haulage Association confirmed that at the level of media perception, such a split did develop: 'at the moment, particularly, the AA and the RAC are tending sometimes to knock the lorry ... publicly, anyway – privately they still talk to us. ... That is not a wise course for them because they are very vulnerable – there are 21 million cars out there, 450,000 lorries: what's your problem?' (Interview, 21st August 1996).

In addition, it is argued that in the Major era a division developed between commercial interests and the general public, centred on the issue of road pricing. Many of the commercial interests began to accept the need for road pricing on a pragmatic basis on the condition that the cost of the tolls were offset by efficiency gains, while the general public resisted such tolls, retaining the view that access to roads was a right which should remain free at the point of use (HC 376-II, pp. 21-32, HC 104-II, pp. 97-103).[1]

Finally, according to the view that significant change in the nature of the roads policy network took place in the Major era, the anti-roads groups became more effectively integrated in the policy process, moving towards insider status. The end of the predict and provide orthodoxy enabled erstwhile outsider groups to gain access to formal processes of government consultation. The impact of this is most clearly illustrated by the change in status afforded to Transport 2000. In the pre-Major period Transport 2000 fell between the categories of a *peripheral insider group* and an *outsider group by goal* according to the typology of Maloney *et al* (1994, p. 32). It attempted an insider strategy which however had little impact on the thinking of civil servants (as described by peripheral insider group theory), while its goals were seen as totally incompatible with those of mainstream policy makers (as described by outsider group by goal theory). In the Major era, in contrast, Transport 2000 enjoyed much easier access to government, with regular contact with civil servants and a greater capacity to influence the priorities of government policy (Interview information, John Stewart, ALARM UK, 23rd November 1995). Thus Transport 2000 moved along the insider-outsider continuum, now being located at a point between specialist and peripheral insider status.[2]

Groups which in the Thatcher period were outsiders by goal also had some success in gaining access to formal processes of consultation:

> When some of the environmental groups [started], they didn't have access, so they had to learn how to get it. And clearly now anyone working with those groups, who have established access to government, and opposition, are not going to have the same or similar sorts of problems. I don't believe that anyone at Friends of the Earth would believe they didn't have easy access to government because they clearly do. They may not have in the past, and it may be worth understanding why they didn't in the past, but I don't think that would be a problem for them in the future. (Interview, Paul Everitt, BRF, 21st August 1996)

Still further outside the political mainstream, the growth of direct action campaigning increased the diversity of the anti-roads groups, further increasing their capacity to affect the agenda. Operating as outsiders by choice, the direct action movement developed during the Major era, undertaking a series of *illegal actions*. These groups emerged in response to a perceived failure of conventional pressure groups, such as Greenpeace and Friends of the Earth, to offer leadership in the protests at Twyford Down in 1992: 'The fact that the Twyford protesters had been disowned by Friends of the Earth, who were fearful of the loss of assets from any court actions arising from illegal protest actions, helped to ensure that the movement developed autonomously, following the counter-cultural and anarchistic form already established by, among others, the network of Earth First! groups' (Doherty, 1997, p. 149).

The scope of the opposition to the road programme also broadened with the rise in activism of groups which enjoyed good access to government and represented a predominantly middle class membership, such as the National Trust and the RSPB. These groups objected to a number of proposed road schemes which they viewed as posing a significant threat to areas of the countryside rich in wildlife or ecological significance (see, for example, RSPB, 1995).

Overall then, according to the hypothesis that change to the nature of the policy network was extensive in the Major era, the anti-roads groups have benefited from a number of parallel developments. Firstly, the breadth of the movement expanded considerably, and anti-roads groups were able to use the full range of tactics available to outsider groups. On the one hand, they gained increased access to policy makers as the predict and provide orthodoxy lost its dominance; on the other, the rise of the direct action groups enabled the opponents of roads to gain greater access to the media and influence the agenda through the use of extra-legal campaigning strategies. Secondly, it is argued that the pro-roads groups became less coherent during this period, with divisions developing between the user groups and construction interests and within the user groups themselves.

Evaluating Actor Centred Models of Agenda Setting

The principal aim of this chapter is to evaluate the hypothesis set out above, that significant change occurred to the roads policy network in the Major era. In the preceding section, I have argued that according to the initial hypothesis, changes can be identified in both the internal cohesion of the road lobby and in the *breadth* and the *scope* of the anti-roads opposition. The remainder of this chapter will examine the extent of these developments and of their impact on the agenda setting process.

Examining the Cohesion of the Road Lobby in the Major Era

Schattschneider's theoretical framework makes it clear that groups which have historically been insiders are unlikely to intentionally externalise policy (see Chapter 2). According to Schattschneider, policy externalisation has high risks: the control which insider groups have historically had over an issue is likely to be lost as a result of policy externalisation, and externalising policy may well result in the fragmentation of the core policy community (1960, p. 39). Thus, insider groups will only externalise policy in extreme circumstances.

Schattschneider's model provides the first theoretical argument in support of the view that the split within the road lobby (between road users and construction interests) is in fact predominantly rhetorical, not being indicative of any fundamental division of opinion. His work rests on two key premises: that actors are aware of their own 'best interests' and that these are best served by remaining within the existing core policy community. Both premises, therefore, raise doubts as to the validity of the hypothesis that the road lobby is increasingly fragmented.

Sabatier's work on advocacy coalitions provides important evidence that both of these premises apply in the transport case. His model also provides support for the view that the importance of the apparent division within the road lobby has been greatly overstated. Overall, Sabatier's work is important because it questions whether significant changes did occur to the nature of the transport policy network in the Major era.

Sabatier's framework suggests that advocacy coalitions form alliances on the basis of deep core (unchanging) beliefs, which all members of a coalition share. Deep core beliefs refer, for example, to perceptions of the nature of man (inherently evil vs. socially redeemable) and the relative priorities attached to certain key values such as freedom, power or love (Sabatier, 1993, p. 31. See Dudley and Richardson, 1996a, for an application of this approach to the transport case).

In addition, groups have near core and secondary beliefs. In most cases these beliefs will reflect the deep core beliefs of the groups, and thus of the advocacy coalition. It is however, possible for members of an advocacy coalition to disagree on secondary beliefs or, less frequently, on near core beliefs. And advocacy coalitions will sacrifice a secondary or near core belief which has been challenged or discredited by a rival advocacy coalition 'before acknowledging weaknesses in the policy core' (Sabatier, 1993, p. 33). Thus in order to evaluate the impact of the conflict between the pro- and anti-roads groups on the stability of the transport agenda it is important to avoid confusing conflict over a near core or secondary belief with conflict over deep core beliefs. I argue that this confusion has been extensive in the transport case.

In looking at Tables 5.1, 5.2 and 5.3, the reasons why the fragmentation of the road lobby has been overstated become clear. As Sabatier's framework suggests, the transport groups are divided into three advocacy coalitions which have fundamentally different core beliefs. In essence these coalitions are divided on fundamental questions concerning the nature of man, the priorities of different social values and criteria of distributive justice. In addition, there are fundamental differences between the pro-roads and anti-roads groups on the basis of their near core beliefs.

Table 5.1   An ideological map of the roads groups

Core beliefs	Near core beliefs	Secondary beliefs
Ultimate values include: High premium on freedom and knowledge	*Scope of Government activity:* Low. Market activity should dominate	*Policy issues:* (i) budgets: Market-led (i.e. roads focused)
Nature of man: Man holds dominion over nature	*Policy Conflicts - economic vs. environmental:* Economic	*(ii) programme performance:* Roads vital to generate prosperity
Distributive Justice: Relative weight of own society/self very high	*Policy Instruments:* Inducements	SACTRA report has marginal impact
	Participation: Elite led	
	Can society solve problems? Very strong belief in technical fixes	
	Government authority: Centralised	

These beliefs are reflected in the following ways:

Capitalism is a positive development model	The predict and provide model *ought* to be the basis of policy	Public transport is not to be encouraged
Transport is integral to economic growth and development	Roads are essential for prosperity	People given the choice would rather use a car
Mobility is important for the promotion of liberty		

(modified from Sabatier, 1993, p. 31)

Table 5.2 An ideological map of the moderate anti-roads groups

Core beliefs	Near core beliefs	Secondary beliefs
Ultimate values include: Balance of values between freedom and knowledge (pro-roads) and love and beauty (direct action)	*Scope of Government activity:* Medium: balance between market activity and government planning	*Policy issues: (i) budgets:* Planning led (i.e. alternatives to roads emphasised)
Nature of man: Man is part of nature	*Policy Conflicts - economic vs. environmental:* Environmental	*(ii) programme performance:* Roads do not generate prosperity.
Distributive Justice: Balance between all peoples, future generations and non-human beings	*Policy Instruments:* Inducements, coercion and persuasion together	SACTRA report has significant impact
	Participation: Elite led	
	Can society solve problems? Belief in both technical fixes and lifestyle changes	
	Government authority: Centralised and local	

These beliefs are reflected in the following ways:

Capitalism must be developed sustainably	The predict and provide model should *not* be the basis of policy	Public transport is to be encouraged
Mobility is important for the promotion of liberty BUT that does not imply car use	Road improvements generate traffic	People given the choice would rather use a car but that is because the alternatives are poor

(modified from Sabatier, 1993, p. 31)

Table 5.3   An ideological map of the direct action anti-roads groups

Core beliefs	Near core beliefs	Secondary beliefs
Ultimate values include: High premium on love, beauty etc. *Nature of man:* Man is part of nature *Distributive Justice:* Relative weight of future generations/non-human beings very high	*Scope of Government activity:* Low. self sufficiency and local activity should dominate *Policy Conflicts - economic vs. environmental:* Environmental *Policy Instruments:* Coercion *Participation:* Public led *Can society solve problems?* Very strong pessimism about technical fixes *Government authority:* None/localised	*Policy issues:* *(i) budgets:* Planning-led (low mobility and local sustainability emphasised) *(ii) programme performance:* Roads generate ecological poverty SACTRA report vindicates need for local sustainability

These beliefs are reflected in the following ways:

Capitalism is a negative development model Transport destroys the eco-system which is symptomatic of the impact of economic growth Mobility destroys liberty, denies children freedom to use the street etc.	The predict and provide model *cannot* be the basis of policy Roads impoverish and destroy prosperity in unquantifiable ways	Local transport/low mobility ought to be encouraged People given the choice would rather not travel

(modified from Sabatier, 1993, p. 31)

These differences are so extensive that, in the Major era, they resulted in real difficulties in reaching compromise between the pro-roads and anti-roads coalitions to the extent that a 'dialogue of the deaf' developed (Dudley and Richardson, 1996a, pp. 76-80):

> I can't get consensus with someone from, I don't know, Friends of the Earth, CPRE, because at heart those organisations have a very different view of how the world should be. In the main, they don't think economic growth is a very good thing because of the environmental consequences of that. Now that is very difficult, I can't accept that, the Federation can't accept that as a basic tenet because every one involved with the BRF is about developing economic ... or growth is good, kind of a thing. We might accept there are limits and we might accept there are ways in which it can and can't be achieved but fundamentally, economic growth is a good thing. And if you come across someone who says economic growth isn't then there is a chasm that you can't really breach. I think it is one of the things that has not come out of the 'great debate' and really about ... around transport issues generally is the degree to which many of the environmental groups, it is less to do with a transport campaign and more to do with, what would normally be, political campaigns because they are about the way in which society is organised and run. Now, normally that would be in the political sphere where you are elected or not elected. The reality is that environmental groups have had very little success in getting representation through the electoral system, therefore, they pursue it in other manners, which tends to blur the issue. (Interview, Paul Everitt, BRF, 21st August 1996)

Lily Matson, transport campaigner with the CPRE, shared this perception, arguing that in essence the capacity for co-operation between the pro and anti-roads groups is severely constrained by fundamental differences in the deep core beliefs of these groups:

> We meet across radio desks and we did have a meeting once (last year I think) with the BRF, and we exchange information. I might send a report I have produced or something like that. There is no obvious attempt at secrecy but there is — we clearly just come from completely different perspectives and one is not going to convince the other of their point of view so in many ways there is not much point. (Interview, 20th August 1996)

The ideological maps thus make it clear that movements between rival advocacy coalitions are difficult (and unlikely) even under circumstances in which disagreements within those coalitions may appear great.

In addition, Table 5.1 also illustrates that the division within the road lobby has been overstated. The acceptance by a number of the road user groups, in particular the AA and the RAC, that people *ought* to use their cars less does not indicate any change to either the deep core or near core beliefs of the actor concerned: in fact, it reflects the change of a secondary belief. As Jeremy Vanke from the RAC has argued, there are commercial benefits to be derived from their members using their cars less but this need not indicate any division of interest within the roads groups:

> The more people use their cars, the more they cost us. Every break down the RAC attends costs us forty quid. Now that is more than a lot of people pay for membership in a year. If people use their cars less they will still join the RAC (this is me being cynical) and we will make more money. But the RAC, as indeed the AA, is a non-profit organisation, there are no shareholders to satisfy. All of the profit is reinvested in the business. There is therefore no vested interest in increasing levels of the number of cars out there on the roads. (Interview, 29th May 1996)

Thus, in this case the change in emphasis from the RAC is based on reshaping a secondary belief following changes to the policy environment. In such circumstances, a change of policy serves to bring the objectives of the policy back into line with the deep core beliefs of the organisation: not changing policy in such circumstances would, in the light of increasing congestion, in fact make the realisation of the RAC's core beliefs more difficult.

Similarly, the public pronouncements by groups such as the CBI and the Freight Transport Association in favour of greater investment in public transport and their demand for more balanced investment across transport modes also represent no more than a reorientation of secondary beliefs by these groups (CBI 1995b, p. 28, para. 136, and CBI 1996, p. 18. For the view of the FTA see HC 104-II, p. 98). Such pronouncements do not indicate any change to core beliefs but instead mark a pragmatic acknowledgement that a policy which does not include greater investment in public transport is ultimately counter-productive to their primary interest, namely that of ensuring the smooth operation of the road network in order to facilitate economic growth:

> It seems to me given the underlying structure of society and the economy that there are not going to be huge changes in transport demand, you have to

try and deliver the quality of transport that people want in a way that is significantly less damaging to the environment ... what you're going to get is what we've always done, which is some form of a compromise, which means that yes, we will see larger areas within city centres as pedestrianised, or town centres pedestrianised, we will see more cycle lanes, more bus lanes, that kind of thing, but we will also see improvements in the strategic network: more bypasses, widening some motorways, some trunk roads, so that we get some sort of balance between the two. That sounds terribly ... but I believe it is a question of compromise, and it's a question of people being prepared to actually develop realistic alternatives, both in terms of alternative combinations of transport that give people the same degree of freedom and access and flexibility that they get from cars and lorries and that kind of thing, alongside measures that actually reduce the impact of that traffic. (Interview, Paul Everitt, BRF, 21st August 1996)

These changes, then, simply reflect changes to secondary beliefs within elements of the road lobby rather than a challenge to core or near core beliefs. But even so, these divisions proved difficult for elements of the pro-roads groups to control. Links began to develop between groups such as the RAC and Transport 2000 and areas of common interest began to form on the basis of secondary beliefs, often excluding the road construction interests. Lily Matson of CPRE provided an indication of the development of understanding between elements of the pro and anti-roads groups:

I think it is important for interest groups to be aware of what the other groups are saying though and if they say something that is true, or it is real, or it exposes some new dilemma with research then you can't ignore that. For example, the RAC commissioned some quite important research on car dependency, and we may disagree with exactly how they interpret it, but that research is important, and we will use that, and I am glad they have done it. (Interview, 20th August 1996)

A further and potentially more fundamental division occurred within the road lobby as a result of the challenge to the 'predict and provide' orthodoxy. A number of the road user groups began to alter their priorities for the road network in response to this change, acknowledging that widespread road building is no longer feasible:

We have in our constitution a duty to protect the motorist's interest: increasing congestion and going the way we are is not in the motorist's interest – even if we consider the motorist as someone who spends twenty four hours a day behind the wheel of a car, and thinks of nothing else. If we

> get real and think about what motorists really want, it's not in our interest to
> promote road building, to promote increased car use and so on. It's in their
> interests for us to promote a balanced and integrated transport policy that
> gives them the choice of how they travel and satisfies their own economic,
> environmental and social requirements. (Interview, Jeremy Vanke, RAC,
> 29th May 1996)

However, a number of interviewees have suggested that the
significance of this apparent division over the predict and provide
orthodoxy has been overstated. In particular, one suggested that the public
pronouncements of a number of the road user groups had been primarily
motivated by commercial necessity rather than a change in core beliefs:

> The changes that I talked about earlier about media presentation, and how
> lobbying goes on, have affected all organisations, not just within the road
> lobby, but within all those kind of organisations. Now some have come to
> terms with that better than others – the way in which the public concern, or
> the way in which the public perceives environmental problems, has created
> problems for the more commercial[ly dependent members] of the road
> lobby, or elements of the road lobby that rely on, basically, public support
> for the purchase of their services ... they're caught in a very difficult
> situation, where – I don't think they're very clear in their own minds as to
> what their public policy objectives are. Because they want, at one and the
> same time, yes, like everybody they want to be environmentally friendly,
> they want to ride that wave, but equally, their commercial success demands
> car use. (Interview, unattributable)

Thus, although a number of the road user groups did acknowledge
the limitations of the predict and provide model in providing sufficient
infrastructure in the long term, they remained committed to the core belief
that the primary function of the road network ought to remain unchanged:
namely, to promote economic development, personal freedom and liberty.
Thus, the changes in the emphasis of policy within the road user groups in
fact represent a division over near core beliefs and not core beliefs.

In contrast, it is argued that elements of the road construction sector
were slower than the road user groups to adjust to the implications of the
challenge to the predict and provide orthodoxy. The continuity of these
groups' beliefs is illustrated by their continued emphasis throughout the
Major period on the importance of developing a strategic hierarchy of roads
which are essential for the economy:

Certainly some of the things that we've been working on are to do with creating a more defined hierarchy of roads, so that you've got heavy traffic focused on a limited number of routes, but those routes would obviously have to be high capacity, with high environmental standards, so that anyone next to them didn't have too awful a life. But the trade off of that is that obviously on other sorts of roads the intrusion by heavy traffic would be significantly reduced thereby protecting people's quality of life ... I think that our task is to ensure that people do fully appreciate that the road improvements of one form or another are part of that broader strategy. Up until now we've heard a lot about sustainable transport or integrated transport, but in the main what those people seem to say is, 'Everything *but* improving the road', and if you've got 90% of all traffic, of all journeys, being undertaken on the road network, then it's fairly stupid really, or fairly short-sighted, to believe that you don't have to address realistically the problems on there. (Interview, Paul Everitt, BRF, 21st August 1996)

However, the primary motive for this emphasis on continued road building by the construction sector was based on a need to protect their commercial income rather than the need to protect a primary belief. This is evidenced by the fact that as the conflict over the road programme became more intense and the predict and provide orthodoxy was increasingly discredited, the construction interests started to change their priorities away from road building towards road improvements and road maintenance in order to protect their commercial interests:

A lot of what we are doing at the moment is about trying to put in place a programme to upgrade the environmental performance of the network. That has nothing to do with increasing capacity, or building new bits, but merely about looking at how you can improve its environmental performance through things like noise barriers, low noise surfaces, landscaping and general planting and management of the verges. (Paul Everitt, BRF, 21st August 1996)

Overall, therefore, while apparent divisions emerged between members of the road lobby as some elements, particularly road users, re-oriented their objectives, no change occurred in the core beliefs of the lobby. As Tables 5.1 and 5.2 illustrate, although the divisions within the road lobby over the implications of the end of the predict and provide orthodoxy seem intense, they do not represent a division in core beliefs, in fact indicating conflicts which are restricted to near core and secondary beliefs.

Examining the Cohesion of the Anti-Roads Groups in the Major Era

In the Major period, a lack of cohesion between the moderate anti-roads groups and the direct action groups further weakened the capacity of the anti-roads lobby to alter the nature of the transport policy network. Tables 5.2 and 5.3 show that the anti-roads 'coalition' is itself divided into two discrete advocacy coalitions, thus weakening its ability to form a coherent group. In particular, considerable differences between the deep core beliefs of the moderate and the direct action groups pose significant problems in the co-ordination of strategy, tactics and communication between the different groups. As Simon Festing, transport campaigner for Friends of the Earth, has reflected:

> Working with the direct action movement is a challenge. When a hierarchical organisation like FoE comes into contact with a loose network of activists with a very different views on radical action, the cultures can clash. The direct action movements have varying views about FoE. Some do not accept we should exist. They see us as part of the system which they are challenging. Some recognise how we feel but feel we are not radical enough – the 'Friends of the armchair' approach. Others do not think about our work, but have their own agendas. At Newbury, a small number of protesters thought FoE should be organising firewood collections for the camps! (Festing, 1997, unpaginated)

Although there is no literature applying Sabatier's advocacy coalition framework to the anti-roads groups in the UK, Doherty's work can be used to provide some theoretical support for the view that real divisions exist within the anti-roads 'coalition' (see in particular 1997). According to Doherty, 'eco-protesters take on planetary concerns, and local and national policy changes; cultural questions about the nature of public space and spiritual relationships with nature as well as detailed technical discourse. Their cultural codes are clearly challenges to the dominant codes' (1997, pp. 154-55). The direct action movement, as Table 5.3 shows, operates with a series of core beliefs which are very different to those of the moderate anti-roads groups.

Furthermore, Doherty argues that differences between the core beliefs of the protesters and local NIMBY groups created considerable obstacles to building partnerships at a grass roots level:

> The medieval character of the battle, with massed lines of security guards with bright tunics moving through the mist, siege engines manoeuvring slowly towards their goal, with a phalanx of police and knights in the form

of police on horseback, reinforced the sense of dislocation from everyday life. While more conventional groups of locals were often portrayed acting in support of the eco-protesters, they were always on the fringes, reinforcing the image that eco-protest had become a technically skilled form of action, which not only required a difficult lifestyle, but also a degree of professionalism, that should not be attempted by amateurs. (1997, p. 152)

This separation between the direct action movement and local NIMBY protesters is symptomatic of a fundamental division between the core beliefs of these groups which, as Simon Festing of FoE has argued, centres on differing conceptions of the relationship between protesting and the democratic system:

The direct action movement can itself be accused of being undemocratic. There are (perhaps legitimate) concerns about the way direct action people can swoop in as sort of rent-a-mob outsiders to do a last-ditch battle with the bulldozers, and the public image of the eco-warrior is rarely backed by clear cut campaign victories. To those who believe in the British institutions of democracy and planning, the anarchic approach goes against their ideas of rational argument. In short, there can be public hostility to direct action, and this can be worrying. (Festing, 1997, unpaginated)

As a result, the credibility of groups which retain strong links to the direct action movement remains low in the eyes of policy makers: they are perceived as dysfunctional, anti-democratic and incapable of accepting the 'legitimate' forums for consultation. As John Stewart of ALARM UK has argued, even those groups which moderated their activity in the Major era and moved from the status of *outsider by choice* towards *peripheral insiders* (Maloney *et al*, 1994) had considerable legitimacy problems as a result of their continuing association with the direct action movement (Interview, 23rd November 1995).

Thus far I have argued in this chapter that the changes to the transport policy network in the Major era were not as significant as they first appeared, as the pro-roads groups and the anti-roads groups in fact remained divided between three discrete advocacy coalitions. Thus, even the so-called 'moderate' anti-roads groups were unable to build links with insider groups in the Major era. In this context, the Major government's launching of a 'Great Debate' on transport in 1994 aimed, according to that government, to reach consensus between transport actors. The next task of this chapter is therefore to consider what effect, if any, this 'Great Debate' had on the status of the anti-roads groups.

The 'Great Debate'

> I wish to see an end to the shouting and insults – sometimes even actual violence – that have characterised arguments about transport in recent years. I want a cease fire; a fresh start. We need to move back to proper informed, rationale argument, respect for opposing views, in the manner more fitting to the democratic traditions of our country. My aim is to define the questions and seek to pose them in as sharp and clear a way as possible. I hope others will contribute to that process and, more importantly, will then help to shape the answers to those questions. (Dr. Brian Mawhinney, 7th December 1994, cited in CBI, 1995, exhibit 22)

The 'Great Debate' was launched on 7th December 1994 (*Financial Times*, 8th December 1994) by the then Secretary of State for Transport, Dr. Brian Mawhinney, who set the parameters of the consultation process in a series of six speeches in late 1994 and early 1995 on the topics of transport and the economy; transport and the environment; freight transport; international transport; the importance of choice, and urban transport (speeches reproduced in Mawhinney, 1995). In June 1995 these were published as a collection which invited responses from interested parties in order to find 'a way forward for Britain's transport policy' (DTp, 1995c).

On the surface, the 'Great Debate' presaged a time of unprecedented consultation over transport policy, which could enable hitherto outsider groups to gain insider status. Mawhinney himself stated that a primary objective of the debate was to increase dialogue and achieve consensus between groups over the future path of public policy. In a speech to the Leeds and Bradford Chamber of Commerce in April 1995 he made his position clear:

> I hope you and others will look at the speeches together, and then get together to suggest some answers to the questions I have raised. Not in comfortable, like-minded groups but in difficult and challenging forums. Only by taking such risks and accepting such challenges can we move forward to the next stage of the debate. (Mawhinney, in DTp 1995b, para. 46)

The 'Great Debate' did increase consultation between the road lobby and the anti-roads groups. However, there are two principal reasons to suggest that the process did not result in any significant change in status for the outsider groups. First, a number of the anti-roads groups expressed general dissatisfaction with the consultation process itself. Lily Matson of the CPRE argued:

> I think that Mawhinney's idea was a bit of cop out really because it is not for pressure groups, which represent different perspectives, to come to consensus, it's about governments who make decisions based on what a range of interests say. (Interview, 20th August 1996)

As I have argued earlier in this chapter, the rival advocacy coalitions have very different core beliefs, thus being unable to reach consensus on fundamental issues of policy. A number of interviewees have suggested that in such circumstances the 'Great Debate' was not actually designed to strengthen the links between groups, but was rather motivated by a desire to manage the transport agenda in the run up to the general election which was scheduled for 1997:

> Mawhinney opened the debate, which was the greatest stalling tactic I have yet to see. I am not saying that was a bad ploy. But the point is that they stop everything while they are doing that. And one is highly suspicious that they are just slicing off that budget [i.e. the transport budget] so that they can feed [it] into tax benefits to buy themselves back into power next time round. (Interview information, senior transport consultant, February 1996)

Second, the capacity of the anti-roads groups to gain insider status through the 'Great Debate' process was restricted by the content of Mawhinney's speeches which, in practical terms, restricted the scope of the debate. In particular, Mawhinney emphasised the government's view of the relationship between the environment and the economy and the importance of consumer choice in transport, both areas of significant division between the anti-roads groups and the Major government.

Mawhinney opened the debate with the view that economic development and environmental protection must inevitably be traded off against one another:

> Perhaps the most fundamental question of all – are we prepared to curtail our rising economic prosperity to some extent – to any extent – to protect the site of historic significance, the rare flower or the great crested newt and all they represent? (Mawhinney, 1995, p. 16)

In contrast, in their submissions to the 'Great Debate' the anti-roads groups rejected this rationale. Both the CPRE and the RSPB, for example, rejected the view that economic development and environmental protection should be seen as policy trade-offs, arguing that central government should develop policy within a model of sustainable development, 'whereby the environment is seen as the framework within which other objectives are set' (CPRE, 1995, para. 3.4. See also para. 2.7).

This view was also reflected within the RSPB's submission, which argued that the government ought to integrate transport, the economy and environmental protection in a coherent package of policy proposals: 'Such a goal [according to the RSPB] requires fundamental shifts in environmental and economic policies and the relationships between them' (RSPB, 1995, p. 4). Thus significant differences between the views of the Major government and those of the anti-roads groups on the relationship between the environment and the economy pervaded the 'Great Debate' from the start.

Significant philosophical differences between the Major government and the anti-roads groups also manifested themselves in relation to the concept of choice. In his fifth speech, *Transport and Choice*, Dr. Mawhinney stressed that a central objective of both the Thatcher and Major governments had been to increase choice, thereby increasing personal freedom (DTp 1995a, para. 1):

> Transport has a vital role to play in increasing and protecting freedom. Easy mobility is a defining feature of a free society. Wherever people live under democracy, they have freedom of movement. In the old communist regimes freedom to travel was restricted to the elite. Ordinary men and women were not permitted to travel freely let alone to leave to visit other countries. In free societies people are free to travel when they want, how they want and wherever they want to go. (Mawhinney, in DTp 1995a, para. 2)

According to Mawhinney, choice had been crucial to the development of the UK economy, increasing access to both housing, retail and leisure facilities and job opportunities (DTp 1995a, paras 18-22). 'This is a healthy requirement: it leads to improvement in service through competition and to higher standards. Government should seek to promote this kind of choice for sound economic reasons as well as to meet the natural wishes of our citizens' (DTp 1995a, para. 5).

Therefore, according to the terms of the debate set out by Mawhinney, the government's role was to encourage choice, with its positive effect on economic and political development. Furthermore, the environmental effects of transport ought to be limited by voluntary changes in the behaviour of transport consumers, rather than from policies which forced changes to behaviour:

If people are genuinely concerned to reduce environmental impacts, they have responsibility themselves to take actions reflecting those views. Calls for the Government to 'show a lead', and to bring about fundamental changes in the way society works, need to be tempered by the knowledge that Government can lead only where people are prepared to follow. Government cannot easily force people to change their lifestyles, at least not without dire consequences. (DTp 1995a, para. 28)

The anti-roads groups' responses to this speech on choice were divided into two distinct views.[3] 'Moderate' anti-roads groups, such as the RSPB, broadly supported the government's philosophy, acknowledging that central government is restricted by the choices which individuals make. The RSPB agreed that the main function of government was to 'lead the way and influence attitudes and decisions' (RSPB, 1995, p. 20). This should be achieved through the full implementation of the measures contained within the 18th report of the RCEP, *Transport and the Environment* (RCEP, 1994), such as land-use planning policy; economic instruments such as fuel taxes and road pricing; and increased spending on alternatives to improve access to walking cycling and public transport (RSPB, 1995, p. 10). Thus, the RSPB supported Mawhinney's view: government can create a framework within which choice is exercised but 'ultimately, it is the attitudes and decisions of millions of individuals and businesses which will determine whether these objectives can be met' (RSPB, 1995, p. 20).

In contrast, more 'radical' groups such as the CPRE were highly critical of the way in which Mawhinney framed the concept of choice. In their submission the CPRE took issue with Mawhinney's view that any action which aimed to reduce mobility imposed restrictions on personal freedom. This was a significant limitation of the terms of the debate, according to the CPRE; following the challenge to the predict and provide orthodoxy it had become increasingly important for central government to integrate transport with land use planning, thus reducing the need to travel. The integration of transport and land-use planning in this way would, argued the CPRE, in fact increase the choices available to all transport consumers, by enabling them to choose from a range of alternative provision for each journey (CPRE, 1995, paras 3.10-3.13).

We can conclude that the consultation process which the Major government launched through the 'Great Debate' did not reflect a genuine desire to achieve consensus between the road lobby and the anti-roads groups. First, the government instigated the 'Great Debate' with a clear sense both of its own objectives and of the parameters within which the debate would be conducted. Furthermore, the 'Great Debate' did not result in any widespread change in the status of the anti-roads groups – which retained their status as either peripheral insiders or outsiders – because the core values of these groups remained quite different to those of the Major government. Thus the 'Great Debate' was largely a cosmetic exercise, designed to retain control over the agenda setting process prior to the general election which was due in 1997.

In the Major era, the capacity of the anti-roads groups to alter the nature of the transport policy network was further restricted by the operation of the structural imperatives of the state. I have argued in Chapter 3 that, historically, government policy was founded on three bases: that a free-flowing road network was essential for economic prosperity; that transport policy ought to be market-based, responding to demands placed on the network (the predict and provide orthodoxy), and that transport policy was important in order to support democratic ideals such as liberty and freedom. These structural imperatives of the state can also be represented using Sabatier's framework, where they show very strong parallels with the beliefs of the pro-roads groups which are outlined in Table 5.1.

Although developments in the problem stream challenged the coherence of the predict and provide orthodoxy during the Major era, as we saw in Chapter 4, the key policy rationale of central government remained intact: namely a commitment, as before, to maintaining free-flowing roads to aid economic development; to market-based policy and to the link between transport and democratic consolidation. Despite the change from 'predict and provide' to 'restrict and provide', these basic structural imperatives continued in full force.

Significant differences remained between the structural imperatives of the state and the beliefs of both the direct action movement and the moderate anti-roads groups, thus preventing the anti-roads groups from gaining insider status. In consequence they were denied access to conventional policy arenas, instead having to seek out alternative arenas which did not reflect either the institutional biases of the road lobby or the structural imperatives of the state. The next task of this chapter is therefore to consider the extent to which such alternative arenas enabled the anti-roads groups to overcome their relative lack of power within the agenda setting process.

Alternative Policy Arenas and the Anti-Roads Groups

Dudley and Richardson's work on policy change in British trunk roads policy is particularly useful for exploring the capacity of the anti-roads groups to infiltrate alternative policy arenas in the Major period (Dudley and Richardson, 1995, 1996a, 1998. I explore their contribution in detail in Chapter 2). John Stewart, of anti-roads group ALARM UK, emphasised the importance of seeking alternative policy arenas for the campaigning of the anti-roads groups at this time:

> Now, I think the key difference, and I think that one of the things that ALARM from an early stage has been advocating, is a different sort of campaigning. And that is campaigning on what we call 'our territory, our group's territory'. So that, you don't wait until the public enquiry. Campaigning on our territory is starting at a very early stage doing two things. One, getting the community behind you, the local community, which is not necessarily what the groups in the '70s did. Some of them did but on the whole it was a handful of individuals who were making a noise. Once you've got the community behind you that's one thing, but the second thing is with the community behind you start campaigning at street stalls, stunts, using the media. Somebody said, 'One picture in a local newspaper for a group is much more important than a thousand words written to a junior official in the Department of Transport, who'll probably never read it anyway.' [So] it's taking the fight to the Department of Transport, not always reacting to them. In a sense the groups that have won, these are the two things that typify the winners; starting early, campaigning on their own territory, and having the community behind them. These are the two key elements and groups that have had that have rarely lost a roads fight in the '80s and '90s. (Interview, 23rd November 1995)

Dudley and Richardson's actor centred account of agenda setting in the transport area hinges on two key premises: that the strategies of the outsider groups opened new arenas to the anti-roads groups, thus creating opportunities for them to challenge the dominance of the pro-roads lobby; and that these changes, in a causal sense, explain the transformation of the transport agenda in the Major era. The following analysis shows that the activities of the anti-roads groups indeed opened a number of new arenas of political conflict in this period, in particular through the relationship between the media and the direct action protests which were undertaken at the construction sites. However, I will argue that these changes have not had as extensive an impact on the agenda setting process as Dudley and

Richardson suggest, because these new arenas have only an arm's length relationship with the policy making process.

The Twyford Factor: The Media and the Politics of Direct Action

A number of studies of the politics of the car have focused on the effect of the interaction between direct action and the media on the policy agenda (Anderson, 1997, Paterson, 1997, Doherty, 1997, Dudley and Richardson, 1996a and Young, 1993). In the 1970s, conflict centred on the highway inquiry process, being explicitly designed to disrupt its operation and thus gain widespread coverage in the mass media (Tyme, 1978, p. 40, Levin, 1979, p. 27, Dudley and Richardson, 1998). By the 1990s, however, the intensity of the conflict between rival interests had increased dramatically. Significant sectors of the anti-roads 'alliance' had lost faith in the highway inquiry process, resulting in a new form of transport protest focused on disruption and physical obstruction of the road construction sites. As was the case in the 1970s, the protests were conducted in ways guaranteed to secure extensive coverage in the media (Doherty, 1997, p. 154).

Doherty argues that these new kinds of anti-roads protests took on the character of 'a form of siege warfare', in which the occupiers build defences in trees, tunnels and houses and the 'besiegers outnumber the occupiers and have greater resources' (1997, p. 150). In spite of the imbalance of resources between these groups, the protesters had considerable success in maintaining media interest in the protests through a process of ongoing technological innovation in the nature of the tactics which they employed. The most significant of these innovations were lock-ons, walkways, tripods and tunnels, all of which depend for their success, and a high media profile, 'upon the risks taken by the protester. By making themselves vulnerable, they require the evictors to take extra care and time, to avoid injury' (Doherty, 1997, p. 153). Protesters were thus able to sustain the interest of the media in the conflict over roads.

The impact of the direct action movement on the media's handling of the transport issue was considerable. In an interview Keith Harper, transport correspondent for the *Guardian* newspaper, suggested that the tactics of the direct action movement had been instrumental in changing the perception of the transport issue from that of a technical and specialist issue to an emotive and public one. The protests at Twyford Down, in particular, were extremely important as for the first time the act of protest became news in, and of, itself. The impact on the editorial process within the media was significant: editors began to report the protests as general news stories, and through association a number of hitherto specialist transport stories gained an emotive aspect and a higher media profile (Interview, 8th May 1996). Another respondent commented on the media's changing relationship to the transport agenda in this way:

> They are commercial organisations and they have to sell their papers ... Now if you come into the technical areas of the specialist correspondents: the transport correspondents – they get squeezed out [by the editors]. If they have got a story running and something big comes on they get pushed out – editors will do that. But if they are going to put something in – yes they will go for the story which has, something different, a bit of bite to it. And what they tend to like will of course be bailiffs lifting people out of trees. Now the relevance of that to the overall issue of Newbury, for example, where the local residents would like a bypass, as would indeed the residents of about 259 other places in Britain, is lost. (Interview, Sydney Balgarnie, Road Haulage Association, 21st August 1996)

These changes to the coverage of the transport issue had significant consequences. Transport increasingly came to be seen by the public in emotive terms, no longer being considered as a specialist issue. As Baumgartner and Jones have argued, when a core policy community loses control over the perception of an issue in this way, it is also likely to lose control over the policy process itself (1991, p. 1050). A senior employee of the British Road Federation reflected these concerns when he argued:

> The fact that you've got protesters or people making statements in such a vigorous or photogenic manner clearly is more appealing from the news editor's perspective. I think that the way in which the media is being used by the environmental groups, in general, has left a lot of the traditional trade associations, campaigning type groups, in a difficult position. They don't know how to respond and clearly you can't ... it would be great if you could get fifty truckers, or a hundred truckers, to drive into central London and block off all the roads and say, 'We want better facilities'. Realistically, that is not going to happen because the people who, if you like, are in charge of those sorts of organisations are traditionally conservative (and that is with a small c). And clearly, their tradition has been to campaign, lobby, in a much more laid back, traditional, style. You know, talking to Ministers; talking to politicians; talking to civil servants, so that they get their message across, rather than, if you like, trying to seize the media attention and set the agenda that way. So that is a change. (Interview, Paul Everitt, BRF, 21st August 1996)

The impact of this change was considerable. Firstly, as the interviewee from the BRF argued, the direct action campaigns of the anti-roads groups utilised a form of protest which was not open to the road lobby at that time. And direct action is not governed by rules of engagement which can be controlled by the pro-roads groups in the way that the highway inquiry process is. Highway inquiries have, by their nature, always restricted the scope of the opposition to a particular road scheme: for example, it is not possible to question the need for a road in the first place or to request that a single road proposal be looked at in relation to the strategic plan for the whole network (Levin, 1979, pp. 23-31). In such conditions, the pro-roads groups enjoy considerable institutional advantages in their dealings with the anti-roads groups.

In contrast, the direct action arena presented considerable problems for the pro-roads groups as, for the first time, the anti-roads groups gained institutional advantage in their conflict with the road lobby. The culture of the road lobby restricts its capacity to deploy outsider tactics in order to get its message across; direct action is a much more rational tactic for groups which are outside the political mainstream. It is highly confrontational, and frequently extralegal, thus appealing to groups which have little to lose in alienating mainstream political opinion.

Secondly, the insider groups' traditional methods of lobbying encountered increasing difficulties in retaining the attention of news editors, with the result that an important line of communication between the pro-roads groups and the public was progressively restricted during the Major era. At the same time, the direct action groups gained unprecedented media access to the public and, therefore, gained a greater capacity to project their ideas to an attentive audience.

However, although these changes have had a significant effect on what Schattschneider would term the 'public' perception of the transport issue, they have had less effect on the 'private' perception of the issue, which remains closed to the direct action movement. From their outsider perspective, policy making is still characterised by frequent contact between government bureaucrats and the pro-roads groups in a core policy community. As John Stewart of ALARM UK has argued, the effect of the media interest in direct action has been double-edged: while it enabled anti-roads groups to gain access to public opinion, it also led to concerns amongst government policy makers over the capacity of these groups to engage in conventional dialogue:

I think it is absolutely true to say that a lot of people in authority, I don't just mean government, but local authorities and a number of the politicians of all parties are very wary of meeting ALARM UK. I think they are not quite sure what they are going to get. Whether they are going to get a protest outside their door or whether we are all going to turn up with dogs on strings. And I think fundamentally they don't actually believe that we've got transport arguments, i.e. anything relevant to say. I think that they partly they want to think that, some of them. Partly, it's the effect of the media. The media has been ... It highlights very much the drama, obviously, the direct action and all that business. So what they think is that we're going to simply come and either chain ourselves to their desks, tempting though it is, or simply at least come charging with our banners our mantra, 'No more roads', and that's it. (Interview, 23rd November 1995)

Thirdly, however, the activity of the direct action groups *was* important in enabling 'moderate' anti-roads groups, in particular Transport 2000, to gain greater access to policy makers (see Figure 3.4 above). Following the increased coverage of the anti-roads protests in the media, Transport 2000 developed 'an unofficial partnership' with sections of the direct action movement, in which they came to be seen as spokesman for the protests, based on their capacity to operate with an insider group strategy which gains access to the machinery of government:

I think we have deliberately worked it that we have got this kind of unofficial partnership with Transport 2000. If they weren't there we would have problems and probably if we weren't here they wouldn't be as strong. Stephen Joseph their director has often said to me: 'Well look. I go and meet officials', he'll say, 'I may have very good arguments, but if they know there are 250 ALARM UK groups out in the country also saying the same sort of thing, then they'll listen much more readily'. So there is this sort of two-way thing. (Interview, John Stewart, ALARM UK, 23rd November 1995)

Cobb and Elder's work on outsider groups provides a theoretical explanation for the increasing capacity of Transport 2000 to gain access to the decision making process. They argue that in order for outsider interests to affect the agenda, they often need a group which is willing to resort to extra-legal activity, violence or direct action to gain the attention of the media and establish their credibility in the eyes of policy makers (Cobb and Elder, 1972, pp. 54-55. See also Nieburg, 1962, and Anderson, 1997, pp. 117-28).

This theoretical contention is well supported in the transport case. The anti-roads groups gained a number of advantages in the Major era which resulted directly from their usage of extra-legal outsider tactics. Before the advent of the direct action protests the 'moderate' anti-roads groups did not have the support of any groups willing to resort to extra-legal activity. There were protests aimed at disrupting the public inquiry process, but no activists directly obstructed the implementation of a road scheme. Following the protests at Twyford Down, however, the anti-roads groups were able to mobilise the full scope of the tactics available to them, opening up wider access to the media and gaining greater public legitimacy.

Increased media attention thus enabled the more 'moderate' anti-roads groups to gain a platform for their message. This was vital in changing the public perception of the transport issue: once seen as a technical, specialist area, it became linked by the public to emotive issues such as nature and health. An important legacy of the direct action movement was, therefore, the development of extra-legal activity to complement the insider strategy of groups such as Transport 2000, thus enabling the anti-roads groups to utilise the full scope of tactics required for a successful campaign by an outsider interest.

Parliament and the Politics of Public Schizophrenia

Parliament also offered new institutional opportunities to the opponents of roads in the Major era. Following the 1992 general election the Parliamentary majority of the Major government was reduced to 21; this majority continued to decrease during the lifetime of the government. The effect of Major's small majority was variable: in general terms, 'the drop in the majority [...] represented more of a potential than an actual threat' to Major's administration, but on certain policy issues, ministers 'had to make concessions to their own backbenchers' in response to a threat of rebellion by a group of MPs (Riddel, 1994, p. 49. See also Ludlum, 1996, pp. 117-25). This weakness in the administration affected a number of proposed schemes within the government's *Roads for Prosperity* programme (Cm 693).

The centrepiece of backbench opposition in the roads case related to a series of schemes proposed in the South-East of England, with the proposal to widen the M25 between the M3 and the M4 to 14 lanes (DTp 1994, p. 18 and pp. 50-53) providing the principal focus of conflict:

> It was going straight to six lanes [on each side of the carriage way] that made us all sit back and say, 'Wait a minute; this is another motorway; where is this policy taking us? Why are they actually doing it?' It is so startling it forces you to stand back and say, 'Does this make any sense?' And then you start talking to other people who say, 'Actually, I don't think it makes sense either'. (Interview, Sir George Pattie MP, BBC, 1994)

This, together with other proposals within the government's roads programme, provided the impetus for a group of MPs to come together and co-ordinate their opposition. A BBC *Panorama* programme, *Nose to Tail*, identified 10 MPs who were instrumental in leading Parliamentary opposition to three principal schemes: the widening of the M25 and the M62, and a proposed East-West route from Harwich to South Wales through Buckinghamshire (BBC, 1994). According to George Walden, MP for Buckingham, these proposals failed to reflect the widespread desire for a multi-modal transport policy:

> You are now getting a national feeling, which I share, that there is a policy for cars but there is not a transport policy. And I think that that is one thing that has inflamed opinion here. It is not just the local aspect, which is very important: they have no idea, any more than I do, where our transport policy is going other than building more and more roads for more and more cars. (Interview, BBC, 1994)

Opponents of the road schemes in Parliament were joined by local government representatives, similarly concerned about the electoral implications of widespread road building. In the South East, the local authorities affected by the government's road proposals formed an alliance (SERPLAN) under the leadership of the transportation director of Surrey county council, Geoffrey Lamb, in order to lobby the government for alternative solutions (BBC, 1994). Once again the sheer scale of the proposed widening of the M25 provided the focal event for the opponents of further road building:

> If you look at some of the things that were proposed: the sections through Surrey. If it had been done incrementally then probably no one would have noticed ... [Laughter] ... That sounds a bit stupid I know. They blew up this huge political balloon and someone was bound to try and prick it. It was just too tempting. And when they saw that ... I think it's because it was done without real thought. And then when you have the stalwarts of the Tory heartland come out against it (you could say they came out on NIMBYism or whatever): counties like Surrey who are very, very powerful. The war

they can rage against proposals like that is pretty substantial. They are not ALARM or even Friends of the Earth, they can mount a terrific campaign. And of course all the others joined them. So, in a way they almost set themselves ... it was almost a sucker punch. They set themselves up to fall. (Interview, senior transport consultant, February 1996)

The importance of this combined opposition of Conservative councils and MPs in South East England, in particular, was considerable. However, the increasing opposition of backbench MPs and local councillors in the electoral arena did not provide the access to new arenas for the anti-roads groups which may have been anticipated. The reason for this is that this opposition to the government's road schemes was motivated, for the most part, by short term electoral considerations based only on a desire to appease the concerns of middle-class voters, not in response to the demands of the direct action movement.

The real interest is that it is people, you know very respectable, middle-class, Conservative voting, car owners who are concerned about the prospect that infinite traffic growth appears to lead inevitably to more and more infrastructure and more and more environmental interference. [The response of government to increasing concern over the environmental impacts of transport] comes not from the sort of Newburian tree hoppers, who frankly, I must tell you, if you want an insight into government nobody here takes the slightest bit seriously, because the only interest they have in a bypass is in a kind of democracy bypass. (Interview, Steven Norris, former Minister for Public Transport, Traffic Safety and Transport in London, 29th June 1996. For similar comments reflecting the impact of middle class opposition on the media see Bryant (1996, p. 192))

The growth of the opposition in 'middle England' to the government's proposals changed the balance of power within a number of constituencies, which moved, electorally, from having a pro-roads lobby to an anti-roads lobby: 'Fifteen years ago every Tory MP probably had some sort of residents' group in his, or her, constituency looking for a road. Now you can guarantee they'll have a pressure group, everyone will have some sort of anti-roads group in their constituency' (Interview, John Stewart, ALARM UK, 23rd November 1995).

In this changed political environment, the anti-roads groups were able to rely on a supportive climate of public opinion in order to project their message to the Parliamentary arena. John Stewart, of anti-roads group ALARM UK, emphasised the importance of this link at this time:

My feeling is that this change, certainly in a lot of this grass roots protest, would not have been successful if it had merely been a few people throwing themselves in front of bulldozers in Twyford Down, or what-have-you. They would have been marginalised. It's been successful because it's had, what I called, I rather like the phrase so I'll use it again, 'The voting classes' behind it. (Interview, John Stewart, ALARM UK, 23rd November 1995)

The capacity of the anti-roads groups to generate links between the media/construction arena and the Parliamentary arena was thus highly conditional. In relying on the support of changing public opinion in order to influence the policy agenda the anti-roads groups were open to real weaknesses in their ability to effect change. The principal problem, as a number of respondents have pointed out, is that public opinion on the roads issue is subject to high levels of internal inconsistency: while road users oppose the building of new roads and show high awareness of the environmental impacts of motor vehicles, they are unwilling to change their own behaviour to reflect this environmental consciousness:[4]

I hesitate to slight public opinion as hypocritical but the truth is that if you probe very carefully you are absolutely right [that there is widespread inconsistency within public opinion]. There is at one level this deeply honest, caring response about the impact of growth in car usage on the environment, but all the evidence is that the elasticity of change is extremely limited. (Interview, Keith Hill MP, 26th February 1996)

The cuts to the roads programme in the period 1995-8 can, therefore, only really be explained as a pragmatic reaction to pressure by governmental actors operating within the Parliamentary arena. This pressure resulted from the contradictory demands of the 'voting classes', combined with the need to reduce public expenditure (Dudley and Richardson, 1996a, p. 80). The cuts to the road programme at this time should thus not lead us to conclude that any fundamental change to the priorities of government occurred as a result of the activity of the anti-roads groups. In fact, a focus on the Parliamentary arena has revealed that outsider groups are still heavily reliant on influencing public opinion at 'arm's length'.

Overall then, parliament's changing attitude to the roads programme during this time was a pragmatic response to public opinion, largely driven by the small majority which the Major administration enjoyed in the last Parliament. Parliament thus was (and remains) an unstable arena for the anti-roads groups, as this analysis shows that it was merely motivated by ambiguous public opinion, trying to balance short term environmental and revenue saving concerns with future demands by the public for further road building.

The position of the anti-roads groups as parliamentary lobbyists is unlikely to improve: their fundamental problem is that, despite a temporary alliance of interests, the movement has had only weak links to local NIMBY groups on the ground. Consideration of Sabatier's work on advocacy coalitions, discussed above, must lead us to conclude that the situation will remain unchanged, for closer analysis shows that the NIMBY protesters and the direct action movement are motivated by very different deep core beliefs. Thus alliance building between them is very difficult, if not impossible.

Conclusion

This chapter has explored the influence of actors on agenda setting in the Major era, focusing on changes to the nature of the transport policy network and on the capacity of the anti-roads groups to open up new policy arenas not dominated by the priorities of the road lobby.

As we have seen, one particular view of developments in the Major era is that changes to the nature of the transport policy network can be used to explain, in a causal sense, changes to the transport agenda. This view argues that during the Major era the road lobby became increasingly fragmented, while at the same time a number of anti-roads groups moved towards insider status. However, this chapter has argued that there are a number of reasons to question the core assumption on which such a hypothesis is based.

Firstly, Sabatier's work on belief systems suggests that the apparent divisions within the road lobby were in fact based only on differences over secondary or near core beliefs; the groups remained unified on the basis of fundamental core beliefs. Thus the likelihood of the road user groups and the more moderate elements of the anti-roads groups forming a new advocacy coalition remains severely limited.

Secondly, the theory of advocacy coalition frameworks has enabled us to suggest that there are significant structural problems for the anti-roads groups in any attempt to form a coherent coalition between the so called 'moderate' groups and the direct action movement in the long term. This chapter has examined the core beliefs of these groups and concluded that significant differences exist between them. The anti-roads lobby is in fact based on an alliance of two quite different advocacy coalitions whose unity was forged on the existence of an extensive road programme around which to rally in opposition; without such a programme real doubts must exist of the extent to which the anti-roads lobby would be able to maintain coherent links between the two advocacy coalitions in the future.

In addition, the theory of advocacy coalition frameworks has enabled us to evaluate the extent to which groups such as Transport 2000, which have historically had outsider status, were able to gain meaningful access to decision makers during the Major period. This chapter reflects the work of Maloney *et al* (1994) on the insider-outsider model, arguing that the anti-roads groups have historically been excluded from the consultation process because their goals are at odds with those of central government.

As I have argued in Chapter 4, developments in the problem stream in the Major period led to changes to the predict and provide orthodoxy which enabled hitherto 'moderate' outsider groups (i.e. outsiders by goal according to Maloney *et al*), such as Transport 2000, to become incorporated within the consultation process. At one level, such a process of consultation reflected a genuine desire of the Major government to build a new consensus which would incorporate some of the ideas of the moderate anti-roads groups.

However, this chapter has shown that there were many aspects of policy in the Major era on which increased consultation did not result in any change to the agenda. In particular, many of the 'moderate' anti-roads groups had policy objectives, such as those related to the implementation of sustainable development, which conflicted with both the core beliefs of the Major government and indeed, continue to conflict with the structural imperatives of the state. Dialogue in these areas was thus largely 'cosmetic', not indicating any significant change to the agenda (Maloney *et al*, 1994, p. 32). The fact that many of the anti-roads groups continued to seek alternative arenas for their challenge to the road programme throughout the Major era provides further evidence that many of them placed only limited faith in the consultation process which followed the launch of the 'Great Debate' in 1994.

Overall, therefore, an examination of the transport policy network in the Major period has revealed considerable continuity rather than change: actors remained closely linked to their traditional associates in three discrete advocacy coalitions, each of which retained their very different orientation as to fundamental core beliefs. This continued division of the actors into three advocacy coalitions suggests three key conclusions. First, that new forms of alliances between traditional members of the road lobby and 'moderate' anti-roads groups are very unlikely to remain stable in the long term unless they are based on policy consensus on the basis of secondary or near core beliefs. Second, that the capacity of even the 'moderate' anti-roads groups to gain more than peripheral insider status on issues related to their core beliefs is limited in the long term. And third, that the anti-roads lobby will find it increasingly difficult to maintain a coherent alliance between the moderate anti-roads groups and the direct action movement in the long term.

The second key objective of this chapter has been to explore the capacity of the anti-roads groups to enter new policy arenas in order to challenge the dominance of the pro-roads lobby.

This chapter has utilised the work of Baumgartner and Jones (1991 and 1993) and Dudley and Richardson (1996a) to explore the relationship between two alternative policy arenas and the agenda setting process.

Looking at the impact which direct action has had on the policy process, I have argued that conflict in the construction sites was very successful in gaining extensive coverage in the media and thus in changing the conception of the transport issue from a dull, technical and private issue to an emotive and public one. This interaction between image and venue corresponds closely to the studies which Baumgartner and Jones have undertaken of policy change in sectors such as nuclear power, suggesting that direct action by the anti-roads groups should have had considerable impact on the policy agenda. However, this has not in fact been the case: although the protests influenced the news agenda (and through that the public perception of the transport issue) they had much less effect on the private perception of the transport issue which remained dominated by the interaction between government and erstwhile insider groups.

This chapter has also examined the Parliamentary arena, in which the opposition of a number of backbench Conservative MPs to elements of the road programme might have appeared to present the anti-roads groups with the potential to secure governmental support for their objectives. However, as with the direct action arena, Parliament offered only limited potential for the anti-roads groups to affect the policy agenda, because the opposition of the affected MPs was based predominantly on pragmatic and NIMBY grounds, rather than on any fundamental opposition to the ethos of the Major government's transport policy.

In conclusion, it appears that actor centred accounts of agenda setting fail to explain developments in the Major era. This chapter has examined two contentions: that changes to the nature of the transport policy community resulted in policy change; and that the anti-roads groups successfully opened new policy arenas in order to change the agenda. But close analysis of these views has questioned their ability to offer a convincing explanation of policy change in the Major era: a central conclusion of this chapter is that the opportunities to influence national policy which opened to the anti-roads groups were in fact limited. The next chapter therefore turns to explore the role of the European Union (EU) as an alternative policy arena, arguing that it took on an increasingly important role in the development of the politics of the car in the Major era. The EU could therefore have conceivably offered a significant alternative arena in which UK anti-roads groups, deprived of alternative national arenas, could have tried to change the transport policy agenda.

Notes

1   I explore this issue in more detail in Chapter 9 (Postscript), which considers the politics of the car in the Blair era.

2   A good illustration of the transformation in status afforded to T2000 is the appointment of Stephen Joseph, its director, to the SACTRA Committee. According to a prominent member of the Committee, this appointment has not affected its cohesion or operation, as Joseph has conducted himself in a manner consistent with the new status afforded to T2000 rather than seeking to politicise his presence (Interview, Peter Mackie, Member of SACTRA Committee, 8th August 1997).

3   The distinction between the responses of the various anti-roads groups to the question of choice provides further evidence that they are best conceived of as forming two discrete advocacy coalitions, with considerable differences between them on the basis of core beliefs.

4   For comments on the inconsistency of public opinion in the Blair era, see Chapter 9 (Postscript).

6 The European Union and National Transport Policy

Introduction

> Competitiveness, growth yes! But I do not want economic growth which leaves out part of our population. I do not want growth which widens the gap between regions. I certainly do not want growth which destroys the environment for us today and for our children. On the contrary, I want growth which implies social solidarity, regional solidarity and solidarity with future generations. This is necessary for reasons of fairness, justice and morality, of course. But also, I repeat, for the sake of economic prosperity. (Address by Santer to the European Parliament, 17th January, 1995, in CEC, 1995a, pp. 9-10)

> Traffic jams are not only exasperating, they also cost Europe dear in terms of productivity ... Networks are the arteries of the single market. They are the lifeblood of competitiveness, and their malfunction is reflected in lost opportunities to create new markets and hence in a level of job creation that falls short of potential. (CEC, 1993c, p. 75)

The increased involvement of the European Union (EU) in the conflict over transport policy can be seen as one of the most significant changes during the Major period with which this analysis is concerned.[1] In the 1990s, the EU published a number of strategy documents which accompanied increasing legislative activism in the transport field.[2] On the one hand, these documents emphasised the importance of an expansion of Europe's transport infrastructure through the Trans-European Network (TEN) programme in order to enhance competitiveness, reduce congestion, aid regional integration and create jobs. On the other, they focused on sustainable mobility, through the implementation of 'fair and efficient pricing in transport' (CEC, 1996) and the development of integrated public passenger transport systems thorough the 'Citizens' Networks' proposals (see CEC, 1995b).[3]

Such objectives are apparently contradictory: thus this chapter, which seeks to evaluate the influence of the EU on the national agenda setting process in the UK, must examine the conflicts which arise as a result of these competing aims. In particular, it considers the conflict between the exercise of subsidiarity (which implies a national mandate for transport policy) and the rise of supranational legislative activism in the transport field which is justified by the Single European Market programme (SEM) and the growth of trans-national environmental pollution and traffic.

Secondly, this chapter outlines the effect which these developments had on the EU's ability to act as an agent of exogenous change in the Major era. While acknowledging the limitations imposed on the EU's role by the primacy of national decision making, this section argues that it was still able to 'Europeanise' certain aspects of transport policy by adopting a regulatory strategy for policy making. Such a strategy was actively supported by the UK government, as it has focused on technical solutions to the transport problem, maintaining the balance of power between erstwhile insiders and outsiders in the UK transport policy network.

Thirdly, this chapter considers the limitations constraining the ability of the EU to undertake an activist environmental or investment strategy which conflicted with the priorities of the Major government. In the period after 1992, following the publication of the White Paper on the Common Transport Policy and the ratification of the Treaty on European Union, the more ambitious proposals of the Commission met with little success (CEC, 1993a). After a successful low politics strategy which emphasised the liberalisation of the transport market in line with the objectives of the SEM, the Commission's attempts to move back into the domain of 'high politics' through an ambitious infrastructure programme (the TENs initiative) faltered.

Initially the development of road TENs, in particular, was actively supported by the UK government. Such support formed part of a strategy of shifting the arena of decision making to the European level, making it more difficult for the domestic anti-roads groups to affect the national agenda and thus helping to maintain the dominance of the insider groups over the policy process.

However, in the medium term, this strategy backfired: the TENs programme, perhaps surprisingly, increased the capacity of the anti-roads groups to influence the national policy agenda. I argue that in order to gain access to European funding the UK government decided to classify a number of road schemes as TENs, despite their really being national projects. As a result, the anti-roads groups were able to successfully damage the policy image of such roads, combining anti-European and anti-roads sentiment to increase the levels of opposition to these schemes and thereby reduce the operational autonomy of central government.

The EU and National Autonomy

This chapter looks at the impact of the EU on national autonomy. Its primary purpose is to evaluate how effective the Major government was in maintaining control over the transport policy process during a time of increasing 'Europeanisation' of domestic policy. In order to examine the effect of this I adopt a model of EU-UK relations which is framed in terms of autonomy rather than sovereignty.

A focus on autonomy is particularly appropriate in this case because it can take account of both formal transfers of UK sovereignty following extensions of EU power (due to the processing of directives, regulations and revisions of the treaties) and of changes in the autonomy of policy networks caused by changes in the balance of power between insider and outsider groups.

I argue in this chapter that in spite of the changes to the EU treaties affecting transport in the Major era, the autonomy of the Major government remained high. As I argue in the next section, autonomy should not be confused with sovereignty: this is very important in the transport case as formal transfers of power have been widespread. The co-decision procedure is now the norm following the treaty revisions at Amsterdam, implying that a significant decline has occurred to the sovereignty of the member states. But, as I will argue in the remainder of this chapter, this change in fact had little effect on the operational autonomy of the UK government or on its capacity to retain control over the mechanisms of agenda setting. The primary reason for this is that, in the Major era, the outcomes of the policy process within the EU were largely compatible with the priorities of the UK government, which thus maintained significant national autonomy over policy making and agenda setting. On occasions when the Major government perceived that the UK's sovereignty and autonomy were both threatened, such as in the proposed development of a carbon-energy tax, the government exercised its national veto where possible.

The EU and National Autonomy: A Review of the Literature

The literature on the impact of the European Union on the autonomy of national government is surprisingly limited in scope. As Kassim and Menon argue, 'despite the claims made about the extent to which power has migrated from national capitals to Brussels, about the freedom of the governments to make policy, and about the "Europeanisation", supranationalisation, communitarianisation and "Europeification" (Andersen and Eliassen, 1993, p. 3) of policy making, the precise impact of EU action on the member states has been curiously under-researched' (1996a, p. 1). In analysing the EU's impact on the capacity of national decision makers to retain control over the transport agenda I share these writers' aim to go 'some way towards remedying this deficiency' (1996a, p. 1. See also Kassim and Menon 1996b).

The result of this deficiency is that theoretical debate over EU-nation state autonomy, unlike the debate on central-local relations (Chapter 7), is often implicit rather than explicit. Many studies of decision making in the EU focus on the constitutional structure governing relationships between so called 'federalist institutions' (such as the Commission, European Parliament and the Court of Justice) and the institutions serving the national interest (such as the European Council and the Council of Ministers), and are divided on the extent to which EU-member state autonomy reflects the evolving constitution of the Union. However, before outlining these models it is first important to provide an overview of the relationship between the EU and member states as contained in the EU treaties.

Until the signing of the Single European Act (SEA), which signified the acceleration of the single market programme, accounts of EU-member state relations were centred on the extent to which policy making reflected the intergovernmentalist settlement contained within the Luxembourg compromise. Focusing on the Luxembourg compromise, constitutionally based accounts of EU-member state relations argued that the desire to secure unanimity, backed up by the national veto, resulted in the predominance of intergovernmentalist decision making. After the SEA, however, national sovereignty was considerably reduced: the principle of unanimity (and with it the national veto) was replaced in many areas with a system of Qualified Majority Voting. National sovereignty was further eroded as the 'federalist' institutions, in particular the European Parliament, gained actual, as well as relative, power (Earnshaw and Judge, 1996, p. 101). These changes fundamentally altered decision making in the EU:

for the regular business of government, now more and more caught up within a multilateral framework of rules and negotiations, the lowering of state boundaries has severely weakened the ability of national governments to define and pursue coherent 'national interests' in their relations with other states. (Wallace, 1996, p. 452)

Many accounts of the EU decision making process tend to assume that the actual working relationship between the EU and the nation states reflects these formal constitutional and legal expectations, and that the growing competence of the EU inevitably reduces national autonomy. In such accounts autonomy and sovereignty are seen as one and the same:

The erosion of national sovereignty means the erosion of the power of the member states to decide exclusively much of their public policy via domestic policy-making processes and institutions. Empirically, it is beyond dispute that the EU level is now the level at which a high proportion of what used to be regarded as purely domestic policy-making takes place. (Richardson, 1996c, p. 3)

In analysis such as Richardson's the nature of EU-nation state autonomy remains conceptualised in formal, legalistic terms, in which sovereignty and national autonomy are conceived of as being eroded in light of 'the rising volume of transnational and transgovernmental activity which has accompanied the intensification of political, economic, and administrative exchanges within the common market and customs union in Western Europe' (Webb, 1983, p. 34).

However the focus of these accounts, on national sovereignty, is inadequate for a number of reasons. Sovereignty is principally concerned with political and legal authority over a specified territorial area (Held, 1989); in contrast, this analysis seeks to ascertain the *actual* capacity for state action, regardless of the constitutional descriptions of power relations found within the treaties of the EC. A focus on 'autonomy'[4] is more useful: this can take account of both formal transfers of UK sovereignty following extensions of EU power (due to the processing of directives, regulations and revisions of the treaties) and of changes in the autonomy of policy networks caused by changes in the balance of power between insider and outsider groups. Autonomy is a 'more subtle instrument' for analysis than sovereignty, overcoming the limitations of the latter concept:

It is too narrow, for instance, for understanding the extent to which EU membership has circumscribed the power of member states, because a change in the *de facto* power of a state may be unaccompanied by a formal transfer of authority. In such cases, although the autonomy of the state has been diminished, its sovereignty remains constant. It is too wide, because, although the formal authority of the state to act in a particular sector may be transferred or pooled in collective decision making at the European level, the Community may not have acted on its competence. In this case, a state's sovereignty may have been diluted, but its autonomy undiminished. (Kassim and Menon, 1996a, pp. 3-4)

Kassim and Menon themselves utilise the concept of autonomy to analyse the impact of the EU on the evolution and processing of national industrial policy (1996b). Although agreeing that the Community has been successful in pursuing a 'fairly uniform picture of European Community initiatives' in this field, their study reveals 'a far more complex and differentiated view of the impact that the Community has had on the industrial policies of the member states': in fact, national governments have frequently been able to operate with considerable autonomy in spite of the EC treaties' provisions for Community competence in this area (Menon and Hayward, 1996, p. 268).

Kassim and Menon's autonomous state model suggests that national governments are able to operate with considerably more autonomy than constitutional accounts would predict. There are a number of reasons for this, amongst which the lack of internal consistency or agreement between the Commission's Directorate Generals (DGs); constraints on resources within the Commission which lead to reliance on outside expertise; and the primacy of national interests in the formulation of EU policy are the most important (Christiansen, 1996, p. 85. See also Cram, 1994).

Overall, Kassim and Menon's study finds that national governments will aim to protect state autonomy according to the perception of the strategic importance of a policy subsector to national government and the perceived effect of greater EU competence on national or Community spending. In the transport case, with which this book is concerned, the fact that national self-interest motivates the perception of both governments and policy networks is clearly illustrated by reactions to the liberalising agenda of the EU. Where national intervention has been supporting a weak national industry, national policy networks and the industrial players within them have favoured protectionism and resisted the liberalising aspirations of the EU, but where transport operators are strong and have thus been able to benefit from liberalisation, the opposite is true (see Kassim, 1996, for application of this to airline regulation).

Kassim and Menon's work is important as it challenges the orthodox approach to EU-member state relations, providing a convincing justification for a focus on autonomy rather than sovereignty when evaluating the impact of the EU on the agenda of national government. Furthermore, their approach is significant as it emphasises the need for models of policy making to incorporate the impact of both 'high' and 'low' politics. In particular, as the growing literature on the regulatory role of the Commission makes clear, models which underestimate the importance of routine decision making can offer only a partial account of the effect of the EU on the autonomy of national governments.[5]

The EU, Policy Making and the Member States

Studies of the policy process in the EU increasingly emphasise that in order to evaluate the impact of the Community on policy making in the member states it is essential to distinguish between 'high' and 'low' politics (see for example Liebfried and Pierson (1996), Cram (1993 and 1994) and Majone (1993)). In making this distinction, Liebfried and Pierson argue that EU policy making occurs in three ways.

The first of these, 'positive or activist' policy, describes attempts to undertake expansive programmes which aim to create uniform standards and operate in the 'high politics' sphere. Examples of such initiatives include the 1992 Social Protocol, the TENs programme and the *Growth, Competitiveness and Employment* White Paper launched by Delors in 1993 (CEC, 1993c). Commission initiatives in this area are hampered by 'formidable obstacles: institutions that make reform difficult, limited fiscal resources, jealous member-state protection of "state building" resources, and an unfavourable distribution of power among interest groups' (Liebfried and Pierson, 1996, p. 187).

The need to establish 'market compatibility requirements' is the second influence on the operation of the EU policy process. This manifests itself in the social sphere, for example, through 'legal challenges to those aspects of national welfare states that conflict with the single market's call for unhindered labour mobility and open competition for services' (Liebfried and Pierson, 1996, p. 188). Parallels with the transport case are clear: much of the EU's regulatory activism aims to facilitate the mobility of goods and people which is a core objective of the single market programme.

Finally, the EU policy process is subject to indirect pressures 'that do not legally require but none the less encourage the adaptations of national policy' (Liebfried and Pierson, 1996, p. 186). In the transport case, indirect pressures such as the commitment to the convergence criteria associated with monetary union helped to facilitate the promotion of private finance for the provision of transport infrastructure across the countries of the EU. Such common pressures enabled the Commission to promote a series of universal solutions applicable across member states.

The remainder of this chapter utilises Liebfried and Pierson's typology of the policy process in order to illustrate that the EU has had a variable impact on the UK policy agenda in the transport field. It argues that EU policy initiatives in the transport sphere are best classified as either market or environmentally motivated, with either a regulatory or 'active politics' mechanism. Thus, EU initiatives fall into one of four categories: environmental regulation; single-market regulation; environmental activism; and single-market activism (see Figure 6.1).

Figure 6.1 Classification of EU transport initiatives

		POLICY FOCUS	
		Regulation	**Active policy**
P O L I C Y	**Environmental**	e.g. vehicle emission regulations	e.g. Carbon Tax proposal
M O T I V E S	**Single Market**	e.g. airline regulation	e.g. Trans-European Network road proposal

Overall, this chapter argues that the capacity of the EU to affect the national agenda setting process in the UK during the Major era was most strong where policies focused on building a regulatory framework (i.e. policies justified on market compatibility grounds).

However, such policies cannot be said to have reduced the autonomy of the UK because, as I shall argue below, the Major government supported their development. As a result, in spite of the fact that expansions in regulatory policy reduced national sovereignty, they did not reduce autonomy. In fact, the focus of the EU on building a regulatory framework for the reduction of vehicle emissions and for the deregulation of transport markets increased the autonomy of central government in the Major era, as it strengthened the domestic political strategy of invoking technical solutions in order to manage the policy agenda which we have seen that that government pursued in response to the increased conflict over transport policy.

The Commission's more ambitious, 'active' policy proposals which inhabit the 'high politics' sphere, such as the TENs programme, have, on the surface, had less impact: in theory national governments should have retained high levels of autonomy either due to their capacity to veto such proposals or due to the reliance of the EU on national governments for the funding of such proposals.

However, in fact the effect on the agenda of the development of such proposals has been less straightforward. The Major government classified a number of domestic roads as European roads in order to get financial support for them from the Community TENs budget (which funds up to 10% of the total cost). Following this, when the conflict between the protesters and central government over a number of the affected roads escalated, the government tried to manage the conflict by arguing that the roads were European roads, and thus of considerable strategic, Community-wide significance. However, this tactic backfired, increasing the capacity of the protesters to mobilise. Thus the political tactics of the Major government once more resulted in a policy disaster, ultimately reducing the autonomy of central government.

The third element of Liebfried and Pierson's typology describes those policies which exert an indirect (or spillover) pressure in other areas. This chapter argues that, in the transport case, indirect pressures were particularly important in two contradictory ways: the indirect pressures of the single market programme aided the Commission in the development of a regulatory framework for transport but, at the same time, moves towards

EMU constrained the capacity of the Commission to fulfil its objectives for activist policy, in particular its objectives for the TENs.[6]

Britain and the EU: Challenging the Awkward Partner Thesis

This chapter rejects the common conceptualisation of Britain as an awkward partner. The overwhelming perception of Britain's relationship with its Community partners is that of the 'awkward partner' and of uncooperative obstructionism; significant opposition to the expansion of Community competence in the development of transport policy might thus be expected from the UK government (see for example, George, 1996, Chapter 7; George, 1999; Gamble, 1994, pp. 132-35. See Buller, 1995, for a critique of the awkward partner thesis).

Recent accounts of the awkward partner thesis have focused on the impact of the Thatcher governments' attachment to the 'free economy and the strong state': British government priorities for a deregulated market economy with minimal state intervention clashed with a continental European emphasis on regulation and market intervention (Gamble, 1994, p. 133). Thus Britain has traditionally opposed the development of Community fiscal instruments, in particular the expansion of the Communities budgetary resources (Wallace, 1996, p. 448-49) and sought to utilise a restricted definition of subsidiarity (Kersbergen and Verbeek, 1994, p. 225).

However, I will argue below that analysis of the transport case in the Major era shows that the awkward partner thesis only proves to offer an accurate portrait of the nature of EU-UK relations in the case of activist environmental policy. In the other cases – activist infrastructure; environmental regulation, and single market regulation – the UK accepted a mandate for community action which on balance increased its operational autonomy in dealing with domestic opposition to its transport policy nationally.

The Transport Case

The post-war history of European transport policy suggests a model of decision making containing both intergovernmentalist and neo-functionalist elements. Since the mid-1980s, the EU has had particular success in developing an incrementalist, regulatory, framework on neo-functionalist lines but it has been hindered in its attempts to implement activist policy 'by difficulties ... in trying to develop a Union policy in the face of diverse practices across its member states' (Baker, 1994, p. 67).

The Common Transport Policy (CTP) is one of only three common policies which are specifically identified in Article 3 of the Rome Treaty (Whitelegg, 1988, p. 6). However, until the mid-1980s, the predominance of intergovernmentalist decision making in the transport sphere meant that 'progress towards the realisation of the CTP was slow, especially when measured against the importance of transport in the Community economy' (CEC, 1993a, para. 2).

The principal reason for this was that the Community's member states had 'different state traditions', and thus different conceptions of the role which market forces 'ought' to play in the allocation of transport, affecting the provision of transport infrastructure and transport finance at both a philosophical and practical level (Whitelegg, 1988, p. 13). Baker argues that fundamental differences exist between the Anglo-Saxon focus on maximising transport efficiency and the continental model which 'treats the provision of transport as a state obligation as well as an instrument in a wider social framework and focuses on the role of transport in achieving larger, usually distributional objectives' (Baker, 1994, p. 71).

The evolution of a common policy was thus hindered by the Commission's emphasis on a market-orientated focus, which the majority of the member states rejected at that time. A memorandum produced by the Commission in 1973 described the aim of the CTP as 'the development of a common transport market based on the principle of the free play of market forces subject to correction only in exceptional circumstances' (cited in Wise and Gibb, 1993, p. 136). For those member states historically committed to a continental model of transport policy, 'to accept the original Community proposals, based on free market principles, would have involved a major change in attitude and, more seriously, the threat of economic dislocation' (Wise and Gibb, 1993, p. 137).

However, following the signing of the SEA the interests of the member states in the transport field began to converge around the need to facilitate the single market programme.[7] The Commission was thus able to exploit the policy opportunities provided by the liberalisation agenda of the single market and the subsequent anticipated rise in cross border traffic. In addition, the expansion of the Community resulted in an increasingly economically and geographically isolated periphery: without effective integration of transport this would undermine the anticipated benefits of the single market.

The EU, the Single Market and Transport De-regulation[8]

> The agreement under the Single European Act to establish an area without internal frontiers in which the free circulation of goods, services, capital and persons is ensured represents the single most important step that the Community has made towards a rational economy and greater prosperity. *Ensuring that this ambitious objective* is translated into practical reality is an essential condition for economic growth, competitiveness and employment in the Community. (CEC, 1993c, p. 68. Emphasis in original)

The abolition of frontiers and the concrete implementation of the freedom of movement for people, goods and capital could not, in fact, be conceived without an internal market for transport. (DG for Research, 1991, p. 21, cited in Lee, 1994, p. 205).

The Commission White Paper of 1985, *Completing the Internal Market* (CEC, 1985), and the agreement of the Single European Act in the same year initiated a flurry of legislative activity in the transport sphere relating to the single market initiative. The first stages of maritime, air and road transport harmonisation and regulation were initiated in December 1986, December 1987 and July 1988 respectively (Baker, 1994, p. 69. See McGowan, 1994, pp. 257-59 on maritime policy, Kassim, 1996, pp. 114-20 on airline regulation and Lee, 1994, pp. 217-21 on road transport regulation). According to the Commission, the strategic nature of the transport sector, combined with its importance in the facilitation of cross-national trade, made attention to the process of liberalisation both inevitable and essential:

> The transport sector accounts for about 7% of the employment and gross domestic product of the Community. It absorbs about 40% of all public investment. It is therefore a very important sector in itself, besides making an essential contribution to economic and social progress: trade and the movement of persons can grow only if the transport system becomes more and more effective. Completion of the Community's large internal market by 1992 therefore makes it all the more necessary to achieve a common policy in this field. (CEC, 1990a, p. 3)

The single market initiative and the associated rise in international traffic thus provided the Commission with a rationale for extending the competence of the liberalisation and harmonisation agenda of the EU (CEC, 1993c, p. 68 and CEC, 1995b, pp. 36-39): 'By its very nature the Single European Market (SEM) seems certain to instigate a large increase in lorry traffic, because it has not only removed physical barriers to freight movement in the form of border controls, but also has done away with technical barriers of standardisation which have excluded one country's products from the market for another and dismantled the fiscal barriers that formerly inhibited trade between member states' (Tolley and Turton, 1995, p. 350).

The legitimacy of Community action was also enhanced by the impact on mobility levels of structural changes to the global economy. In particular, a number of manufacturing and service industries relocated from urban to non-urban 'green field' sites, increasingly using 'just-in-time' delivery methods to reduce storage space and hence costs (CEC, 1996, p. 51). As transport costs form only a small proportion of the total value of most products, on average 'only account[ing] for 2.8% of final product prices in the Union' (CEC, 1996, p. 51), cost savings can often be made by industries which service their whole market from a smaller network of warehousing facilities and plants (Tolley and Turton, 1995, p. 350).

Such changes in the operation of the macro-economy have occurred across the nations of the Community, even if the extent of their impact has varied. Thus both the legitimacy of Community action to prevent discrimination in the transport market, and the acceptance of such action by national governments, has increased.

The principal focus of the Community's initiatives regarding road transport has historically been the carriage of freight, with initiatives on public transport only gaining significance with the publication of the Community's *Citizens' Network Initiative* in 1995 (CEC, 1995b). The Community's action was governed by the need to remove the bilateral agreements on international haulage which had previously characterised relations between member states, resulting in the imposition of quotas and encouragement of disparities in the quality of service which hindered the completion of the single market (CEC, 1990a, p. 6).

According to Lee, the motives for national regulation of the road haulage industry were twofold: to reduce the levels of competition between road and rail freight, and to restrict competition in the road haulage industry itself. The latter was deemed to be particularly important as cost-cutting measures could compromise safety and create considerable instability in the market place (1994, p. 217). Regulation sought to maintain standards of service and regulate prices – with measures including restrictions on the areas or types of goods an operator might carry; restrictions on charging levels and on the number of registered vehicles; and finally, restrictions on the numbers of vehicles able to transport goods to or from other member states or their ability to undertake the commercial carriage of goods on the return journey ('cabotage') (Button, 1984, cited in Lee, 1994, p. 217).

It was only following the moves towards the single market programme, the adoption of Qualified Majority Voting in matters affecting the extension and implementation of the CTP, and the rulings of the European Court of Justice in the mid-1980s that the Community was able to overcome the resistance of protectionist governments such as Italy and the Federal Republic of Germany and to propose a threefold strategy designed to open up the transport market. The harmonisation of technical and social standards and financial regulations, the deregulation of freight transport charging and the removal of cabotage restrictions, and the abolition of quotas and licensing restrictions formed the pillars of this approach (Lee, 1994, p. 218-20).

The community has played a much more limited role in the market liberalisation of passenger road transport. Such liberalisation is of relatively little importance to the single market programme, while 'a high proportion of bus and coach travel is of a local or regional nature, which, except in border areas, does not pass from one Member State to another' (Lee, 1994, p. 220). As with the market for road freight, the bus and coach industries have historically been highly regulated, to protect them from competition from private cars and ensure that they are able to maintain their obligations of public service.

The cross-border nature of the international coach market means that the Commission has been more active in developing regulatory policy for the sector. The EU passed two regulations in 1992 which had the combined effect of removing 'the requirements for authorisations for certain inter-member state coach services' and allowing 'a limited form of cabotage to be practised by international coach operators' (Lee, 1994, p. 221. See CEC, 1995b, pp. 49-53 and Bulletin of the EU, 12/97, pp. 61-62 for a list of the regulations passed by the Community applicable to public passenger transport).

Overall, although the measures undertaken by the Commission at this time 'stop well short of full immediate liberalisation' (Lee, 1994, p. 221) they provided an important spur to the process of greater integration in the transport sphere which has had a significant impact on both the process of European integration and the agendas of the member states.

Single Market Regulation and National Policy Autonomy

Perhaps unsurprisingly, both the Thatcher and Major administrations supported the EU's focus on the liberalisation of transport markets. As I have argued in earlier chapters within this book, the UK government's policy was driven by the predict and provide orthodoxy: the development of a Community regulatory framework would provide significant support for this strategy at a supranational level. Furthermore, throughout the 1980s and 1990s, the Thatcher and Major governments undertook significant de-regulation of public transport nationally, subsequently implementing a policy of privatisation of bus and rail services. EU action thus reinforced the activities of national government. In her memoirs, former Prime Minister Thatcher illustrates the rationale for her government's support for the development of EU single market regulation:

> I had one overriding positive goal. This was to create a single Common Market. The Community's internal tariffs on goods had been abolished by July 1968 ... What remained were the so-called 'non-tariff' barriers ... [which] served to frustrate the existence of a real Common Market. British businesses would be amongst those most likely to benefit from an opening-up of other countries markets ... Transport was an important area where we were stopped from making the inroads that we wanted. The price which we would have to pay to achieve a Single Market with all its economic benefits, though, was more majority voting in the Community. There was no escape from that, because otherwise particular countries would succumb to domestic pressures and prevent the opening of their markets. (Thatcher, 1993, p. 553)

EU liberalisation of air transport was also welcomed in the UK. Although state aid had historically been granted to UK flag carriers, governments 'had been prepared to allow independent airlines to compete on international routes wherever it was able to negotiate traffic rights. It [the UK] had a liberal charter policy, had liberalised its domestic market and privatised British Airways' (Kassim, 1996, p. 121). Thus, the initiatives which the Community developed for the liberalisation and harmonisation of transport policy were clearly related to domestic policy initiatives and, as a result, the UK government supported greater Community competence in this area.

I argue in the next section on the development of EU environmental regulation that the effect of increased Community activism in the development of regulatory policy has been to increase rather than decrease the autonomy of national government, thus increasing their control over the national agenda setting process.

The EU and Environmental Policy: The Qualified Rise of EU Legitimacy

> Increasing transport delays have brought down travel speeds in a number of major European cities to levels which prevailed in the age of horse-drawn carts. Air pollution problems (e.g. ozone) in summer are requiring that, on more and more occasions, citizens across Europe have to refrain from outdoor activities. It is estimated that thousands of European citizens die each year from just one form of air pollution (particulate matter) ... congestion will increase to unparalleled levels if no further action is taken. Whereas technical progress has made transport much safer and the total of road accidents is slowly declining further, society is realising that the cost in terms of suffering, misery and lost productivity is unacceptably high. (CEC, 1996, p. 13)

Turning from the single market policy motivation for Commission action on transport, the impetus for greater supranational regulation of domestic transport markets has also been justified by the integrationalist institutions of the EU on what may broadly be termed environmental grounds (see Figure 6.1, Classification of EU transport initiatives). The multi-faceted nature of the transport problem has led to a dual strategy approach by the Commission: first by regulation, which focuses on the harmonisation of technical standards such as vehicle emissions, and second by activist policies, such as the carbon-energy tax proposal. These two strategies are seen by the Commission as complementary in achieving its parallel goals of sustainable mobility, personal autonomy and economic development. However despite this, and the despite the cross-national nature of the transport problem, the Commission's impact on the agenda of the member states has been mixed. Considerable regulatory success has been achieved, but attempts at activist environmental policy have met significant resistance.

The EU and Environmental Regulation

The first moves to impose limits on emissions from new cars were taken in 1970 with a general Community directive on air pollution from gasoline cars (Directive 70/220/EEC). Subsequently a number of directives have targeted emissions of specific substances such as lead, carbon monoxide, hydro-carbons and nitrogen oxides. The cumulative effect of these directives has been to reduce the permitted emission levels of carbon monoxide by 90% since 1970; since 1983 hydro-carbons and nitrogen oxide emissions from vehicles affected have reduced by 65% and particulates from diesel engines by a third (Cm 3234, chart 12b, p. 78).

After implementing 'Stage 1' of the Community's plans to reduce vehicle emissions in 1993, the process of tightening emissions levels for new cars accelerated considerably through development of the 'Stage 2' standards for vehicle emissions. The Stage 2 standards cut:

- carbon monoxide emissions from 3.16 to 2.20 grams per kilometre for petrol engines, and from 3.16 to 1.00 for diesel;
- hydro-carbons and nitrogen oxide levels from 1.13 to 0.50 grams per kilometre for petrol and to 0.70 and 0.90 grams per km for indirect and direct injection diesel engines respectively;
- particulate emissions from 0.18 to nil for petrol and to 0.08 and 0.10 grams per km for indirect and direct injection diesel cars (cited in RCEP, 1994, table 8.1, p. 121).[9]

This strategy of targeting emissions from new cars was complemented by directives to reduce emissions for light goods vehicles (93/59/EEC) and heavy goods and passenger vehicles (91/542/EEC).

In his work on regulation in the EC, Majone emphasises the reasons for the Commission to focus on such a regulatory strategy for policy making (Majone, 1993, pp. 160-61. See also Cram, 1993, p. 137). As I shall argue below, the Commission does not have the budgetary resources required to pursue an activist transport policy on even a modest scale, but while a lack of financial resources served to constrain activist policy in the Major era it had no comparable effect on regulatory policy:

> In fact, an important characteristic of regulatory policy-making is the limited influence of budgetary limitations on the activities of regulators. The size of non-regulatory, direct expenditure programmes is constrained by budgetary appropriations and, ultimately, by the size of government tax revenues. In contrast, the costs of most regulatory programmes are borne directly by the firms and individuals who have to comply with them. Compared to these costs, the resources needed to produce the regulations are trivial. This general feature of regulatory policy making is even more pronounced in the case of the Community, since not only the economic, but

also the political and administrative costs of enforcing EC regulations are borne by Member States. (Majone, 1993, p. 161)

A focus on European wide regulatory policy making was also preferred by the Commission with a view to extending its own policy competence. At least initially, according to Cram, this approach was supported by a number of multi-national firms:

> This pre-emptive federalism is seen as a means of eliminating inconsistencies between national standards while avoiding the potential knock-on effect of increasingly more stringent national legislation. The adoption of a single European standard will, the companies hope, prevent the continued upwards escalation of national standards. (1993, p. 137)

Although Cram's comments are primarily directed at the rationale for the trans-national support of regulation by multi-national companies in the social field, there is considerable evidence to suggest, initially at least, that the multi-national, export-oriented nature of the motor vehicle industry did support European wide regulation of emissions and safety standards for the same reasons.

Initially, the Community's focus on strengthening emission standards reflected these two core aspects of Majone's explanation of the rationale for a focus on regulatory policy. Firstly, as with the regulation of freight and passenger transport markets the Commission justified the supranational regulation of transport-related air pollution in order to avoid disrupting the functioning of the internal market. Writing in 1996, the Commission argued that, 'for internal market reasons, it is obvious that product standards for vehicles should be set at the European level' (CEC, 1996, p. 39. For comments applicable to social policy see Cram, 1993, p. 141).

Secondly, there is strong evidence to argue that vehicle manufacturers have an incentive to ensure Community wide regulation of emissions standards. (For comments applicable to social policy see Majone, 1993, p. 161 and Cram, 1993, p. 141). Vehicle manufacturers are heavily dependent on export markets, producing high value products which are particularly vulnerable to changes in national regulations of safety or emissions standards. In addition, as Paterson argues, most EU national governments are closely associated with the energy and transport sectors in their countries and as such have strong incentives to protect domestic industries in this area (1996, p. 160). As a result, these companies are universally 'worried about the competitiveness effects of unilateral action'; for example, the Society of Motor Manufacturers and Traders in the UK urged that action should only take place in a 'framework of international co-operation' (SMMT, 1990, cited in Paterson, 1996, p. 160).

Aware of the need to secure multi-lateral co-operation between national governments and the energy and vehicle industry in the management of vehicle emissions, in 1993 the EU instigated 'an unprecedented three year collaboration' between vehicle manufacturers, the oil industry and the Commission which aimed to devise a framework for tighter emissions standards and cleaner vehicle fuels (*Financial Times*, 26th June 1996, p. 20). This collaboration, known as the 'Auto-Oil' programme, had two primary objectives: to agree proposals to reduce vehicle emission levels and to remove the need for vociferous lobbying by vehicle manufacturers and the oil industry.[10]

Initially, both the vehicle and oil industries actively participated in the Commission initiative, investing ecu 10m in a joint research project entitled the 'European Programme on Emissions, Fuels and Engine Technologies' (EPEFE, 1995). This programme identified three priority areas for research:

> To quantify further reductions in road traffic emissions which may be needed to achieve agreed air quality objectives; to identify sets of measures – including improvements in fuel/vehicle technologies as well as other measures such as inspection and maintenance programmes, [and] traffic control – that can achieve such reductions; to evaluate them from a cost/effectiveness point of view and to search for the most cost-effective proposals. (EPEFE, 1995, p. 2)

The research reached two important conclusions: that 'both fuels and engine technologies are important determinants of motor vehicle emission levels' (EPEFE, 1995, p. 2); but also that although the relationship between fuel properties, engine properties and emissions was complex, 'the spread in emission levels related to vehicle technologies was wider than the variations due to fuels' (EPEFE, 1995, p.6). Consequently, the EPEFE study concluded that 'it was possible to have a greater impact on emissions by varying vehicle technology than by improving fuel' (*Financial Times*, 26th June 1996, p. 20). Such findings were particularly damaging for the vehicle manufacturers: if the primary aim of policy was the adoption of the most effective means to reduce emissions levels, then most of the burden of tightening standards would fall on them. As a result, although the Commission proposed parallel strategies to cut the emission levels from vehicle engines, to improve the quality of petrol and diesel fuels and to strengthen inspection and maintenance tests, the vehicle manufacturers would bear ecu 4.1bn of the total annual cost (ecu 5.5bn) of these proposals.

The recommendations had a pronounced impact on the EU transport policy agenda in a number of ways; in the UK, as we shall see, such effects were not always predictable. First, and perhaps most predictably, they weakened the co-operation between the Commission, oil and vehicle industries. The car producers in particular, argued that 'they have been unfairly burdened with most of the clean-up costs'. ACEA, the European vehicle manufacturers' association, called for a 'balanced contribution' from both the oil and vehicle industries to the financing of emissions reductions. In particular, they argued that the impact of improving fuel technology would be immediate, with all cars benefiting from cleaner fuels, whereas improvements in engine design, being targeted at new vehicles, 'would take years to permeate the vehicle fleet. But the oil industry, which support[ed] the measures, counter[ed] that they [were] ... in line with the Auto-Oil conclusions'. As Europia, the European oil industry body, argued in June 1996, 'the car industry cannot deny that what the Commission has proposed is in line with [the conclusions of] the study' (*Financial Times*, 26th June 1996, p. 20).

In evaluating the influence of the Commission strategy, the divisions within the Auto-Oil partnership would seem, initially, to imply failure. However, if the Commission's objectives are perceived as primarily being to establish an institutional framework to provide the data for development of future regulatory policy, and not with the building of consensus in the long term, then their strategy can be seen as successful:

> Regulation is not achieved simply by passing a law, but requires detailed knowledge of, and intimate involvement with, the regulated activities. Thus, a commitment to regulation implies, sooner or later, the creation of specialised agencies capable of fact-finding, rule-making and enforcement. (Majone, 1991b, p. 30 cited in Cram, 1993, p. 144)

The incorporation of the technical expertise of the oil and vehicle industries in a tripartite arrangement designed to find solutions to the growth of vehicle-related air pollution was a significant step towards the creation of just such a specialised agency. By developing this framework the 'Commission could be said to be shaping the future environment in which the development of EC regulation might take place' (Cram, 1993, p. 144).

Second, the building of this tripartite relationship enabled the Commission to acquire greater political authority to formulate policy in this area. Historically, the Commission has been hindered by an inability 'to provide effective leadership, without the support of the member states, and learning from this past experience, the Commission has increasingly learned to expand its powers through the manipulation of its skills as a bureaucracy' (Cram, 1994, p. 143). Consequently, in order to ensure that the Commission does not alienate national governments it has used 'marginal, relatively innocuous measures' (Spicker, 1991, p. 9) combined with the incorporation of industry experts in a purpose built epistemic community. This has cumulatively increased 'the scope of Community competence without alienating national governments' (Cram, 1993, p. 143. See Haas, 1992, for an overview of the concept of epistemic communities).

Finally, although perhaps less obviously, the Commission's strategy demonstrated a commitment to the facilitation of enhanced mobility across the European continent. The focus on improving the quality of the environment through tougher emissions standards helped to insulate the pro-roads groups from the life-style implications of the growth of traffic volumes. Once again we are in the realm of the 'technical fix' which successive UK governments have deployed to manage transport policy problems (see Chapter 3 in particular). The Commission's strategy of incorporating the oil and vehicle manufacturers in a technical network designed to 'identify which new measures may be required to meet rational air quality objectives in the most cost effective way, derived from scientifically sound data' (EPEFE, 1995, p. 1) was explicitly designed to exclude the opponents of road-based transport from the policy process and to avoid the lifestyle implications of rising traffic volumes on transports contribution to air pollution. Community level initiatives thus aimed to manage the challenge of the anti-roads/environmental groups by facilitating a trans-national issue attention cycle invoking technical solutions to manage the political agenda (Downs, 1973). There are thus considerable similarities between the Community approach and the Major government's domestic management of policy problems.

Britain, Europe and Environmental Regulation: Britain Belies its 'Laggard' Status

Britain is commonly seen as an environmental 'Euro-sceptic' by commentators; as such the UK government might have been expected to rigorously oppose the Commission's regulatory strategy on vehicle emission levels (Sbragia, 1996, p. 250). Britain, it is argued, has had a tradition of management of environmental pollution which is perceived as incompatible with a European stance. This manifests itself in a 'definition of pollution which [has] differed fundamentally from Continental conceptions of pollution' (Golub, 1994, p. 37 cited in Sbragia, 1996, p. 250). The 'precautionary principle', it is argued, has been the driving force behind most Continental conceptions of environmental policy. This approach justifies going '"beyond science" in the sense of being required to make decisions where the consequences of alternative policy options are not determinable within a reasonable margin of error and where potentially high costs are involved in taking action' (Weale, 1992, p. 80). In contrast, the British style of environmental policy making 'has been to emphasise the importance of balancing cost, risk and benefit factors in order to elucidate the most efficient use of the environment's innate capacity to absorb waste. The British "approach" is characteristically pragmatic rather than radical; tactical rather than strategic; reactive rather than proactive' (Jordan and O'Riordan, 1995, p. 71). In its 1990 White Paper, *This Common Inheritance*, the UK government stressed the importance of acting on facts, not speculation. Environmental decisions, they argued, needed to:

> Look at all the facts and likely consequences of actions on the basis of the best scientific evidence available. Precipitate action on the basis of inadequate evidence is the wrong response. (Cm 1200, p. 11, para 1.16)

This orthodox view of the UK's environmental traditions has, however, now been challenged by a number of scholars who argue that the government began to soften its approach in the early 1990s. In particular, the 'precautionary principle' has been adopted in 'situations where there are significant risks of irreversible harm' (Jordan and O'Riordan, 1995, p. 71). The 1990 White Paper also contains examples of this new approach:

> Where there are significant risks of damage to the environment, the Government will be prepared to take precautionary action to limit the use of potentially dangerous materials or the spread of potentially dangerous pollutants, even where scientific knowledge is not conclusive, if the balance of likely costs and benefits justifies it. The precautionary principle applies particularly where there are good grounds for judging either that action taken promptly at comparatively low cost may avoid more costly damage later, or that irreversible effects may follow if action is delayed. (Cm 1200, p. 11, para 1.18)

This new approach began to influence the thinking of the Department of the Environment, resulting in the UK government's active endorsement of the strategy of the Commission in controlling air pollution from vehicles through the strengthening of the regulatory framework on engine emissions and oil quality. Central government support for the Commission's proposals during the Major era was thus entirely consistent with its strategy for managing domestic transport 'problems' which was described in Chapter 4's analysis of the impact of policy problems on the UK transport agenda.

Firstly, the strategies of both the Commission and the UK government were shaped by the need to ensure that policy is formulated using technical experts. Writing in the 1996 Green Paper, *Transport: the Way Forward*, the UK government argued that the framework for its *National Air Quality Strategy* would be based on the input of technical experts:

> The standards and objectives will be soundly based taking account of advice from experts on the effect of emissions on human health and the environment. The strategy will encompass pollution from all sources and transport measures will be a key element of the strategy. (Cm 3234, para. 12.5)

This desire to incorporate technical expertise and industry representatives by the UK government closely paralleled the strategy adopted by the Commission through the 'Auto-Oil' partnership described earlier. As such it provides the first explanation for UK support for the Commission's regulatory strategy.

Secondly, the Commission's focus on technical management of air pollution levels through the strengthening of the European regulatory framework was supported by the UK on economic grounds, as it ensured market compatibility for UK vehicle exporters across the EU, protecting them from unilateral action by environmental 'leader states' designed to strengthen domestic environmental regulation (Sbragia, 1996). The technical management of air pollution levels by the EU did not challenge the market-orientated focus of UK policy which has historically relied on transport consumers to cost in environmental factors in the process of making transport choices:

> Government measures can set the context for individual behaviour. But a great deal rests on the choices people make within that context. People are increasingly conscious of the need to behave responsibly in order to protect the environment, and this is starting to be reflected in travel choices as well as in activities such as recycling and choices of consumer goods ... Other important choices include the choice of which car to buy. Fuel efficiency can vary significantly between models: motorists who are concerned about

the environmental impacts of travel will wish to buy a more efficient car, perhaps sacrificing other areas of performance such as higher top speed or more rapid acceleration. (Cm 3234, paras 5.13 and 5.15)

Thirdly, the EU's focus on regulation of vehicle emissions was compatible with the UK government's desire to localise the management and responsibility for air pollution through a strategy of devolving responsibility to local government (see Chapter 7). Local government has been given a 'key role' in the management of local air quality since the passing of the 1995 Environment Act (Cm 3234, para. 14.7). This role was re-emphasised in 1996 with the publication of the government's *National Air Quality Strategy* (Cm 3587) and its Green Paper, *Transport: the Way Forward* (Cm 3234), both of which emphasised that local authorities should take the lead in the management of local air quality 'hot spots' (Cm 3234, paras 12.5-12.12). In order to facilitate this central government suggested that local authorities should use a variety of measures which 'include parking controls, speed limits, traffic calming, bus priority measures as well as traffic regulations and traffic bans' (Cm 3234, para. 12.9). As I will argue in Chapter 7, these restrictive measures were not, during the Major period at least, accompanied by the means to develop sufficient public transport alternatives.[11]

Overall, this analysis has shown that the UK government's support for the EU's regulatory strategy in the Major period was pragmatic. The Commission's focus on the technical management of the transport problem and of the incorporation of technical experts in the decision making process enabled the UK to continue a market-orientated approach to transport policy, retaining high levels of national autonomy, and consequently, extensive control over the agenda setting process.

I now examine the development of 'activist' EU policy which is motivated by the single market programme. The Major government's actions in relation this EU activity resulted in a policy disaster, which in fact reduced the autonomy of national government and affected its control over the agenda.

The EU, the Single Market and Transport Infrastructure

Europe's ascendancy in the past was due to the quality of its communications networks, which gave its inhabitants easy access to natural and technical resources. By developing the movement of people and goods, Europe has been able to marry economic prosperity, quality of life and commercial efficiency ... We need to continue along this road, to enter a new phase and to visualise other frontiers in the light of the globalization of markets, the growing mobility of capital and technology and the investment needs which are becoming apparent in the East and the South. The development of trans-European transport, telecommunications and energy infrastructure networks answers this need which all the Member States emphasised in their contributions. (CEC, 1993c, p. 28).

Following the acceleration of the single market programme, the need for a developed infrastructure policy to complement the Commission's regulatory activism became increasingly clear. However it was not until the signing of the Treaty on European Union that the Commission's proposals gained a legislative basis, through the commitment to 'contribute to the establishment and development of trans-European networks in the areas of transport, telecommunications and energy infrastructure' (Treaty on European Union, A129b).

Throughout the 1970s and 1980s the Community produced a number of policy statements on the significance of transport networks for the further integration of Europe, with striking similarities to the TENs initiative which now governs EU infrastructure planning. Analysis of the Commission's 1979 policy document, *A Transport Network for Europe* (CEC, 1979), and the TENs initiative show that both have similar rationales: both provide a strategic plan for the Commission to respond to increased international traffic flows anticipated from rising levels of trade between the member states (CEC 1979, cited in Whitelegg, 1988, p. 20, CEC, 1993b, pp. 15-25 and CEC, 1993c, p. 75). And in both cases the Commission's solution focuses on greater cross-national co-ordination of funding and transport planning at the Community level (CEC, 1979, cited in Whitelegg, 1988, p. 20 and CEC, 1993b, p. 31).

Further, the Commission's thinking in the 1970s and the TENs initiative use similar criteria for the generation of a list of priority projects: the overcoming of bottlenecks and strengthening of links between member states; the strengthening of links with peripheral regions, and the aiding of economic development in the less developed regions; the overcoming of natural obstacles such as mountain ranges and the sea; the increased harmonisation of, in particular, motorway standards between member states; and the optimising of the network's efficiency by improved traffic management (see CEC, 1979 cited in Whitelegg, 1988, pp. 21-22 and Christophersen Group, 1995, p. 35-36).

Thus, the overall picture is one of considerable continuity over time. The criteria for investment decisions, the policy process utilised and many of the programmes themselves remain unchanged since the 1970s. However, the signing of the Single European Act resulted in the creation of an environment conducive to a greater Community role in the provision and co-ordination of transport infrastructure programmes. In Kingdon's terms, a 'policy window' opened up which enabled 'advocates of proposals to push their pet solutions, or to push attention to their special solutions' (Kingdon, 1996, p. 165).

Common Problems and Common Solutions: National Convergence and the Rise of Community Competence

The acceleration of the single market programme, and the resulting increases in international traffic, forms the primary rationale of the TENs programme (see CEC, 1993b, pp. 15-25 and CEC, 1993c, p. 75). Market liberalisation and technical standardisation have enabled transport operators to operate across national borders more easily, resulting in rising volumes of cross-national road freight (Ross, 1995, p. 116). Following the ratification of the Single European Act, international road freight levels between EC member states grew 84.4% on average in the period 1984 to 1989 (CEC, 1993b, p. 12). Furthermore, forecasts of a three to four fold rise in traffic levels between the EU and the Central and Eastern European countries (CEC, 1994c, p. 69) have created a new east-west transport axis with its own infrastructure demands.

The impact of this internationalisation of traffic growth has affected all of the countries in the geographical core of the EU, to the extent that the member states are now in almost universal agreement with the Commission's view that 'many of the policies associated with the road network have nowadays such an international resonance that policies at merely national or local level cannot yield a real solution' (CEC, 1993b, p. 27).

At the same time, high speed rail has become a credible transport alternative (see Ross, 1994, pp. 194-95 for an explanation for the evolution of Europe's 'railway renaissance'). The prioritisation of rail networks, and the transformation of rail from a marginal to an 'essential Community interest', was extremely important in securing support for Community co-ordination of the TENs initiative. In particular, those countries committed to a 'continental model' of transport provision were able to overcome their objections to the emphasis on market instruments underlying the TENs in order to rationalise Community action on a pragmatic basis.

Perceived distortions in the transport market also aided the opening of the 'policy window' (CEC, 1996, p. 3). According to the Commission Green Paper, *Towards Fair and Efficient Pricing in Transport*, the total cost of externalities such as congestion, accidents, noise and air pollution is ecu 250bn annually (CEC, 1996, p. 9). The Community estimated this annual sum as 4.1% of annual GDP, with congestion, accidents, air pollution and noise accounting for 2.0%, 1.5%, 0.4% and 0.2% respectively. As over 90% of these costs are attributable to road transport, according to EU estimates (CEC, 1996, p. 14), the promotion of 'fair and efficient pricing' enabled moves by policy makers towards a dual strategy of increasing road transport costs through road tolls and promoting less environmentally damaging alternatives, in particular rail.

Finally, prior to the signing of the TEU, activist infrastructure initiatives were constrained by a lack of cross-national consensus on the strategic priorities for European action, as the conflict between the 'Anglo-Saxon' focus on transport efficiency and the 'Continental' focus on transport as a tool of social engineering weakened the ability of the Commission to build consensus between the EU member states. By the early 1990s, however, the commonalty of the problems confronting those states had blurred the distinctiveness of the two transport orthodoxies to the extent that the TEU could reflect a consensus around the Commission's proposals.

In particular, the increased trade between the EU member states, with its creation of common transport problems and common solutions, combined with the economic austerity measures implied by the post-Keynesian economic order and the move to economic and monetary union reduced the 'Continental' states' capacity to continue their commitment to state-led infrastructure investment. This created pressure for convergence between the 'Anglo-Saxon' and 'Continental' transport traditions, thus opening a policy window for proponents of Community action. On the one hand, consensus around the priorities of the 'Anglo-Saxon' model, focused on public/private partnerships and policy outcomes founded on a commercial basis, increased: the failure of the continental model to reverse the relative rise of private transport and the decline of rail and inland waterway use across Europe added further to pressure for co-operation between the private and the public sectors to secure infrastructure funding in an economic climate in which national governments no longer had the capacity for independent action.

On the other hand, the countries operating on the 'Anglo-Saxon' model have also adjusted their position to enable the building of a

Commission-led consensus surrounding the funding of infrastructure projects. They recognised that high costs, combined with high levels of uncertainty concerning risk and profitability, restricted the projects which were viable for private contractors – a partnership of public and private finance was required to achieve their objectives (Christophersen Group, 1995, pp. 68-69. See also interview information, Tim Pope, Highways Agency, 6th November 1997).

In conclusion, then, it is plain that the single market programme, the growth of international traffic (and its consequent impacts), and the development of multinational consensus on priorities for Community investment and appropriate mechanisms for funding have weakened the capacity of national governments to control the governance of transport policy in the EU. Across the EU a number of member states have reoriented their transport strategies around the need to strengthen market competition and increase the scope of public-private partnerships: both aims mirror the thinking of the Commission, striking a compromise between Anglo-Saxon and Continental models of transport policy. Thus we can see, in Kingdon's terms, that these changes to the policy climate opened up a policy window which enabled the Commission to pursue activist transport policy for the first time.

Britain, Europe and Infrastructure Provision: Anticipating Policy Awkwardness

In this particular case, moves by the EU to develop activist infrastructure policy might have been expected to provoke UK opposition. Although both the Thatcher and Major governments supported Community proposals to develop the single market (Wallace and Young, 1996, p. 132 and Moravcsik, 1991) and to improve transport links in order to facilitate market integration, as the House of Lords 1994 report, *Common Transport Policy*, emphasised, Britain's geographical location means the TENs are of only peripheral importance to national objectives:

> We note that the Trans-European Road Network (TERN), is considered of very great importance to some countries, especially those countries in central and Eastern Europe whose infrastructure is undeveloped and who want to increase links with the European Union. But this argument is of much less relevance to the United Kingdom. (HL 50-I, para. 58)

In addition, the TENs programme was justified not only in terms of the liberalisation of the Community's transport market and the reduction in congestion levels, but also as delivering substantial social benefits. The Commission's *Growth, Competitiveness, Employment* White Paper suggested that:

> Time wasted because of traffic congestion, under utilisation of the new communications media, environmental damage owing to the failure to use the most efficient technology are all to some extent contributory factors in the present malaise of our cities and the rising social discord. The same is true of the thinly-populated rural areas, whose isolation is a threat to their very existence. (CEC, 1993c, p. 29)

Thus, according to the White Paper, the TENs programme aimed to reduce congestion and pollution, strengthen the links between the economic and geographical periphery and aid the process of job creation. The 1993 White Paper proposed an ecu 400bn investment programme which, according to the Commission, was designed to protect the vulnerable from the dynamism unleashed by the single market programme:

> Experience has also shown, however, that the market is not without its failings. It tends to underestimate what is at stake in the long term, the speed of changes it creates affects the different social categories unequally, and it spontaneously promotes concentration, thereby creating inequality between regions and towns. (CEC, 1993c, p. 15)

This association of the TENs proposals with the development of Keynesian social and regional policy objectives, perhaps predictably, encountered strong rhetorical opposition from the Conservative government in the UK. In response to the Commission's 1993 White Paper, it argued for minimalistic state-led intervention, emphasising job creation through greater labour market flexibility:

> It is primarily for Member States to establish the right framework in which labour markets can operate. But the Community has a role in complementing and supporting action by Member States. It should co-ordinate exchanges of experience and views on how to improve labour market flexibility; ... encourage flexible working arrangements, so that people can adopt the working patterns that they need; and encourage a more flexible approach to the contractual relationship between employer and employee, where unnecessary restrictions can limit labour market efficiency. Above all, the Community must avoid imposing labour market regulations that increase costs, lock member states and employers unnecessarily into exiting rigidities or make it harder to create new jobs. (H.M. Treasury and Department of Employment, 1993, p. 291)

Further grounds for opposition to the Keynesian principles underlying the Delors' White Paper and the TENs programme were also found in UK concerns that the EU's structural funds have often been used as politically motivated 'side payments'. According to Majone, 'from the start, regional subventions were viewed less as redistributive measures than as side payments to obtain unanimous approval of efficiency-enhancing reforms of the Community system' (1996a, p. 131). According to this view, regional aid is thus designed to reduce the opposition from the poorer countries to the integration process and 'maintain cohesion *for the entire Maastricht set of reforms and, above all, EMU*' (Lange, 1993, p. 24. Emphasis in original. See also Marks, 1992, pp. 194-204). Utilisation of Community finance in this way would have been expected to encounter strong opposition from the Major government in the UK.

However, despite these particular grounds for the UK to have remained an 'awkward partner', objecting to the evolution of these supra-national infrastructure proposals, such opposition did not materialise. Community action was supported by the Major government for a number of reasons. Firstly, the TENs initiative was supported as facilitating the development of the single market:

> It is a matter of great concern to the Department of Transport that what the single market should provide for transport, both for us who provide transport and for those who use it, should in fact come about. (John Henes, DTp, in evidence to the House of Lords Select Committee, HL 50-II, p. 1)

Secondly, both the Commission and the UK government have, historically, been influenced by the belief that investment in infrastructure will facilitate economic development (see Chapter 3). The 1994 DTp review of the road programme, *Trunk Roads in England: 1994 Review*, argued that: 'We need an efficient road system to enable industry and commerce to deliver goods and services on which we all depend. A programme of new construction to improve our roads is one of the many ways in which the Government meets this need' (DTp, 1994, para. 2.1). Investment in links to peripheral regions in order to reduce economic dislocation formed a key part of this policy for both bodies:

> While trans-European networks should help to bring about a truly single market, under the Treaty, they are also assigned the explicit role of promoting harmonious development of the Community as a whole. They should enable connections with peripheral regions, whether islands or isolated areas on the mainland, to be improved. (CEC, 1994c, p. 55)

The UK government's 1995 review of the road programme reflected similar concerns. Two of the five criteria used to evaluate the need for a new road in *Managing the Trunk Road Programme* were connected to 'the significance of the road for regional and economic competitiveness' (DTp and Highways Agency, 1995, p. 4).

Thirdly, Community co-ordination of infrastructure provision was supported by the Major government as being compatible with its perception of subsidiarity (DTp, in HL 50-II, p. 2). Community funding of a TEN proposal is limited to 10% of its total cost, with the balance coming from either the public or private sector (Cm 3234, para. 11.15). This was compatible with the UK government's twin desires, to ensure that Community control operated on an 'arm's length' basis, and for increased private investment in the transport sector:

> Investment in new transport infrastructure and services can massively widen the choices available both to individuals and to businesses. But Governments concerned with the management of the economy at large, are inevitably constrained in the amounts of public money they can make available for new transport investment ... The private finance initiative is bringing a sea-change in the delivery of major transport investment. It is allowing a wider role for the private sector, not just in design and project management, but also in the operation of transport infrastructure and services. This means capturing the benefits of private sector skills and efficiencies, while transferring significant risk away from the Government where it can be better managed by the private sector ... This promises to result in value for money investment at a higher quality than would otherwise have been possible. (Cm 3234, paras 7.10 and 7.12)

Subsidiarity is also protected due to the limited financial resources available to the Community for infrastructure investment: the subsequent emphasis on national funding for the TENs prevents the EU obliging member states to build any particular scheme. In 1995 a total of ecu 240m was allocated from the Community budget to the TENs initiatives, of which only ecu 182.1m was available for the priority projects identified by the Essen Council (DTp, 1995, p. 1). Although the UK received over 15% (£22m) of the total funds available under the TENs initiative, making it the principal beneficiary of Community funding, 'that is still not a great deal of money set against all the needs of and all the present expenditure of the Community' (John Henes, Head of International and Freight Directorate, Department of Transport, in HL 50-II, p. 2). As a witness for the DTp argued in evidence to a House of Lords select committee on the European Community in 1994:

The significance of a road or a proposed road being or not being on the network is not yet clear. It is not yet an obligation on the member states, and it is unlikely to become one, that any road on the network, or indeed any other piece of infrastructure on the network, would have to be developed by some particular time. (DTp, evidence to HL 50-II, p. 2)

Consequently, the mandate for Community action, although enhanced by the incorporation of a commitment to the TENs in the TEU, continued to remain conditional on the financial support of the member states. The fact that the transport, telecommunications and energy sectors have all been privatised in the UK meant that the response of the Major government to the UK TEN proposals was not constrained by consideration of public finances, instead being conditional upon sufficient investment by the private sector. In its 1996 Green Paper on transport policy, *Transport – The Way Forward*, the Major government argued that:

Recent years have seen added pressure on public spending, which have strengthened the need to seek private sector investment. A great deal of progress has been made in developing new partnerships between [the] public and private sector, and attracting significant new resources which the public sector would not have been able to afford ... Privatisation of the railways will free the industry from having to compete against other priorities in the annual public spending rounds, allowing rail businesses more freedom to back their judgement about the case for new projects. (Cm 3234, paras 11.5 and 11.8)

Finally, support for Community competence within the framework of the TENs initiative was motivated by the Major government's desire to increase its national autonomy by weakening the coherence of the domestic opposition to roads.[12] This political tactic, and the problems which resulted for central government, can be illustrated by discussion of the conflict surrounding the proposed 'East-West route' between Aylesbury in Oxfordshire and the A120 at the port of Harwich.

The origins of this conflict can be traced to the 1989 White Paper *Roads for Prosperity* (Cm 693) which contained proposals for a series of bypass schemes which would form a central part of a proposed 'East-West' route. The government identified four schemes which it proposed to build to dual carriageway standard, at an estimated total cost of £123 million (Cm 693, table 1). One of these proposed schemes, and the subject of this analysis, was the construction of a dual carriageway on the A418 from the west of Aylesbury in Oxfordshire to the east of Wing in Buckinghamshire.

According to the proposal within *Roads for Prosperity* the East-West route, terminated at Aylesbury in Oxfordshire. However, a number of influential figures in the Oxfordshire and Buckinghamshire area felt that the proposals in fact formed part of a plan to develop a trunk road incrementally, a road which would link the port of Harwich to the M40 north of Oxford. As proposed within *Roads for Prosperity*, the road:

> terminated on the [Oxfordshire] county boundary near to Thame and terminated on a minor country lane. It was quite obvious that that could not physically terminate at that point and that it had to continue, and there had been no discussion with Oxfordshire as to where that route would continue, and how it would be routed within Oxford. (Interview. Roger Williams, Chief Transport Planning Officer for Oxfordshire County Council, 3rd June, 1997)

This engendered a strong feeling amongst local people that the plan was to continue the route to the north of Oxford around the North Oxford ring road as part of a strategic route across England towards South Wales. This perception was shared by Sir Frank Layfield, who stated in an interview that:

> It began to be a very serious suspicion, not just of myself but of hundreds of others, including the local authorities, I think, to the last parish council, that this scheme, or these two schemes, had a purpose far beyond relief to anything that might be being experienced in traffic in Oxford and around it. It began to be evident to us that there must be some other, much larger, project lying behind it, of which this was an incidental component. (cited in BBC, 1994)

This suspicion was confirmed by a BBC *Panorama* programme in 1994 which obtained documentary evidence that the then transport secretary John MacGregor had been lobbying for the inclusion of just such an East-West route within the TENs priority projects (BBC, 1994). However, according to Roger Williams, Chief Transport Planning Officer, Oxfordshire County Council, this action was motivated primarily by a desire to obtain EU financial support for what was in reality a domestic road scheme: it did not indicate the development of any coherent strategy amongst UK policy makers for the development of a network of 'Euro-routes':

> I don't think there was a clear strategy. It was enlightening because I went to a Lords' committee where I was cross-examined and then the Minister

was cross-examined on the country's strategic European route network strategy and it was clear that there was no firm, fully justified philosophy behind the European transport strategy thinking in relation to Britain. There was a debate about how does traffic from Western Europe get to Ireland and there are a number of alternatives. And they couldn't answer: the government officials couldn't answer what their strategy was. So it was being formed at that time and was evolving and had not been established. So, it was very difficult then to argue that the East-West road at Oxford could be justified as part of a strategic route. (Interview, 3rd June 1997. See also interview, Brian Simpson MEP, 3rd April 1998)

However, in response to developing domestic opposition to the scale of the bypass proposals, and to the increasing local perception that they formed part of a strategic 'East-West' route, the government attempted to manage the agenda by classifying a number of these domestic road proposals as part of the proposed TENs. By classifying these roads as part of the TENs the government aimed to retain control of the roads issue by ensuring that discussion of these proposals was shifted to a European venue which was less accessible to domestic anti-roads groups (see Baumgartner and Jones, 1991, pp. 1045-47, for a discussion of the concept of policy venues):[13]

It isn't a case, or wasn't a case, of Europe imposing a particular solution on Britain. I believe it was the British officials, and possibly politicians, who were using Europe to justify what they were wanting to achieve. So, they were hiding behind Brussels, using Brussels as a mechanism – as a Trojan horse – to get what they wanted. (Interview. Roger Williams, Chief Transport Planning Officer for Oxfordshire County Council, 3rd June 1997)

The effect of this government action was in fact detrimental to their aims, as local roads protesters were able to exacerbate the conflict, harnessing a more general opposition to Europe onto their opposition to particular schemes. Brian Walden, MP for Buckinghamshire, captured the effect of this when he argued:

The strength of my constituent's case, and I hope, of my own case, is that when a string of bypasses are conveniently linked together into, not only a trunk route, but a major European trunk route, and then when people are in effect told that either they agree with this, or they don't get the bypass, then that comes very close to blackmail. (Interview, cited in BBC, 1994)

The cumulative effect of the promotion of these schemes as 'Euro-routes' was thus to increase the scale of the conflict over them, ultimately leading to the withdrawal of bypass proposals for North Oxford in 1994 and Wing and Aylesbury in 1995 (See DTp, 1994, p. 54 and DTp, 1995, p. 23). Hence, once more the political tactics of the Major government served to create a policy disaster, increasing the capacity of the anti-roads groups to mobilise against the road programme.

Overall, then, the result of the attempts by the Major government to utilise the European arena when confronted with growing opposition to a proposed domestic road proposal was to reduce rather than increase the autonomy of central government. Thus, in a tactical sense such a policy strategy can be seen as a policy disaster as its effect was to reduce the capacity of the government to fulfil its objectives.

In concluding my comments on the effects of EU activist policy with single market motives, I have argued that overall the UK government in the Major period supported the increasing 'Europeanisation' of transport infrastructure policy for a combination of pragmatic and ideological reasons. The emphasis by the UK on the principle of subsidiarity, the building of partnerships between the public and private sectors, the facilitation of greater market integration and the management of domestic opposition to UK road schemes (even though it subsequently backfired politically) were all compatible with the Community's objectives. Therefore, as I argue elsewhere, the failure to implement the TENs programme in Europe can not be attributed to opposition from an 'awkward' UK government on either an ideological or symbolic basis, but can instead be explained by *de facto* pressures on the transport budgets of the member states, caused by protracted economic austerity linked to the move to economic and monetary union (Robinson, 1997b).

In the final section, I will argue, through an examination of the EU's proposal for a carbon-energy tax, that the support of the Major government did not extend to activist EU environmental policies. Proposals such as the carbon-energy tax, which were designed to directly interfere with the operation of the market for transport, were met with outright hostility, achieving only a limited impact on the autonomy of UK transport policy networks or the national agenda setting process.

The EU and Activist Environmental Policy: Still the Autonomy of National Government

> The Community and its Member States have a special responsibility to encourage and participate in international action to combat global environmental problems. Their capacity to provide leadership in this field is enormous. (CEC, 1990b, p. 18)

The carbon-energy tax proposed by the EU in 1991 was designed to complement energy efficiency measures, the promotion of renewable energy sources and the regulatory strategy of the EU in order to enable it to stabilise carbon monoxide emissions at 1990 levels by the year 2000, as it pledged at the Rio Earth summit in 1992 (Paterson, 1996, p. 88, and Maddison and Pearce, 1995, p. 123). The EU proposed a Community administered tax applying across all fuels, with the exception of renewables, levied 50:50 on carbon content and energy content 'on the grounds that a pure carbon tax would have favoured nuclear energy' (Haigh, 1996, p. 165). The levy would be introduced across the EU at an initial rate of US $3 per barrel of oil equivalent, rising to US $10 by the year 2000, in annual $1 increments (see Paterson, 1996, p. 88).

This proposed tax would have had a profound effect on the transport sector. Looking for example at the UK, figures by the DTp show that transport's contribution to carbon emissions in the UK rose from 23 million tonnes of carbon (mtC) in 1970 to 38 mtC in 1990, with future traffic growth resulting in a projected rise to 45 mtC in the year 2000 (cited in Cm 2427, para. 3.65). Of all the options available to policy makers to counteract these trends, 'many would have judged such a tax to have been the best available option' (Maddison and Pearce, 1995, p. 138). The proposal would, according to research by Barker *et al*, have 'reduced UK carbon emissions by 10.7 mtC relative to the year 2000 baseline', thus providing the impact necessary to stabilise emissions at 1990 levels as agreed at Rio (Barker *et al*, 1993. Research findings cited in Maddison and Pearce, 1995, p. 138).

Despite its effectiveness, opposition to the carbon-energy tax proposal was considerable. Studies by Skjaerseth (1994), Paterson (1996), Haigh (1996) and Maddison and Pearce (1995) have identified the industrial lobby and a number of national governments as among the most influential sources of such opposition.

According to Skjaerseth, the industrial lobby focused on two key principles: that the tax should be conditional on similar measures being adopted throughout the OECD, and that exemptions should be granted to certain energy intensive industries (1994, p. 28). The lobbying campaign conducted by European industry against the tax proposal through their employers confederation (UNICE), was particularly vociferous, being described in the *Economist* as the most intensive opposition to a Community policy proposal ever expressed (9th May 1992, p. 91), and motivated by concern that the tax would damage the competitive position of EU business in the global economy. 'With regard to the energy/carbon tax: "UNICE stresses that such plans run completely counter to the need ... for concerted international action"' (UNICE, 1991, p. 155, cited in Skjaerseth, 1994, p. 29).

The industrial lobby's opposition was aided by sharp division within both the Commission and the Council, in which opponents of the carbon-energy tax were, like UNICE, concerned with the costs to European competitiveness which would occur with unilateral EU action. Such was the extent of this division that, as a compromise, the tax proposal was subsequently 'made dependent on similar measures being introduced in other industrialised countries' (Paterson, 1996, p. 88). Given the strength of, in particular, US opposition, the adoption of a conditionality clause to the proposed carbon-energy tax, effectively killed the proposal dead (Paterson, 1996, pp. 130-31).

But even with this compromise the UK government, together with Spain, Portugal and Greece, still opposed the Commission's proposal. The latter three countries feared 'the tax would hamper their industrial development' (*Financial Times*, Survey on Energy Efficiency, 5th December 1995, p. III) unless the cost of its implementation was offset by a Community programme of financial assistance (Skjaerseth, 1994, pp. 19-30). In contrast, the UK did not appear to be motivated by fear of the implications of the proposed tax on either competition or employment levels, with the government itself acknowledging that its impact on the macro-economy would only be 'slight' (Cm 2068, p. 43). 'Rather it appears that attempts to establish an EC wide policy on global warming coincided with a period of conflict over moves to greater political and economic union and the EC carbon tax breached the highly sensitive subject of EC influence over national taxation issues ... The British government was concerned about the symbolic dimensions of any decision on an EC wide tax. The EC carbon-energy tax proposal had to be sacrificed' (Maddison and Pearce, 1995, p. 138).

Thus in this case the decision by the UK government to veto the proposed tax was taken in order to prevent a perceived decline in both sovereignty and autonomy. In addition, the action by the UK ensured that the anti-roads groups were unable to utilise the EU as a forum for the pursuit of an alternative policy discourse based on sustainable development which, as I have argued in Chapter 4, would require the implementation of measures designed to fundamentally alter the behaviour of transport consumers.

The UK government's veto of the proposed carbon-energy tax had a dual impact. At an EU level, the Commission was forced to abandon its activist environmental strategy and to re-emphasise the tightening of regulations applying to emissions levels. The Commission thus proposed the strengthening of the 'Stage 2' emissions standards with a further regulatory programme which aimed to cut 'current exhaust emissions by a further 20 to 40 per cent from 2000, with additional costs from the second step to apply from 2005' (*Financial Times*, 26th June 1996, p. 20).

On the domestic stage, the UK government had to pursue a national strategy for reducing greenhouse gases. Central government thus focused on increasing road fuel duties, imposing VAT on domestic fuel, incorporating Community regulatory instruments on emissions standards, and on what Maddison and Pearce describe as a combination of 'direct regulations, subsidies, the provision of information and moral exhortation' (1995, p. 135. See Cm 2427, in particular chapters 3 and 10). Despite these programmes, the government itself remained far from optimistic as to its ability to maintain CO_2 levels at 1990 levels beyond the year 2000:

> With the measures in this programme in place, UK emissions of most greenhouse gases should decline beyond 2000. However, this may not be the case for the most important gas, CO_2 ... the range of scenarios in EP59 [DTI Energy Paper, 59] indicates that CO_2 could rise steadily beyond 2000 ... Even with the measures in this programme in place, on the basis of the scenarios, it is likely that UK emissions of CO_2 would increase beyond 2000. (Cm 2427, para. 10.6)

The principal reason for this is that the Major government failed to implement any policies designed to change lifestyle and reduce the predicted growth of road traffic levels (Chapter 4). This failure to reduce traffic growth 'will continue to put pressure on the ability of the UK to curb levels of CO_2 emissions'(Cm 2427, para. 10.8). The management of rising CO_2 emissions was, in practice, restricted to domestic measures, such as raising fuel prices, and a pragmatic acceptance of EU regulatory measures aimed at increasing vehicle efficiency and reducing emissions. This latter strategy was, as we have seen in the analysis of the regulatory strategy of the EU, endorsed – but only with the caveat that the costs of Community proposals should fall upon vehicle manufacturers and the oil industry, and not on national governments or transport consumers. The EU was thus relatively powerless in preventing the rise of transport related greenhouse gases in the UK.

Conclusion

A primary concern of much academic and media comment is the extent to which the sovereignty of the UK has been diminished by the process of greater integration in Europe. At the outset of this chapter I argued that a narrow, legalistic focus on sovereignty is of limited use in an attempt to study, in practical terms, the capacity of a particular state to act on its own priorities. In order to evaluate the ability of a state, such as the UK, to retain control over its domestic transport policy, I suggested that a focus on autonomy is more instructive.

Such a focus on autonomy is particularly important to a consideration of the impact of the EU on the agenda of UK transport policy for a number of reasons. Firstly, as I have argued, a commitment to a Common Transport Policy was incorporated in the Treaty of Rome. Subsequently a commitment to an ambitious activist programme of TENs was agreed at Maastricht and incorporated in the TEU. But the success of these policy initiatives, as I have shown, has been limited despite their treaty status. While these examples are illustrative of a decline of state sovereignty over transport, they have in fact had little effect on either the autonomy or the agenda of UK transport policy makers.

Regulatory policy initiatives, in contrast, have profoundly affected the political landscape in which domestic policy makers operate, having had a significant and lasting impact on the scope of the alternatives and agenda open to them. Although in a technical sense the rise of EU regulatory policy has restricted the autonomy of UK policy makers, the commonality of focus between the UK government and the EU has in practical terms had the opposite effect, with the EU's prioritisation of technical solutions to the transport problem helping to insulate the government and pro-roads groups from pressure from the anti-roads groups.

Finally, the autonomy of the UK government has been enhanced by the EU's lack of action on the environmental implications of traffic growth, which has closed an important arena to the opponents of roads.

This chapter has thus provided a number of arguments which question the assumption that the European Union has been a positive influence on the development of environmental policy in the member states, instead suggesting that the development of EU environmental policy in the transport field has on balance been damaging in a number of ways. This, this chapter contends, is a result of an imbalance in the development of policy instruments available to the Union for management of environmental problems, with a well developed regulatory framework set alongside an almost total failure of activist policy. This imbalance has had the following results:

Firstly, the single market initiative of the European Union, and the associated deregulation of the transport market, has resulted in considerable increases in cross-national road transport. However, these initiatives have not been accompanied by either improvements to the road network, to reduce damage locally, or the provision of alternatives to encourage mode switching. Consequently, the result of the Community's initiatives has been to substantially increase mobility, with all of its associated environmental problems;

Secondly, the environmental initiatives of the EU have themselves had only mixed success. On the one hand, the development of a Community framework for the reduction of vehicle emissions has had a significant impact on ambient air quality, playing an integral part in the reduction of a number of pollutants associated with the deterioration of public health and the management of local air quality. But on the other hand the EU has presided over significant increases in emissions of greenhouse gases. The failure of the carbon-energy tax proposal and the rise in mobility encouraged by the single market have been significant factors in the rising emissions of CO_2, the principal greenhouse gas;

Finally, the environmental movement's challenge to the road programmes of a number of member states is undermined by the European Union's transport policy stance. The EU's regulatory strategy works to reduce the political salience of the transport problem by creating a technical framework for its solution: in consequence issues of sustainability, land-use and mobility are largely removed from the political agenda. And further, the EU's plans to develop a strategic network of European roads undermine the opposition of national road protests:

> The single market in Europe, as you well know, is the driving force behind the Trans-European Road Networks. And when they talked about the environment it was almost to hell with the environment. We're going to get these roads in ... At the time of Oxleas wood, and one or two of the other

things, Europe seemed the great green hope and it ain't that! (Interview, John Stewart, ALARM UK, 23rd November 1995)

Notes

1   There are strong parallels between the Major and Blair eras in the area of EU-UK relations in respect of the politics of the car. Thus, while Chapter 9 focuses explicitly on the politics of the car in the Blair era, it should be read alongside the analysis within this chapter for a complete understanding of the effect of the EU on the autonomy of the UK in the 1990s.

2   Of particular relevance to this analysis are: the Commission White Paper *Growth, Competitiveness, Employment* (CEC, 1993c); the Green Papers *The Citizens' Network'* (CEC, 1995b) and *Towards Fair and Efficient Pricing in Transport* (CEC, 1996); and the Commission's 1993 transport strategy document, *The Future Development of the Common Transport Policy* (CEC, 1993a).

3   The TENs programme was introduced within the Maastricht Treaty (Art 129b-d) and is intended to aid the facilitation of the Single European Market (SEM) programme through proposed expansion of Europe's transport, telecommunications and energy infrastructure. The transport proposals involve the strategic linkage of 54,000 kms of roads (of which 37,000 kms were in use on January 1992 and 12,000 kms are improvements or new roads) and 29,000 kms of railway (of which 14,000 are improvements and 12,500 are new lines) at a cost of ecu 120 bn for the road programme and ecu 240 bn for the rail projects (see CEC, 1993b and CEC High Level Group, 1995). For the clearest illustration of the link between the TEN programme and Keynesian objectives see the Commission White Paper 'Growth, Competitiveness, Employment' (CEC, 1993c).

4   This typology is taken from Kassim and Menon (1996a, pp. 3-4).

5   The growth of literature focusing on the role of trans-national lobby groups is also important, moving beyond constitutionally based analysis of policy making to emphasise the importance of routine, technocratic decision making (see for example Mazey and Richardson, 1993 and 1996 and Greenwood *et al*, 1992).

6   Due to the nature of this book, this chapter does not cover the ultimate incapacity of the EU to implement the TENs programme. However, I cover this is some detail in Robinson (1997b).

7   A number of commentators have argued that an impetus to the development of community policy also came from rulings by the European Court of Justice (ECJ) which enabled the institutions of the EU to make up for their historical lack of 'institutional authority'. In particular, the ruling by the ECJ in 1985 on the alleged failure of the Council of Ministers to act on its obligation to provide a CTP was important in providing the EU with legitimacy for political action. (See Ross, 1995, p. 120 and Aspinwall, 1996, p. 5).

8   The EU has developed regulatory policy covering the operation of road, rail, shipping and air transport. However, due to the nature of this research this analysis focuses on provisions for road transport.

9   In addition EC directives passed in 1980, 1982 and 1985 set legal air quality limits for sulphur dioxide and suspended particulates (directive 80/779/EEC), lead (82/884/EEC) and nitrogen dioxide (85/203/EEC).

10   This strategy of incorporating the affected parties and encouraging them to initiate
      policy finds strong parallels with the strategy adopted by the Commission in the
      formulation of European social policy, where trade unions and employers are
      encouraged to reach consensus and initiate policy proposals through the creation of
      'social partnerships' (Hantrais, 1995, pp. 6-7).

11   I argue in my analysis of the Blair era (Chapter 9) that this is arguably one of the
      most significant areas of policy change between the Major and Blair periods, with
      the Blair government acknowledging that revenues from restrictive measures such as
      road pricing must be hypothecated in order to enable local government to provide
      public transport alternatives.

12   This section takes its initial inspiration from a BBC *Panorama* Programme, *Nose to
      Tail* which was broadcast in 1994. I have followed up a number of the themes which
      this programme raised in a number of interviews, in particular with Roger Williams,
      Chief Transport Planner, Oxfordshire County Council (3rd June, 1997).

13   See also Putnam (1988) for a discussion of 'two level games', in which he argues
      that politicians will often attempt to realise their domestic objectives within an
      international arena and vice versa.

7 Local Authorities and the Transport Agenda Under Major: The Qualified Rise of Power Dependency in Central-Local Relations

Introduction

The issues to be addressed when dealing with transport demand in urban areas are in many ways the most intractable, since there is a widespread desire to improve accessibility while, at the same time, minimising environmental impact. But they are not insoluble. The key to finding the right solutions rests with local authorities, because they are best placed to strike the right balances, given the local knowledge available to them. But local authorities cannot shoulder this burden alone. Central government must not only [create the] right policy framework, but must also be prepared to offer support, to share expertise, to ensure the necessary powers are available, and promote a national vision of a quality environment. (Cm 3234, para. 14.88)

The government's response to the transport debate, published in April 1996 in the Green Paper, *Transport: the Way Forward* (Cm 3234), outlined both the opportunities and limitations which local authorities faced in their relations with central government in the Major era.[1] On the one hand, local authorities gained legitimacy and policy competence as central government acknowledged that local government was well equipped to attend to a number of policy problems caused by transport, such as congestion and pollution. On the other, local authorities lost legitimacy, as they were charged with introducing a number of politically unpopular policies such as road pricing and parking restrictions (Cm 3234, para 14.2) which none of them wished to implement:

I do not know at the moment of a town or city which would be prepared to say politically, 'Yes, we'll go for it' [i.e. implement road pricing] ... It is a very difficult political decision to take, and I say this very much as a layman in political issues but inevitably it is. What one needs, if this particular idea is to get anywhere, is an authority that has the political will and the political courage to take risks and try it. (Prof. May in evidence to the House of Commons Transport Select Committee, HC 104-II, para. 261)

This chapter seeks to evaluate the impact of these apparently contradictory pressures on local government, arguing that they simultaneously both created opportunities and imposed restrictions on the capacity of local government to affect the national agenda setting process. In order to substantiate this view this chapter concentrates on two primary tasks.

First, it outlines the ways in which local government increased its ability to influence the transport agenda in the Major era, exploiting instability within the problem stream in order to increase its mandate for action. During the Major period central government increasingly recognised that many transport problems have a significant local dimension, thus requiring local solutions and expertise. In consequence, the Major government developed important pieces of enabling legislation which increased the capacity of local authorities to introduce measures designed to restrict road traffic, such as road pricing and car parking controls.

In addition, in the period after 1993 local authorities gained increased influence over the national transport agenda as a result of changes to the funding formula for all discretionary transport projects costing under £2m through the introduction of the so called 'package approach'. This 'package approach' increased the capacity of local authorities to fund alternatives to road schemes, thus enabling them to develop multi-modal transport programmes.

Finally in considering the increased opportunities open to local authorities in this period, I argue that they were able to gain increased influence over the national transport agenda through a process of developing what I term 'financial advocacy coalitions' between local government, private business interests and the European Union.[2] These coalitions were able to exert considerable pressure upon the DTp and Treasury for 'top up' grants under the Major government's Private Finance Initiative (PFI). The construction of coalitions in this way was particularly significant in the success of the light rail bids for Manchester, Birmingham and Sheffield.

The second part of this chapter focuses on the limitations and constraints on local authorities within the sector. First, I argue that while enabling legislation presented local authorities with the tools for action, they still lacked the political will to take the risks associated with implementing policies such as road pricing, even on an experimental basis. I argue that the Major government was in fact concerned to use the introduction of enabling legislation primarily as a tool to manage the policy agenda, deflecting the problem away from central government.

I examine this view through an evaluation of the political debate which surrounded the proposals to introduce urban road pricing and motorway tolling, both of which are acknowledged as crucial tools for the management of road traffic levels. This chapter argues that significant inconsistencies can be seen in government policy regarding urban road pricing and motorway tolling as regards the issue of revenue hypothecation, with DTp officials in the Major era rejecting the idea in principle for urban roads while endorsing it for motorways. I argue that the reluctance of the Major government to consider the principle of hypothecated urban road pricing effectively ended all local authority interest in experimenting with it, supporting the view that the creation of the enabling legislation in this area was motivated primarily by a desire to manage the policy agenda.

In addition, the impact of local authorities on the agenda setting process was restricted by the limited financial resources available to them for policy innovation. Although the Major government made a number of policy pronouncements which supported an increased mandate for local initiatives in transport, the rhetoric was not matched by any significant increase in local government finances: the package approach only accounted for between 1-2% (or £79m) of the total transport budget in 1996-97 (Figures from Cm 3206, p. 59 and DoETR, 1997, p. 21); central government remained reluctant to increase government grants for capital projects; and the PFI did not deliver the level of investment which policy makers had anticipated.

Finally, I argue that the impact of local authorities on the agenda as a force for change in the Major period was limited because a number of those authorities still remained strongly committed to the 'roads for prosperity' orthodoxy. In particular, a number of authorities in the geographical periphery of the UK continued to emphasise the benefits which new roads could bring to the local economy. In these authorities the changes in the perception of the transport problem following publication of the SACTRA report in 1994 (see Chapter 4) have had even less effect on the thinking of local policy makers than they had on national ones. Consequently, a confused picture emerged from local government, which thus exerted two significant and contradictory pressures on the centre: 'progressive' authorities responded to, and facilitated, changes to the transport agenda away from road building and towards a multi-modal approach, while 'traditional' authorities continued to emphasise the need for road improvements in order to aid regional integration and economic development.

Central-Local Relations Theory: A Review of the Literature

The literature on central-local relations in the UK is strongly focused on the constitutional status of local government, with theorists divided over the extent to which the actual working relationship between central and local government reflects the formal, constitutional, legal relationship. A number of models of central-local relations have been developed of which two, the *agency model* and the *power-dependency* model, provide the focus for this analysis as they provide the most plausible explanations of central-local relations in the transport case. However, before outlining these models it is important to first describe the constitutional structure governing local authority autonomy in the UK.

Accounts which focus upon the constitutional relationship between central and local government emphasise that local government is heavily dependent on the centre, with its functions, powers, duties and structures outlined in acts of Parliament. Local government operates within a state system with a single source of constitutional power and authority, namely the Westminster Parliament (Judge, 1993, pp. 160-63). 'Thus, Parliament – or rather the government of the day acting through Parliament – can, by simple majority vote, restructure local government in any way it pleases and even abolish units of local government' (Wolman and Goldsmith, 1992, p. 71). Such power is well illustrated by the implementation of the 1985 Local Government Act which led to the abolition of the Greater London Council and the six Metropolitan County Councils.

The policy competence of local government is similarly constitutionally restricted: local authorities operate under the doctrine of *ultra vires* through which they may only undertake tasks explicitly bestowed upon them by an act of Parliament (Allen, 1990, p. 22). 'Local authorities depend upon statute and are subject to a strict interpretation of the legal role of *ultra vires*. That is, they may only act – with certain limited exceptions – if they can find positive authority for their actions in a specific law. They have no general competence to act for the benefit of the people of the local area. Silence on the part of the law is not enough; specific authorisation must be given' (Hampton, 1987, p. 2 cited in Wolman and Goldsmith, 1992, p. 72).

The practical implications of this constitutional relationship between the centre and local authorities provide the justification for the *agency model* of central-local relations. According to this approach, local government is little more than an arm, or agent, of the centre with limited discretion in policy implementation. In the transport case, this model serves to emphasise the constraints which the doctrine of *ultra vires* has imposed on the delivery of many local transport services, particularly following the programme of deregulation which the Thatcher government implemented in the transport sector.

The growth of the 'informal local government system' during the Thatcher and Major eras also worked to reduce local authority autonomy in the transport sphere (King, 1993, pp. 203-15). Bonefeld *et al* capture this view:

> The process of 'agentification' has a number of common features such as the centralisation of power to the central state at the expense of local government autonomy, and the enhanced role given to private sector business interests at the expense of public sector provision and trade union involvement. (1995, p. 159)

The agency model focuses on the transfer of power from local authorities to central government as a result of Parliamentary legislation since 1979. 'The aim of these reforms is to marginalise local government as a political institution by creating alternative local agencies to deliver policy and by denuding its representative role' (King, 1993, p. 194). This process, according to agency theorists, accelerated during the Major era:

> None of the requirements of the pre-Major years were abated: the scope of compulsory competitive tendering continued to be extended and financial stringency became still tighter, while important changes in community care and education were pressed forward. Overall, the first years of Major['s] government coupled new initiatives to an acceleration of policies which were already in place when he entered 10 Downing Street. (Young, 1994, p. 84)

A number of other developments also strengthened the control of central government over local authorities during this period, further weakening their autonomy. First, the abolition of the community charge strengthened control over local finance (Young, 1994, p. 96). Second, the role of quangos and informal local government continued to grow annually (King, 1993, p. 205). Third, local government elections were increasingly dominated by national issues, leading to unprecedented losses for the Conservative party which 'represent no kind of judgement on Conservative policies for local government. Their significance is to the contrary: the fewer Conservative councillors there are to offend, the fewer inhibitions on radical action' (Young, 1994, p. 96).

In contrast to this limited picture of local government power offered by the agency models, *power-dependency* models seek to emphasise the interdependent nature of the relationship between central and local government, providing a critique of the perceived inadequacies of the agency model's constitutional focus. Rhodes, who has written extensively from this perspective, argues that central-local relations are best characterised by bargaining. While local authorities may be dependent on the centre for a number of resources, in particular legal and constitutional power and for much of their finance, they in turn have a number of resources such as knowledge, control over local policy implementation and employees, flexibility in priority setting and service charging and a local electoral mandate, which they can use to redress the centralising tendencies of the constitution (1988, p. 42).

Power-dependency also stresses the growing influence of the European dimension in UK central-local relations, as local authorities are increasingly aware, through the developing influence of subsidiarity, of the potential for partnerships between local authorities and EU actors to exert pressure on central government. Under this approach, policy making is personified by 'a complex web of policy networks indicating and even stronger role for SCG [sub-central (i.e. local) government]' (Ward, 1995, p. 102. See Mawson and Gibney, 1985 for a classification of models of inter-governmental relations).

In the transport case, utilisation of power-dependency models highlights two key developments during the Major era. First, I argue below that during this period policy making became increasingly complex due to the growth of financial partnerships between the EU, local authorities and business which placed pressure on central government for 'top up' funding. Second, as I have argued in my earlier discussion of the role of problem centred analysis (Chapter 4), the Major government produced a number of publications which argued that local authorities were 'best placed' to find solutions to local problems (see in particular DoE and DoT, 1994, Cm 3234, ch. 14, and Cm 3188, ch. 18).

Overall, the difficulty for models of central-local relations has been to provide an accurate account of such increasing policy complexity. The problem is that models of central-local relations by implication focus on institutional relationships, which do 'not always provide an adequate account of policy systems'. As a solution to these problems Rhodes suggests that a focus on intergovernmental theory 'with its emphasis on fragmentation, professionalisation and policy networks' is 'more appropriate' (1986, p. 28). This chapter argues that Rhodes' analysis is important for its emphasis on the complexity of central-local relations and the consequent recognition of local government's ability to influence the agenda in this area. However, I also argue that there are serious limitations with such an approach in the transport case. This chapter thus argues that useful insights can be drawn from both the power-dependency and agency models of central-local relations when applied to the transport case in the Major era.

The Transport Case

On the surface, the macro-political environment within which local authorities have operated since 1979 suggests a model of central-local relations closer to that of agency theory than to power-dependency in the transport case. Chapter 3's historical analysis showed that decision making has been dominated by national actors in a process in which a clearly defined and skilfully managed policy community developed around the road programme.

A number of studies of local government transport policy have emphasised that local policy outcomes have tended to be dependent on national priorities, with road building professionals effectively excluding the opponents of roads at the local level through their monopoly over complex technical knowledge (Dunleavy, 1980, pp. 112-23 and Laffin, 1986, cited in Wilson and Game, 1994, p. 126):

> In the old regimes all County highway/City highway engineers, wanted pre-eminence and wanted to fight for their own patch. Clearly, the most important thing was to dual this particular highway, or improve that junction, or put a bigger roundabout in there ... They weren't zealots, they were doing their jobs. They clearly saw this as a way out of problems. (Interview, Philip Hunt, DoETR, 6th November 1997)

As Rhodes has argued, control of the policy process at a local level by professional interests is unsurprising as they are:

> organised as 'learned societies', in which capacity they recruit and train personnel, organise conferences and seminars, produce research and publications and, as with any other organised group, proselytise and lobby for their interests. [In addition they are also] trade unions and ... can use working to rule and strikes as a means of influencing the government. In effect, therefore, the professions can have three bites at the cherry of political influence. (Rhodes, 1988, pp. 214-15)

Throughout the post-war period the domination of decision making by national priorities, combined with the local influence of highway engineers, has resulted in considerable local authority pressure for maintaining and extending the road programme. Such pressure is particularly pronounced in the geographical periphery of the UK, from local administrations which are typically Labour controlled:

> There is enormous pressure, particularly in Labour dominated areas like South Wales or Scotland. There is enormous pressure from local authorities there for better road infrastructure because they believe, although without any proof in many cases, that they are missing out economically because there are not enough roads. So there is going to be a lot of pressure on a Blair government from almost their internal road lobby, local councils, and people like the Transport and General Workers Union, to build more roads. (Interview, John Stewart, ALARM UK, 23rd November 1995)

Finally, the tightening of financial controls on local government since the mid-1970s, the imposition of Compulsory Competitive Tendering (CCT) in the maintenance and construction of highway work, the deregulation of the bus services outside London, and the escalation of political conflict between Labour dominated metropolitan councils and central government throughout the Thatcher and Major eras have all combined to limit the ability of local government to provide alternatives to the private car (Wilson and Game, 1994, p. 327). The legitimacy of local government action has also been called into question through court action taken by central government to ensure that local authorities do not act *ultra vires*, most notably in the legal challenge posed to the Greater London Council's 'Fares Fair' policy in 1982 (see Grant, 1986, pp. 198-200). Such developments are all indicative of the weakening of the autonomy of local government in this area and are 'the direct and inevitable product of worsening central-local relations' (Grant, 1986, p. 203).

Local Transport Finance: A Brief Portrait

Historically, local transport spending has been financed by a combination of the DTp, the DoE, local authority spending and the transport operators themselves. The division between the DoE and DTp reflected the particular roles which the two departments had in transport planning: the DoE being concerned, in general, with current or day to day spending and the DTp with funding strategic capital investment (personal communication, DTp, 2nd July 1996).

This functional division placed responsibility with the DoE for current expenditure, principally local roads maintenance and financial support for buses and metropolitan rail services and concessionary fare schemes. In contrast the DTp's role was to support capital expenditure on roads and public transport which were designed to improve the local infrastructure (Cm 3206, p. 59, para. 6.2). In practice, this functional separation of roles between the two departments did little to counteract the predominance of spending on road building and maintenance. Taking a typical year such as 1994/5, the DTp's own figures show that of the £3.98 bn projected for transport spending by central and local government, almost £3 bn was earmarked for either road improvements or maintenance. The figures for capital spending (i.e. excluding current spending) show an even greater bias in favour of investment in roads, with £1.25 bn of the total of £1.48 bn earmarked for roads in 1994/95 (DTp, 1995, p. 28, table 1.17). As a result 'most investment in the infrastructure [for public transport] is carried out by the service operators' (Cm 3206, p. 62, para. 6.9); local authorities which wish to provide public transport projects are thus restricted in their ability to do so.

Historically, the scope for local authority action has been further restricted by the funding mechanism used by central government. Although there are a wide variety of sources of discretionary funding which local authorities can apply for, they all fall into one of two categories: non-repayable grants and credit approvals entitling the authority to borrow.

The most significant of the non-repayable grants at this time was the Transport Support Grant (TSG) which in 1994/5 accounted for £329m of the DTp's total grants of £349m (figures from Cm 3206, p. 58, figure 25). It was only available for road projects:

> Allocations of TSG must, by law, be made available to specified highway authorities, and can only be paid in support of accepted expenditure on highways and traffic regulation. The Secretary of State cannot delegate this function. In the light of experience gained from introduction of the package

concept the Government will in the longer term consider with the local authority associations the value of changing the existing legal powers for grant-aiding transport infrastructure expenditure. (DTp, 1993, para. 39)

The TSG remained restricted to road projects throughout the Major era. Public transport projects could only seek funding under the 'public transport facilities grant', payable under section 56 of the 1968 Transport Act (S. 56). These grants were payable to local authorities with 'large' transport projects which could be 'justified by benefits to non-users, such as reduced congestion' (Cm 3206, para. 6.9). At first sight, the range of projects benefiting from these grants during the Major era is impressive, including Manchester Metro Link, South Yorkshire Super Tram, Midland Metro and the Robin Hood line in Nottinghamshire.

However, the impact of S. 56 funding was not as significant as it might at first seem. Figures from 1994/5, for example, show that it accounted for only £13m of total central government grants of £349m (Cm 3206, p. 58, figure 25). In addition, the stipulated requirements of these grants restricted the capacity for local authorities to secure discretionary central government finance:

> To be eligible for S. 56 grant, projects will need to represent a substantial addition or improvement to local public transport facilities and will need to be large enough for it to be reasonable that the costs should be spread beyond users and local charge payers. It is unlikely that any project costing significantly less than £5m in total would be accepted for grant. This does not, however, imply that expenditure above that level would by itself constitute a case for a grant. It is also unlikely that grant would be given for a project likely to require continuing subsidy. (DTp, 1989b, para. 3)[3]

These conditions imposed significant constraints on the discretionary powers of local authorities to finance projects in the pre-Major period. In particular, the stipulation that only 'large projects' were eligible for S. 56 grants limited local authorities' capacity to bid for them and they became caught in a catch-22 situation: in need of non-repayable grants in order to increase local transport investment but without the discretionary resource base to 'top-up' the grant as stipulated within the S. 56 criteria. As a result, most public transport schemes had to compete for finance through repayable credit approvals. Yet here again, as in the case of grant-financing, credit approvals for local roads have historically predominated: in 1993/94, for example, £513m of the DTp's budget of

£645m was allocated to roads, with public transport securing only £122m of the budget (Cm 3206, p. 58, figure 25).[4]

Overall therefore, until the middle of the Major period the scope for local authority transport initiatives was limited by the funding formula which central government used for transport projects. First, transport projects which central government was willing to fund were overwhelmingly roads based. Second, the formula limited the capacity of local authorities to gain access to either non-repayable grants (such as S. 56) or to borrow money through credit approvals. Thus, their capacity for policy innovation in the transport sphere was highly restricted.

The Major Effect: Local Government Regains Some Initiative

> In the long run some difficult choices may have to be made about traffic in our towns. It is simply not possible to cater for unrestricted growth of traffic in our city centres, nor would it be right to accept a situation in which traffic congestion found its own level, with inefficient use of road space and increased fuel consumption. Eventually it may be necessary to consider the rationing of road space by road pricing, but this approach is largely untried and there would be difficulties in ensuring an enforceable and fair system. (Cm 1200, para. 8.20)

Until the early 1990s, the domination of transport policy making by national actors, the strong influence of highway engineers on local government decision making and the general hostility of central government to the aims of 'progressive' local authorities limited the capacity for local government to influence the agenda. During the early 1990s, however, a number of developments enabled local authorities to begin to affect the national transport agenda.

In particular, as I have argued in detail in Chapter 4, one of the most pressing policy problems during the Major period was increasing congestion. DTp concerns with the impact of projected traffic growth were particularly significant in urban areas, becoming more acute following the publication of research on car dependency by a number of organisations (see for example the annual *Lex Reports* on motoring and RAC (1995), cited in Cm 3234, p. 128. See also Taylor, 1997, pp. 131-32 for commentary on the British Social Attitudes Surveys). These reports revealed a growing reliance on the car for journeys of under two miles, and highlighted the impact that such journeys have on local congestion:

Journeys to school are a key example of where changes in behaviour could make a real difference. 52 per cent of journeys to school were under one mile in the period 1988/94 and, although more than half of children do walk to school, the proportion travelling by car has increased from only 12 per cent in 1975/76 to 23 per cent in 1989/94. Whilst these trips account for only about 1 per cent of all car mileage, they are strongly concentrated during the morning peak travel period: school trips make up nearly 20 per cent of all car journeys in the height of the weekday morning peak in urban areas and can therefore have a significant impact on traffic congestion. (Cm 3234, para. 14.48)

Trends such as these are indicative of a growing recognition by central government during the Major era that many transport problems are local in nature and thus require local solutions and expertise:

The government believes that the most appropriate package of measures for a particular area is something best determined at a local level, by locally accountable politicians. It follows that, in principle, if a local authority considers that an effective traffic management strategy for its area requires more restrictive measures than it is currently empowered to implement and it is satisfied that such steps would not have an unduly harmful effect on local economic and social vitality, then it should be enabled to take that action. (Cm 3234, para. 14.68)

In response to these concerns central government supported local authority action in this area, encouraging the inclusion of cycling and walking in their bids for capital funding (Cm 3234, para. 14.40 and para. 14.47. I discuss the impact of the package approach in the next section).

In order to evaluate the extent to which the sentiments expressed in the Major government's transport Green Paper actually had an effect in increasing local authority autonomy in the transport sphere this section now focuses on two key issues: the financial resources which local government had to implement its policy objectives; and the scope of the legislation available to it to enable restrictions to the behaviour of transport users.

The Package Approach and Increasing Interdependency in Transport Provision

The Major era witnessed some significant changes to the funding of local authority transport initiatives, enabling local authorities to exercise greater influence on the national transport agenda. In particular, in 1993 the 'package approach' to transport finance was launched.[5] 'Under the package approach local authorities bid for resources to implement a cohesive, area based, *cross-modal* strategy, targeted on meeting local transport needs against a clear set of objectives' (Cm 3234, para. 14.76, emphasis in original). The aim of the package approach was, according to the DTp, to offer local authorities an opportunity to develop an overall plan for dealing with their transport requirements in the context of strategic land use and economic and environmental objectives (DTp, 1993, para. 4). To facilitate these aims this approach offered 'greater flexibility, within the constraints of existing legislation, for local authorities to switch resources between different forms of transport in urban areas' (DTp, 1993, para. 3). Following the scheme's launch the total finance for bids nationally rose from thirteen schemes totalling £12.6m in 1994/5 to fifty three schemes totalling £78.7m in 1996/7, with the range of successful bidders covering the whole rubric of local authorities from urban conurbations such as Greater Manchester to rural areas such as the New Forest (Cm 3234, para. 14.77).

Although the funds available under the package approach were relatively small, by the end of the Major period it accounted for all discretionary bids of under £2m for minor works made by local authorities (Cm 3206, para. 6.4). Consequently it effected a significant change in the way in which local authorities could build their transport strategy:

> One of the things that has happened in the last couple of years [i.e. since 1994/5] is that local authorities' programmes now have to be part of a package rather than individual road schemes. They put forward a strategy for their local authority and submit bids for funding for it which means they have to give attention to the needs of public transport, pedestrians and cyclists rather than just building roads. So that's a definite change to the culture. (Unattributable interview information)

In order to aid the compilation of package bids the Secretary of State identified nine objectives which any proposed spending on local roads and public transport should fulfil: to improve safety and the economy by reducing road congestion; to encourage modal shift from private to public transport; to improve traffic management; to conserve and improve the environment; to divert through traffic away from unsuitable roads; to improve maintenance of key strategic routes; to reduce the numbers of road accidents; to improve facilities for pedestrians and cyclists; and to facilitate urban regeneration through the improvement of access to cities (DTp, 1993, para. 18).

The creation of the package approach was indicative of the Major government's increased recognition of the legitimacy of local authority action to promote alternatives to the car. To this end, during this period local authorities were encouraged to seek funding for transport projects through the package approach which:

> encourages local authorities bidding for capital support for transport projects to take a strategic overview of transport needs and to look beyond road-based options, countering what some had seen as an incentive in the earlier system to focus on roads spending. (Cm 3234, para. 14.75)

Progressive local authorities were thus presented with opportunities to regain policy competence. In particular the package approach enabled them to undertake multi-modal programmes which would not have been possible under the old funding regime with its emphasis on road schemes as solutions to local traffic problems (DTp, 1993, paras 3-4). Historically, local authorities had to justify the finance for a road scheme by demonstrating a need to improve traffic flow. Thus the local rationale for policy was driven by the 'predict and provide' orthodoxy, reflecting the national rationale for policy with its focus on widening local arterial routes, expanding the by-pass programme and removing through traffic from town centres.

In theory, the predict and provide ethos became much less important under the package approach as road schemes were seen as only one of a number of possible solutions for tackling congestion on a particular route, and as such, they remained in competition with alternatives such as bus priority, park and ride, rail improvements and demand management strategies such as congestion charging or parking restrictions (DTp, 1993, para. 33).

The packaging of transport bids in this way enabled local authorities to promote 'green' alternatives to the car, in particular strategies for cycling and walking, and was broadly welcomed by both the pressure group community (in particular by members of the anti-roads groups) and the local authorities, both of whom saw it as a genuine policy innovation: 'We welcome the positive steps the DTp has taken in strengthening the environmental content of the TPP guidance and the introduction of the "package" approach' (CPRE, 1995, para. 4.30).

In particular, the CPRE felt that the development of the package approach provided policy makers with the opportunity to develop a policy framework which fully integrated transport and land-use planning:

> CPRE believes the development of 'packages' has unlocked huge potential to develop integrated approaches to tackling transport problems. In

particular, we feel there is much to be gained from the wider preparation of packages in rural areas. In our view, the potential of the package approach would be further enhanced if transport planning was set firmly within a land use context and national roads no longer distorted the process through their priority status. (CPRE, 1995, para. 4.33)

Local authorities shared this positive view, arguing that the development of the package approach was vital in enabling them to build links with neighbouring local authorities and develop multi-modal transport policy on a regional basis. The West Midlands conurbation has been at the forefront of experiments with the package approach through its transport arm, Centro, and argues that:

> The Balanced Transport Package is an agreed strategy with clearly defined priorities for investment ... Investing in transport in the West Midlands is now viewed as one of a number of strategic programmes designed to support better land use, encourage economic and environmental improvement and open up work and leisure opportunities to a wider community. (Centro, 1994b, unpaginated)

However, in spite of this general enthusiasm for the package approach concept, a number of commentators have criticised its actual implementation by the Major government. First, the CPRE in their submission to the 'Great Debate' (see Chapter 5) argued that the criteria for funding under the package approach should be changed to take more account of the government's objectives for sustainable development and of Local Agenda 21, to which it committed itself following the Rio Earth Summit:

> We *recommend* that objectives for TPPs (and individual packages) should be set within the overall objective of environmentally sustainable development. Specific objectives could include reducing the need to travel or encouraging less damaging forms of transport such as walking and cycling. This is consistent with the environmentally-led approach to transport planning [to which the CPRE is committed] and would follow a cascade of transport objectives from national and local level. (CPRE, 1995, para. 4.31)

Second, the CPRE also expressed concern at the limited scope of the package approach, arguing that it showed an overwhelming bias in favour of urban conurbations: 'The discrepancy is huge at the moment. If you look at where the local transport budget (the packages) went last year: less than one percent went to rural areas and over ninety nine percent was for urban areas' (Interview, Lily Matson, CPRE, 20th August 1996).

Finally, and arguably most significantly, the implementation of the TPP suffered from a lack of finance. As I have argued, the package approach commanded low levels of central government funding when compared to other DTp programmes. As a senior civil servant suggested in an interview, there were real concerns that the lack of resources for packages would undermine the relationship between the centre and locality:

> To produce these glitzy documents every year and to go through all this paraphernalia, to be honest, for increasingly poor returns, or small returns, is something which ... I mean, we kept them on board, to be frank, but we do begin to wonder that you can't keep saying, and telling people, that they are on the right lines, but unfortunately we have been unable to fund this year, but keep trying. (Interview, senior civil servant, DoETR, Local Planning Division, November 1997)

In order to evaluate the effects of the limited finances available through the package approach, the next section of this chapter examines in detail the implications of such constraints and evaluates the initiatives employed by local government in order to overcome them.

Funding Complexity as an Agent of Political Change: Sabatier's Advocacy Coalition Approach

During the Major era local authorities became increasingly innovative in forming partnerships with private interests and the EU in order to overcome the funding limitations imposed by central government on the package approach. The Major government actively encouraged local authorities to seek such sources of funding, in line with its belief that entrepreneurial practice 'is bringing a sea-change in the delivery of major transport investment ... This means capturing the benefits of private sector skills and efficiencies, while transferring significant risk away from the Government where it can be better managed by the private sector' (Cm 3234, para. 7.12).

Sabatier's work on advocacy coalitions provides a useful theoretical framework by which the construction of coalitions between local government, the EU and private business can be explained. The mainstream view is that the advocacy coalition framework assumes that 'actors can be aggregated into a number of advocacy coalitions composed of people from various organisations who share a set of normative and causal beliefs and who often work in concert' (Sabatier, 1988, p. 133). According to this perspective, coalitions only form between actors who share core beliefs; secondary goals (in particular provided by the profit motive) will be insufficient to found a coalition.

However, an alternative interpretation is offered by Jenkins-Smith and St. Clair in their study, 'The Politics of Offshore Energy' (1993). They argue that considerable variation can be identified in the importance of policy beliefs to material groups and to value based groups. According to Jenkins-Smith and St. Clair:

> Material group representatives *do not* appear to be constrained by an hierarchical system of beliefs, as was proposed by the [advocacy coalition] framework. For these groups the orientation of beliefs – and willingness to change policy positions – appears to be anchored on a bottom line representing the critical interests of the represented groups. Outside that concern, considerable flexibility is evident in positions taken. Representatives of purposive groups, in contrast, appear to be more tightly constrained in the expression of beliefs. (1993, pp. 171-72, emphasis in original)

According to this view, for material groups 'commitment to material self-interest (profit) is primordial, with more abstract policy core beliefs (for instance, commitment to local versus national control) adjusted as necessary' (Sabatier and Jenkins-Smith, 1993b, p. 225).

The analysis of partnership building between local government, the EU and private interests suggests a pattern of coalition formation more accurately described by the view of Jenkins-Smith and St. Clair rather than through the mainstream concept of the advocacy coalition framework. For the purpose of this analysis, and to aid clarity of distinction between these two models, I have labelled coalitions which form primarily on the basis of financial motives *financial advocacy coalitions*.

Developments in central-local relations during the Major era suggest that the financial advocacy coalition model provides a useful framework by which the increase in local government influence on the national transport agenda can be explained. At this time, in response to initiatives such as the package approach and the private finance initiative, local authorities tried to build financial advocacy coalitions to develop both small scale and large scale projects, experiencing considerable success in relation to small scale projects but only mixed success in respect of larger ones.

At a general level, the construction of financial advocacy coalitions became more common place in the Major era. According to Tony Bosworth of FoE, local authorities had to come up with 'more innovative ways of getting more funding, certainly saying to the government all we are needing from you is a small percentage ... I think local authorities, in the current climate, are increasingly having to find those new ways. I am not saying that they should but I think that they are having to' (Interview, 12th December 1995). Furthermore, through building coalitions in this way local authorities had some success in pressuring central government into providing the balance of finance for transport schemes, as an interviewee made clear:

> There is no doubt that if you can link all these things up that the government will assist ... They will give SCA [credit approvals] for areas were they have got European funding. So the whole thing builds up as an accumulation which is how they tend to be successful. (Interview, senior transport consultant, February 1996)

In the Major era, local authorities were relatively successful in building financial advocacy coalitions for small projects (i.e. those projects which qualify for funding under the package approach and are of £2m or less in value). The process of coalition building for such projects was facilitated, according to a senior transport consultant, by two key developments. First, financial austerity 'crowded out' large projects, in particular road projects:

> As you know, local government allocation has probably been lopped off by between five and ten percent every year. It's the major schemes that are taking the brunt of the cuts. I think there were, I can't remember how many new highway schemes, but it was not more than twenty, I think it was about fifteen. But it is because they are a big lump of money whereas the amount that can be put into soft traffic management, if you want to call it that, you can get an awful lot for the same amount of money. (Interview, senior transport consultant, February 1996)

Second, the development of the package approach itself helped to institutionalise coalition building as part of the bidding process, as local authorities and private companies were 'forced' into greater co-operation in order to participate. Through the changes to the funding criteria the package approach reoriented the priorities of a number of transport businesses away from local road schemes and towards a multi-modal transport approach, based on small scale local transport projects:

The size of our projects is coming down all of the time. In this section our median project is £10,000 – I mean we do have multi-million pound ones as well but most of those are overseas – and in fact we recruited this year a cycling specialist because a large part of our work still is local authority services, and the money being given out under TSG, TPP, SCA funding is very much more directed towards cycling and pedestrianisation. We foresaw this sometime ago and we pay for the right intelligence. We have to be that much ahead. So we recruited to cater for that market. (Interview, senior transport consultant, February 1996)

Overall, the development of financial advocacy coalitions surrounding small projects had a significant cumulative impact. A practical example of this effect was described by a senior transport consultant in relation to the development of policy initiatives on Merseyside, where Mersey Travel are developing a wire guided bus scheme in order to increase access to the centre of Liverpool. This scheme has been totally dependent on the construction of a financial advocacy coalition between the local authority, the EU and the local transport operator:

They wouldn't be able to do this [i.e. develop the wire guided bus scheme] without their 'objective one' status we are sure of that. Nobody's actually told us that but I would be surprised if they could fund that without that. And there is some good work going ahead there, which will be successful. (Interview, senior transport consultant, February 1996)

In addition to the pressure for such small scale projects, financial advocacy coalitions also attempted to exert pressure on central government to fund large scale projects, such as new road schemes and light rapid transit (LRT) schemes, for a combination of reasons. First, many local authorities attempted to secure funding for such projects for predominantly political reasons:

They tend to be light rail schemes because local authorities don't run buses – buses are in the private sector – the rail system is highly regulated and it's all franchised: local authorities can actually enter into joint ventures in order to develop a light rail system. And, what I've said before, members like large things which focus on Bradford, or focus on Hull, or Bristol, or wherever it is: they want their name in lights – figuratively speaking. And if they can't build a new urban motorway but they've got a tram they think well ... [laughter] No, this is true. Now what we've really got to do is to cut through that and say, 'Hang on a minute – you don't buy Rolls Royce if a Morris Minor will do' – and that's a very hard lesson, and something which is having to be made, and we're having to make it clear. Light rail is obviously exceedingly expensive and we have lots of questions about whether in fact patronage levels will be reached and whether they are worthwhile. (Interview, senior civil servant, DoETR, Local Planning Division, November 1997. See Ross, 1994 for similar comments with reference to the European Union)

In contrast potential private partners remained financially motivated to push for large scale projects as a result of the high costs associated with putting together bids for either central government or EU funding under schemes such as the PFI and ERDF. Many of the costs associated with the competitive bidding process must be paid regardless of the size of the bid, so many private firms have an incentive to pressure central government to fund larger rather than smaller projects. In interview, a senior transport consultant reflected on the effect of this bidding process for private firms such as his:

There are great difficulties for firms such as ours because of the way the thing is remunerated. It means really that any company has to be prepared to put quite a substantial investment in ... there is so much involved in the submission and you have to have the right partners and you have to try and get what is called industry funding ... The amount of work by very senior expensive people that is actually required, and then you may not even be accepted. At the end of the day the out-turn, perhaps covers 25% of the costs, and consultancies in this country work on wafer thin margins ... I think that that has been an inhibitor to people being prepared to invest in this country in the knowledge and the research that goes into it .... There are a number of firms who have got involved and the ones who can generally survive are either the very small ones or the very, very big ones. The great body in the middle can't actually afford it. It's a bit like legal aid, if you like. It's only the very poor and the very rich who can actually afford legal services, one way or the other. (Interview, senior transport consultant, February 1996)

During the Major era, a number of financial advocacy coalitions were successfully constructed, illustrating the potential for local authorities to build coalitions and secure financial concessions from central government. The most instructive recent case is that of the Midland Metro scheme. 'Midland Metro is a light rail, rapid transit system that is planned to link many of the key destinations within the West Midlands. Quiet, clean and quick it will give the region one of the world's most advanced forms of passenger transport' (Centro, 1993, p. 4). The scheme envisages a network of 200km of dedicated track by the year 2010 encompassing routes between

Birmingham and Wolverhampton (Line 1); Birmingham and the International Airport via Solihull (Line 2); Wolverhampton and Dudley via Walsall (Line 3), and, in the longer term, a number of supplementary services radiating from Birmingham and Coventry (p. 4).

As of June 1996, the West Midlands Passenger Transport Authority (WMPTA) had secured Parliamentary approval for the building of Lines 1, 2 and 3 but had only secured S. 56 grant, on which the project was dependent, for Line 1. The S. 56 grant of £40m was matched by credit approvals for £40m of local authority borrowing, £22m in EU grants and £10m from an international private consortium, Altram, which was 'taking on virtually all construction risks and will operate the 23 stop line without public subsidy for 20 years' (Centro, 1994a, p. 6, figures from *Financial Times*, 6th May 1994, p. 8).

Examination of the proposal to build Midland Metro seems at first to endorse the power-dependency thesis of central-local relations, illustrating as it does the failure of local authority PTAs to ' bring government around to providing policies and the investment that will enable PTAs to modernise and bring up to acceptable standards the public transport infrastructure and services in the areas they serve' (Cllr Worrall in Centro, 1994a, p. 2). Writing in 1994, Cllr Worrall, Chairman of the WMPTA, emphasised the frustration which the planners of Midland Metro had suffered as a result of the governments delay in approving Lines 2 and 3:

> The government has nothing at all to say yet about the more ambitious projects for Lines 2 and 3 that would provide us with the basic core network for Birmingham and the Black Country. (Centro, 1994a, p. 2)

However, despite Cllr Worrall's understandable pessimism, this case also illustrates the capacity of local authorities to construct financial advocacy coalitions and to pressure central government. The DTp set 'the most rigorous appraisal that any project has ever had to endure' (Centro 1994a, p. 6) but the project did succeed in gaining the payment of a £40m S. 56 grant in the Budget of November 1994. Midland Metro constructed a coherent advocacy coalition comprising cross party support, the EU, the private consortium scheduled to operate Midland Metro and the local business community, 'endorsing its significance in improving traffic links, regenerating under used and derelict land, creating economic re-generation and providing and alternative traffic congestion' (Centro, 1994a, p. 6): it was the strength of this financial advocacy coalition which pressured central government into granting approval for Line 1.

First, as a senior civil servant in the Government Office for the West Midlands argued in discussing the process of granting central government support for Midland Metro, the macro-economic and political climate placed significant pressure on the budget of the DTp:

> We got into the present squeeze on resources and there was a real question of whether the government could afford a scheme costing a hundred and forty odd million. And that became quite a political process (with a small 'p') in the sense that the government was saying well, 'We are convinced that there is a good case for doing this but we're not satisfied with the concept of central government paying the whole cost, you've got to go out and find money from other sources'. (Interview, senior civil servant, Government Office for the West Midlands, August, 1997)

As a result an extensive bargaining process developed between central government, the West-Midlands region in the shape of the PTA, the EU and the private contractors:

> There was a bargaining process, yes, and it was very much as I've described it – that the government said well, 'We can't afford a full hundred and forty odd million because that's equivalent to (I don't know what figures are used) 20 bypasses or something; and if we were going to spend that sort of money, we would rather spend it on the 20 bypasses; thank you very much. (Interview, Peter Langley, Government Office for the West Midlands, DoETR, 28th August 1997)

Second, the promoters of Midland Metro also benefited from 'luck'. According to Cllr Worrall, central government support for LRT was restricted to one scheme per year, and in the West Midlands they happened to be the next authority in the queue for financial support from central government:

> They had this 50 million a year set-a-side and wasn't it that the spending on Sheffield was coming to an end and therefore, you know, it was time to think about funding others – so, it was us and Croydon. (Interview, Cllr Richard Worrall, Chair WMPTA, 11th June 1997)

Finally, the construction of a financial coalition of private, local authority and EU partners was shown to be vital at the end of the bidding cycle. According to an interviewee, the Major government tried to cancel the project at the end by announcing a central government grant which left a shortfall of £5m; it was only because the EU could make up that shortfall that the project came to fruition at all:

> In my opinion the government, right towards the end, tried to spike the whole project. There was a package put together – you know, private sector, government money, European money – and the day that the government eventually got around to announcing it it became clear that the government input into it, I think, was going to be about £5 million less than had been foreseen. My view [is] that was quite deliberate at the time; that the government had decided, OK, you drop it by £5 million – you know for good and understandable arguments about controlling public expenditure – but at that sort of notice that would just frighten the public sector; nobody was going to come in for another ... Industry were frightened, was the extra £5 million coming from – I mean, it was more likely to lead to people dropping out than coming in. The assumption was, that Europe wouldn't do anything about it. [However following protracted bargaining within the EU, the EU was able to make up the shortfall]. I think what we would of had without that extra £5 million is sums that didn't add up. You had a financing package that was £5 million short. And I think if that had ever come into the public arena, and announced to the public as a financing package that was £5 million pounds short – you could kiss goodbye to the project. That's my view. (Interview, unattributable).

Thus, as this case shows, financial advocacy coalitions are highly precarious and, in spite of Midland Metro Line 1's success, the pressures which local government, the EU and the private sector exerted on the Major government for funding large projects were in general much less successful in securing central government finance. The principal reason for this, as I have suggested earlier, is that an over-arching policy objective of both the Thatcher and Major governments was the implementation of measures to reduce state spending and continue financial austerity – thus reducing the capacity of local government to secure funding from central government for large scale and expensive infrastructure projects (see also Chapter 3 for the reasons historically used by central government to rationalise spending on road projects in spite of their cost).

As a result of this over-arching framework of macro-economic austerity, even in situations in which local government has successfully secured backing from the private sector, European Union and central government – such as in the case of Manchester Metro Link – this has often come on terms which favour private investors rather than the local authority:

If you look at the Manchester MetroLink one of the ways, I believe, they can actually get more finance for the MetroLink is by putting it through the Trafford Business Park, which is maybe not the route they would have picked if they'd been wanting to talk about serving the greatest number of people. They've picked a scheme which is probably going to be favourably regarded by the business community and therefore they are going to be more likely to get the business finance. So it's affecting the sort of schemes and the sort of routes that they are picking for those sorts of projects. (Interview, Tony Bosworth, FoE, 12th December 1995)

Further reflection on the advocacy coalition framework is useful in considering the nature of the difficulties which local authorities faced in the Major era in seeking to develop financial advocacy coalitions with a view to changing the policy agenda. As I have argued, in creating financial advocacy coalitions between local government, the private sector and the EU, local government attempted to create a rival coalition which challenged central government. But the coalitions constructed by local government were highly unstable, because they were based on financial interests rather than on normative beliefs. During this period local authorities and the EU often had policy objectives which were at odds with one another, while in addition both local authorities and the EU polity displayed significant internal inconsistencies, particularly between their objectives for sustainable development, on the one hand, and for economic development and greater personal mobility, on the other (see Chapter 6 for comments related to the EU). Furthermore, financial advocacy coalitions have also suffered from internal weakness due to the fact that the private companies traditionally involved in the PFI bids for transport projects tended to be from the construction industry, historically closely tied both politically and philosophically to the road lobby.

The reliance on EU and private finance thus had a considerable effect on the kind of programmes which could be developed to ameliorate local transport problems during this period. The propensity of the European Regional Development Fund (ERDF) and PFI to favour medium-sized flagship projects posed problems for local authorities, operating with limited discretionary funds, which attempted to use this money to pressure central government to provide the balance of resources. The cost and bureaucracy involved in placing an ERDF bid or in securing a private consortium of interests led to the pursuit of high cost, 'heroic' projects. Although such projects may promote a sense of European or regional identity, they come at a high cost and may not ameliorate the problem which they were designed to solve.

Historically, the focus on capital projects has tended to favour the provision of road infrastructure but with the argument for road-based solutions to congestion problems now seriously compromised, particularly in urban areas, private interests and the EU are promoting alternative projects which are unlikely to serve the best interests of either the local authority or its citizens. In particular, the only projects which consistently attracted EU funding during the Major period were LRT projects which are high cost, inflexible and often unsuitable for local needs. The methods by which the EU assesses local government transport schemes for ERDF monies mitigated against the small scale, low cost solutions most in line with the sustainability aims of Agenda 21, such as the provision of cycle and pedestrian walkways or technological projects designed to make the bus more consumer friendly.

Finally, investment in replenishable resources was also discouraged by the use of PFI/ERDF monies. ERDF funding, in particular, was not available for replenishable capital such as buses. With local authorities confronted with a deregulated and predominantly private bus network, both they and private interests (excepting the operators themselves) were reluctant to form partnerships for investment in bus priority measures or improved vehicle fleets, further reinforcing the inefficient use of both local and EU resources. So, although the EU does not have any mandate for direct control over urban transport investment, its financial influence still had a strong effect 'on the ground' at a local level: an effect which in many cases undermined rather than facilitated the aims of Local Agenda 21.

Overall, then, although local authorities had some success in building financial advocacy coalitions during the Major period, they remained significantly short of resources in most cases. In general, the successes which local authorities achieved came when they built coalitions surrounding small scale projects, which they were able to submit through the TPP bidding process. Large scale projects, which local authorities, private capital interests and the EU all favour, had much less success in securing central government support, being 'crowded out' by government austerity measures and the domination of the transport budget by the road programme. Thus the capacity for local authorities to generate alternatives to the car were constrained. The next section of this chapter focuses on the capacity of local authorities to develop measures which complement these so-called 'carrots', investigating the effect which the granting of enabling legislation by the Major government had on the development of 'sticks' by local authorities designed to force changes to the behaviour of road transport users.

Restricting Traffic: Local Government and Enabling Legislation in the Major Era

Historically, local government has been able to utilise a number of initiatives to regulate and restrict the level of traffic in congested urban areas. They have had the power to regulate the provision of on-street and public car parking; to close roads to traffic at peak times or to restrict access to certain vehicles, such as buses and essential vehicles; to reallocate road space from cars to, for example, bus or cycle use; and to implement traffic calming measures (Cm 3234, para. 14.15).

Of all of these measures, parking controls have historically been the most important traffic management tool for local authorities 'since availability of parking spaces, and the cost of parking to motorists, can have a major influence on the level of traffic entering a town' (Cm 3234, para. 14.16). In the recent past, however, this strategy has proven insufficient to maintain control over traffic volumes, as Professor May argued in evidence to the Transport Select Committee:

> The real difficulty with parking is, if one looks at a typical city centre, about a third of the traffic that comes in goes straight through and is not affected by parking controls at all, and another third, possibly more, parks in private parking, so anything you do to increase the costs of public parking hits no more than a third of the traffic. It is very easy indeed for the other elements, the through traffic and the private parking to increase to fill up the road space. (HC 104-II, p. 86, para. 227)

The difficulties which local authorities have experienced in stabilising traffic growth have provided an argument for additional local instruments, principally through proposals for urban road or congestion charging.[6] The case for the implementation of urban road pricing has been further strengthened as policy makers have come to be more concerned with measuring the externalities of road transport:

> The theoretical case for what has come to be termed 'road pricing' derives from the rationale that the users of roads, like the users of any other valuable resource, should pay all the costs arising from their use. Only then will the decisions on whether, when, where and how to travel be made correctly and only then will the maximum productivity of the road system, and indeed the transport system more generally, be obtained. (Chartered Institute of Transport (CIT), 1990, para. 3.1, cited in HC 104-I, para. 45)

A number of reports published during the Major era strengthened the rationale for road pricing by emphasising four principal deficiencies with the present taxation system which it would overcome (see Newbury, 1995 and for a useful overview see HC 104-I). First, road pricing would ensure that the psychological differentials in the pricing of transport alternatives diminished (Freund and Martin, 1993, p. 130). Under the existing system, 'once somebody acquires a car .... it gets cheaper every mile for every extra mile the car is used' (Dr. Adams, UCL, in evidence to HC 104-I, para. 45). Road pricing would ensure that all transport consumers pay a cost for each journey which is more closely related to its true marginal cost. In particular, marginal cost pricing would overcome problems with the existing taxation system which, 'whilst it ensures that road users as a whole make a net contribution to public expenditure, is very poor at promoting the efficiency of the national transport system' (CIT, 1990, cited in HC 104-I, para. 45).

Secondly, road pricing would ensure that road users were more aware of the environmental and social costs of the transport decisions that they take. In particular, it would encourage car users to pay the costs of the externalities of private motoring (Newbury, 1995, pp. 19-21).

Thirdly, road pricing was said to be less draconian than other forms of traffic restraint, thus remaining compatible with the market orientation of transport policy emphasised by successive post-war governments, and by the Thatcher and Major governments in particular. According to the Chartered Institute of Transport, 'road pricing is entirely in line with the move towards greater economic freedom: it will establish a market mechanism where hitherto one has been lacking' (1990, cited in HC 104-I, para. 47). By applying variable charging based on demand for road space, road pricing would have two effects: it would influence and manage demand, thereby spreading the peak period; and would inform, through the price mechanism, the road user of the cost of congestion:

> The point about road pricing is that it would give the use of roads to those who most value that use. Those who value time savings on a particular trip highly are given a means to pay for a quicker journey. This is how the road space comes to be used more efficiently. (City Research Project, 1993, p. 71, cited in HC 104-I, para. 47)

Fourthly, a new realism developed in urban areas. In the first place, even the pro-roads groups began to acknowledge that it was not possible to provide for the predicted growth in traffic levels (Newbury, 1995. See also interview information, Paul Everitt, BRF and Sydney Balgarnie, RHA, both 21st August 1996):

I was at a public meeting not so long ago and somebody from the BRF was there and he was talking about [the] need [for] better public transport in London. He had all the old ladies in tears in the front row. [He was saying,] 'We need buses with conductors and all the rest of it'. Now, I thought bastard, he's stolen my lines! I wanted all the old ladies nodding at me! ... The significance is that, certainly in urban areas, the British Roads Federation, and with them the AA and the RAC, now realise they can't go on forever building roads. They are not quite saying what we are saying in urban areas because I think if they had a choice they would build roads ... All of us are calling for more investment in transport in urban areas and there's not that big a difference between us because, I think, they realise realistically road building's off the agenda. (Interview, John Stewart, ALARM UK, 23rd November 1995)

The second aspect of this new realism focused on the impact of road pricing. A number of opinion makers began to acknowledge that road pricing is the only measure which will sufficiently reduce traffic:

There was one major reason why I was interested in road pricing which was that that actually did seem, on all the evidence, to be the one factor which really could do something about road use in a significant fashion. I think the public has to have more than simply the promise of an attractive, modern and accessible public transport system. It seems to me that the exigencies of transport change demand that sort of approach. (Interview, Keith Hill MP, member of the Transport Select Committee, 26th February 1996)

In response to such developments the Major government offered a guarded welcome to proposals for road pricing initiatives. In its Green Paper, *Transport – The Way Forward*, it stated that it would create the necessary legislation for practical experiments by local authorities:

The Government believes that most of the issues that remain outstanding [such as equity and the effectiveness of road pricing as a tool for demand management] would be best considered in the context of designing an actual charging system, rather than through further research in the abstract. The Government therefore proposes to discuss with the Local Authority Associations the case for taking the necessary legislative powers to enable interested local authorities to implement experimental schemes. (Cm 3234, para. 14.70)[7]

Thus, following the transport debate the Major government was willing to support experimentation with road pricing by local authorities. However, as I now argue, the commitment of the Major government to road pricing was severely limited even during this proposed period of experimentation: its reluctance to allow local authorities to retain the revenues from road pricing removed their incentive to attempt the experiment.

Putting this into Perspective: No Move on Revenue Hypothecation

> Without perceived improvements in public transport there is unlikely to be any clear public endorsement of further traffic restraint ... The public discussion that has taken place so far suggests that it will be almost impossible to develop any proposal that does not entail parallel improvements in public transport and a re-investment of any revenues from any charging system. Indeed, any form of further control will need to be accompanied by these improvements. (Memorandum from Lothian Regional Council, Transportation Department, to HCTSC, cited in HC 104-II, pp. 74-75, paras 12 and 17)

The preceding analysis has revealed two main trends in the Major period. First, that local government was constrained in its objective of developing transport alternatives by stringent financial limitations. Second, that acknowledgement grew that some form of road pricing would prove the most effective mechanism for changing the behaviour of road transport users.

In the final section of this chapter I argue that for local authorities in the Major era to overcome 'the unacceptable face of road pricing' they had to be permitted to retain the revenues raised through any pricing system through the local hypothecation of revenues. This would have enabled road pricing to develop 'as part of an integrated, local transport package' in which 'revenues [could] ... be used locally, initially for public transport investment' (Memorandum from Cambridge County Council to HCTSC, in HC 104-II, p. 70, para. 3.3).

Such local revenue hypothecation would have overcome the funding problems which local authorities experienced under the funding regime which existed in the Major era. For example, Edinburgh had proposals to combine urban road pricing with a comprehensive LRT network comprising two lines, one east-west and one north-south costing approximately £200m-£250m per line. They foresaw few problems in gaining the necessary private finance for these schemes but predicted considerable problems in securing the requisite public sector finance:

Only through the medium of congestion charging as part of a wider package were traffic levels forecast to be reduced. We have also the problem that the level of public transport investment to support a package of this nature appears to be beyond the funding capacity of the private sector and conventional sources of finance from the public sector available within Scotland which is the third reason for being interested in some form of congestion charging. (HC 104-II, p. 87, para. 232)

The potential revenues raised from road pricing 'without seeking punitive charge levels' would have been substantial. In Edinburgh a net surplus of between £25m and £50m was predicted annually, with projections of £1.5bn expected for central London (HC 104-II, p. 74, para. 11). In his memorandum to the Transport Select Committee Professor May suggested that in Edinburgh alone:

It would be possible to use congestion charging revenue to finance two new light rail lines and a road scheme, together with a 10 per cent fares reduction, at no net financial cost to the local authority. The reduction in car traffic would permit closure of a quarter of the city centre's road capacity, to achieve environmental improvements. Despite this, speeds would still rise by 20 per cent in the centre and 6 per cent elsewhere, thus improving conditions for road users generally. (HC 104 II, p. 81, para. 30)

Such a promise of local financial autonomy and of the potential for widespread urban redevelopment from locally raised revenues has encouraged pressure from local authorities to seek 'an extension of local authority powers to implement restraint policies' (AMA, 1995, cited in Cm 3234, para. 14.67) despite the political ramifications which led Cambridgeshire County Council to christen it a 'poll tax on wheels' (HC 104-II, p. 71, para. 5).

However, local authorities' calls for local revenue hypothecation had only a limited impact on central government during the Major period, with the Treasury reluctant to endorse the hypothecation of revenues from transport taxes. In his evidence to the HCTSC in February 1995, the then Secretary of State for Transport emphasised that the government 'would see the money raised from road pricing as a levy which would be absorbed by the Treasury' (HC 104-I, para. 100). Under the Secretary of State's proposals, local authorities would not be able to treat revenues from road pricing as a charge for a service rendered, and so they would be unable to earmark those revenues for transport related expenditure. However, this did not stop the Major government from making policy pronouncements 'that

[they] would allow some or all of that money to revert to the area which raised it' (Secretary of State for Transport in HC 104-I, para. 100).

As has already been argued, the hypothecation of revenues is essential as the 'carrot' to encourage local authorities to implement unpopular restrictive measures in their areas. The HCTSC argued in its report on urban road pricing:

> The Government's view, we believe, removes the main incentive for local authorities to introduce road pricing, which is somewhat curious in view of the fact that the Government currently encourages local authorities through the grant system to assemble transport 'packages' of the sort that road pricing could allow to a much greater extent. (HC 104-I, para. 101)

Why then was the Major government reluctant to permit the hypothecation of urban road pricing revenues? The principal explanation is that central government was reluctant to provide local authorities with extensive revenue raising powers and increased interdependency in central-local relations. This is illustrated by the inconsistencies which can be seen between the Major government's views on hypothecated urban road pricing and motorway tolling. In a comparable proposal to introduce motorway tolling, central government emphasised that the proceeds from such tolls would be classed as a charge, hypothecated and reinvested in the motorway network (HC 376-II, paras 722-26). The HCTSC was 'puzzled' by this apparent inconsistency of central government thinking, arguing that there was 'no difference in principle between a motorist paying electronically to use an urban road and paying electronically to use a stretch of motorway'. Consequently, it recommended that Government 'reconsider its view that the proceeds of road pricing would be treated as a levy rather than a charge' (HC 104-I, para. 101).

The explanation for the inconsistencies between these two cases is clear. Motorways remain under the jurisdiction of national government and are a key element of the 'roads for prosperity' orthodoxy which has historically governed national transport policy. Under a nationally administered charging regime motorways could be marketed as a premium service available to those willing to pay, with revenues protected from the Treasury in periods of economic austerity. A continued revenue stream for the maintenance and expansion of the motorway network would thus be secured.

In contrast, urban road pricing cannot be used in this way: the revenues from road pricing cannot be directly invested in roads because of both the physical restrictions within urban environments preventing network expansion and the environmental costs which more roads, and hence more traffic, would inevitably bring. Hypothecation of urban road pricing revenues would inevitably lead to the provision of more public transport and to improvements to the cycling and walking network. Investment in a local modern transport network will be electorally popular locally, strengthening the autonomy of local government in direct opposition to the policy of both Thatcher and Major governments.

Despite the growing consensus over the role that road pricing ought to play in resolving urban transport problems, a number of significant questions (in addition to the issue of revenue hypothecation) remained unanswered in the Major era. These concerned, in particular, the issues of equity and traffic displacement.

Concerns over the equity of road pricing reflect both the predict and provide orthodoxy and the liberal state orthodoxy which have historically governed UK transport policy. Together these orthodoxies are founded on the view that growth in the volume and scope of car ownership is indicative of growing economic prosperity and the development of greater social equality and liberty. Thus, a policy such as road pricing designed to price vehicles off the road will restrain the freedom and liberty of the least well off. This is both unequitable and regressive:

> Everyone seemed to be perfectly happy with the motor car when white, middle-class men, in full-time occupations had one between the wars. As soon as the elderly, women, young people and ethnic minorities have cars, they start introducing systems to price people off the roads so that only white, middle-class men, in full-time occupations can drive around. That's not my idea of a sensible policy. (Interview, Peter Bottomley MP, Member of the Transport Select Committee, 26th February 1996)

The AA voiced similar concerns in its submission to the HCTSC. Both affluent motorists and commercial road users (who would increase prices to offset it) would pay the charge. 'But many lower and middle income car-owning households, whose motoring costs are usually their third largest expenditure after housing and food, will not be able to pay. Road pricing is specifically targeted at this vulnerable group' (AA memorandum to the HCTSC, cited in HC 104-II, p. 95).

Supporters of road pricing, particularly on the left, are sympathetic to these concerns. However, for them, liberty can be improved by the package of measures accompanying road pricing. Such a package can improve the liberty of society as a whole by offering greater access to a variety of transport modes to those previously without transport:[8]

That concern about road pricing being, as it were, a regressive form of taxation is one which is certainly widely perceived within the Labour party ... That it will actually become a form of perk for the longer distance commuter and actually it will be all of those less privileged elements in our society: women, ethnic minorities, the less well-off, who will in fact bear the brunt of this policy. So, I think there is a real challenge and a real anxiety along these lines. The countervailing argument, of course, is that, actually, the corollary of road pricing (which I think that everybody accepts as being integral to the argument) is that you have a better and more efficient public transport system, which will actually benefit those without access to a car on a much more significant scale than the damage done to those less privileged coming into car ownership. (Interview, Keith Hill MP, 26th February 1996)

Discussion of road pricing proposals has also left another crucial question unanswered: that of traffic displacement. In Chapter 4, which focused on the role of problems on the transport agenda, I discussed the problems caused by a market-led planning policy, in which three discernible waves of out-of-town development have undermined the viability of many town centres. Road pricing proposals also entail serious problems which develop from market-led policy.

The Major government's transport Green Paper (Cm 3234) stated that the government was 'prepared to consider' enabling local authorities to implement congestion charging 'on an experimental basis' (para. 14.20) relying on voluntary co-operation between neighbouring authorities:

Co-ordination is particularly important in urban areas, where several local authorities may cover a relatively small, densely populated area. Individual authorities may be wary of applying any restraint measures for fear of the competing attractions of nearby centres, however much they promote complementary policies. (para. 14.82)

In practical terms, however, the local authorities were much less positive about the effectiveness of voluntary co-operation, fearing widespread traffic displacement. This would displace traffic into neighbouring areas, increasing congestion problems there, to which neighbouring authorities would understandably object (HC 104-II, p. 135, para. 383). Further, road pricing would detrimentally affect trade in the short term, and regional investment and development in the longer term:

Were road pricing, as you are suggesting, to be put in for the City, you are actually imposing a toll, a cordon around that area. All movement to some degree is related to economic activity. It is actually putting a cost on business, because the alternative is actually not to do business in that area. (J. Weiss, Assistant City Engineer, Corporation of the City of London, evidence to the HCTSC, HC 104-II, p. 134, para. 377)

Such questions concerning equity and ethics, traffic displacement, the electoral implications of road pricing, and most importantly, the jurisdiction over the revenues from road pricing, raised considerable difficulties in building an elite-led consensus for action, with local authorities confronted with political pressure to act but refused the tools which would enable them to do so. In reality, however, the appearance of local authority inertia had little to do with concerns of equity or traffic displacement, instead being driven by conflict between the centre and locality. While the centre, rhetorically at least, recognised the legitimacy of a local mandate for action, in practical terms it failed to do so, as this study of financial relationships between central and local government in the transport sphere has shown.

Conclusion

This chapter has explored the influence of local government on transport agenda setting in the Major era, focusing on its capacity to influence the national transport agenda. I have suggested that important insights can be drawn from work on central-local relations theory, which offers two key accounts of the relationship between central and local government: the agency model (in which local government is seen as heavily constrained by central government) and the power-dependency model (in which local government and central government operate with significant inter-dependence). According to the literature, these models offer 'ideal types' which operate at either ends of a central-local relations continuum. However, this study of central-local relations in the transport field during the Major era has revealed that the actions of local government demonstrate trends from both of these models, in spite of the fact that they are commonly seen as contradictory.

During the Major era the rise of policy problems such as congestion and the general deterioration of the urban environment increased the potential for local government action, as the Major government acknowledged that a number of local problems required local solutions. I have argued that as a result of this, local authorities gained some increased financial autonomy, enabling them to produce new policy alternatives (i.e. to develop the 'carrots').

In particular, the development of the 'package approach' enabled local authorities to develop multi-modal transport strategies. This initiative has been seen by both local government and the anti-roads groups as a genuine policy innovation, although the lack of resources undermining its implementation has been criticised.

The package approach encouraged the development of small projects, but such projects have a number of associated problems. First, the cost of bidding for programmes in such partnerships is often prohibitive, creating strong incentives for both the private sector and local authorities to push for large scale projects instead. Second, local authorities tended to push for prestigious, high-profile projects, often encouraged by the propensity of the European Union to favour such projects. Thus, for a combination of financial and political reasons local authorities have been relatively slow to shift the focus away from large scale, prestigious projects towards small scale projects.

In addition, local authorities gained further autonomy through their capacity to develop financial advocacy coalitions through alliances with private and European interests. The development of such coalitions was actively encouraged by the Major government as it fitted into their broader objectives for the development of public-private partnerships as prescribed in the PFI.

This chapter has explored this ability to develop financial advocacy coalitions through a focus on the case of 'Midland Metro'. In this case I have argued that the WMPTA was particularly successful in building an alliance of EU, private and local authority money which exerted effective pressure on central government for 'top-up' funding. However, this case has also illustrated that 'luck' and timing are very important to the successful realisation of the objectives of a financial advocacy coalition. The project happened to be 'next in the queue': if that had not been the case, it is unlikely that it would have been successful. Thus the capacity of local authorities to build financial advocacy coalitions for large projects is still subject to macro-economic and political constraints imposed by central government.

The second principal aim of this chapter has been to evaluate the capacity of local authorities to develop strategies to change the behaviour of transport consumers (i.e. to implement the 'sticks'). Historically, local authorities have had a variety of tools at their disposal designed to change behaviour: the capacity to restrict car parking, to develop pedestrianisation schemes, or to create bus lanes, for example. However, during the Major era the growth of urban transport problems created a perception among policy makers that such powers were insufficient, resulting in the view that some form of urban road pricing was key to the successful management of transport levels. This chapter outlines the theoretical case for road pricing, arguing that, on the surface, it would seem to have been a particularly desirable policy strategy for the Major government, fitting as it does the market-orientated focus of government policy emphasised by successive Conservative administrations.

However, I have shown that the Major government in fact refused to enable local authorities to develop urban road pricing schemes accompanied by revenue hypothecation. As I have argued, it is essential for local authorities to have revenue hypothecation from road pricing if they are to both provide public transport alternatives and 'sell' the idea to their local electorate. Without the hypothecation of local road pricing revenues, the introduction of charging for road space would, as far as the local authorities are concerned, be the electoral equivalent of the 'poll tax on wheels'. However, the Major government rejected the principle of hypothecated urban road pricing, thus effectively undermining the road pricing concept itself.

I have argued that this was not due to political pressure from the Treasury, but instead because of a general desire by central government to manage the policy agenda. This is demonstrated by the inconsistency in government thinking with regard to the development of motorway tolling (in which the Major government supported the view that the revenues from such a toll would be seen as a charge to be re-invested in motorways) and the development of urban road pricing (in which this principle was rejected).

The explanation for this apparent inconsistency in central government reflects both a differing conception of the right of access to motorways and urban roads and a desire for central government to retain pre-eminence within the operation of central-local relations. Motorways are seen as a premium service, so the government can justify charging for their use. In addition, the physical space still exists to build new motorways with the revenues such a charge would raise. In contrast, a general perception remains of a right of access to urban roads which the government was reluctant to question. This is unsurprising given the historical emphasis of the transport orthodoxy which this book has shown to have dominated government thinking in the post-war period, in which road use and mobility *should* be encouraged due to a desire to enhance mobility and freedom.

Furthermore, the physical space for more roads is not available in many urban areas. Thus, any revenues raised from urban road pricing would, in practical terms, be spent either on local public transport initiatives or on other civic projects locally. In the long term the impact of this would be to significantly increase the autonomy of local authorities; a shift which central government has opposed in principle throughout the Thatcher and Major years. Hence I argue that the rejection of hypothecated urban road pricing by the Major government was entirely political.

Overall, the study of central-local relations in the transport case during this period has revealed two contradictory trends. On the one hand, local autonomy increased as local government gained a greater capacity to develop innovative strategies as a result of the introduction of the package approach and the construction of financial advocacy coalitions. On the other hand, local autonomy was reduced in two ways: by the worsening of the local transport situation due to increasing congestion and deteriorating environmental conditions, and as a result of the reluctance of central government to allow local authorities to develop charging regimes which enable them to ameliorate these problems.

Notes

1   This chapter concentrates on central-local relations under Major, covering the capacity of local government to provide transport alternatives and change behaviour in their areas. For comments on the management of local air pollution see Chapter 4. For comments on the Blair era see Chapter 9 (Postscript).
2   I discuss this concept in detail later.
3   The DTp criteria for eligibility for S. 56 funding were that the submission should be for a major capital project which contributes to urban regeneration (such as LRT); that the project should be innovative, or that it should have the backing of a number of local authorities (DTP, 1989b, para. 3).
4   Unfortunately no comparable figures for the scale of credit approvals are available for the period since 1994/95. This is due to the development of the package approach to transport funding which emphasised multi-modal applications from local authorities. However, in practice this led to similar proportions of the total sum being allocated to roads and public transport in the latter years of the Major administration (personal communication with DTp, 2nd July 1996).
5   This approach is formally termed 'Transport Policies and Programmes' (TPP).
6   Although differences do exist between the nature of charging regimes for road space – for reasons of clarity I will adopt a generic term 'road pricing' to refer to any form of charging regime which is developed to impose costs on the use of road space.
7   This process resulted in enabling legislation being passed, but no local authorities were willing to act on it due to the failure of central government to support accompanying road pricing with revenue hypothecation.

8   I explore the political conflict over road pricing in the Blair era in Chapter 9 (Postscript).

8 Conclusion

> Government does not come to conclusions. It stumbles into paradoxical situations that force it to move in one way or another. There are social forces that you can identify, but what comes out of them is just accident. (Interview information, cited in Kingdon, 1995, p. 189)

> Continual defeat gives rise not only to the conscious deferral of action but also to a sense of defeat, or a sense of powerlessness, that may affect the consciousness of potential challenges about grievances, strategies, or possibilities for change. Participation denied over time may lead to acceptance of the role of non-participation, as well as a failure to develop the political resources – skills, organisation, consciousness – of political action. (Gaventa, 1980, p. 255)

As the comments of the two analysts cited above illustrate, there is little consensus on the dynamics of political change. Reflecting this diversity of opinion, there is significant disagreement over the impact of the increased political salience of the transport issue in the Major era. Commentators are divided as to the extent to which new forms of social protest and increasing concern with the environmental impact of transport have created instability in the transport agenda.

How are we to account for the increasing political salience of the transport issue in the Major era? This question has, thus far, remained largely unanswered in the politics literature. This study has aimed to remedy this situation by giving an account of the development of UK transport policy in this period. In addition, a key aim of this study has been to place the transport case within the broader literature on the Major period and examine the extent to which it marked a continuation of policy from the Thatcher era. On the surface, this case appears to mark a significant break with the Thatcher government. Major's administration presided over the reversal of the 'roads for prosperity' orthodoxy, a considerable reduction of the scale of the road programme and significant conflict over the future development of transport policy.

In the introduction to this study I posed three key research questions which were designed to enable an evaluation of different models of agenda setting. These were to examine the extent to which a policy network approach proves useful; to consider which if any model of agenda setting provides the most plausible account of political developments; and to examine the applicability of the literature on non-agenda setting in this case. What conclusions can we draw on the basis of the study in this book?

The Research Questions Re-Examined

Is the Network Approach a Useful One?

A constant theme throughout this analysis has been the argument that while policy networks provide a useful device for labelling actors, the approach is too restricted to account for the increased political salience of the transport issue under Major. Dowding argues that the network approach is most useful for 'cataloguing the policy world into different types of network' and that the 'approach will not, alone, take us much further' (1995, p. 136). This study shares Dowding's view (Chapter 2).

Policy networks provide a particularly useful metaphor by which groups in the transport area can be classified as insiders or outsiders. Actors can be characterised in terms of their relationship to a policy making core, which helps to account for the different tactics which they use. Insider groups, for example, have a privileged position in the policy making process which enables them to have a 'significant influence' on consultation, and ultimately, policy formulation (Maloney, Jordan and McLaughlin, 1994, p. 19). Outsider groups, in contrast, have goals which cannot be readily accommodated by decision makers. Consequently, they remain outside the consultation process and their influence on policy making will be conditional on their ability to pressure decision makers through 'publicly active' campaigning (Maloney, Jordan and McLaughlin, 1994, p. 32). This distinction between insider and outsider groups has proven particularly valuable in the transport case when identifying the contrasting tactics used by the road lobby and the anti-roads groups in their attempts to influence the decision making process (Chapter 5).

The network metaphor is also extremely useful in characterising the nature of the policy process. Marsh and Rhodes have developed the concept of a policy network continuum in which networks are categorised based on size and type of membership; level of integration; and access to resources.

Thus networks which are dominated by a limited membership of professional or economic interests, with frequent, high quality interaction and centralised control over decision making are located at the policy community end of the network continuum, while networks with a large number of participants, lack of consensus on outcomes and diffuse control over decision making are located at the issue network end (Marsh and Rhodes, 1992a, p. 251). Marsh and Rhodes' network continuum has also proved particularly useful when describing the impact of the conflict over transport policy on the cohesion of the core, pro-roads, policy community, and the extent to which this conflict has altered the character of the roads policy community.

However, the problem with the network approach is that it is too narrow to provide an explanation for the increased political salience of transport policy in the Major era, tending as it does to assume that changes to the agenda are explained by changes in the balance of power between actors inside and outside the network and reflect conflict between them. However, in this case, as the preceding chapters have shown, change has been driven by a combination of external events, the increasing conceptualisation of transport as a policy problem (both of which insider and outsider groups had little control over) *and* growing conflict between insider and outsider groups. Thus, the increased political salience of transport policy in the Major era has been caused by a wide variety of factors, many of which cannot be accounted for by a network focus.

Which Model of Agenda Setting is the Most Useful?

External (Systemic) Models of Policy Change

This book argues that the network approach is also too narrow in that it fails to account for the importance of the external environment on network stability. In the Major era the balance of power within policy networks was affected by both dynamic and stable systems events. This study supports Sabatier and Jenkins-Smith's view that dynamic systems events are extremely important in changing the balance of power between erstwhile insiders and outsiders (1993b, pp. 221-22). For example, the increasing international co-ordination of environmental policy in response to the problem of global warming was important in promoting the objectives of the anti-roads groups and undermining the pro-roads groups. Such changes also increased the impact of other policy sectors on the core policy community: for example, the Department of the Environment became progressively influential, resulting in a significant reduction to the operational autonomy of the pro-roads groups and increased support for the initiatives of the opponents of the road programme.[1]

There is also a strong link between network stability and the existence of external conditions which are supportive of the insider groups. Throughout the post-war period both Conservative and Labour governments have supported a policy orthodoxy in which improvements to the road network were seen as a crucial precondition to continuing economic development. In such a political climate the pro-roads groups' interests have been dominant regardless of their level of organisation or the sophistication of their lobbying. The status of the anti-roads groups as policy outsiders has also been conditioned by their relationship to the external environment. Historically, these groups have urged a model of economic development which has been at odds with central government; consequently they have been marginalised regardless of the sophistication of their lobbying or the coherence of their opposition (Chapter 3).

Stable aspects of the external environment have thus been extremely important in shaping the historical distinction between insider and outsider groups in the transport case. Consequently, the status of these groups, as Dowding has argued (1991, pp. 152-57), is based on 'systematic luck' rather than being a reflection of the exercise of political power (Chapter 5). A focus on networks alone is, therefore, unable to explain either the historical stability of the core policy community or the apparent failure of the outsider groups to alter the balance of power with that community.

Actor Centred Models of Agenda Setting

A constant theme throughout this analysis has been that actor centred models are also too restrictive to account for the increasing political salience of the transport issue in the Major era. Although changes to the relationship between insider and outsider groups were significant this can only provide a partial explanation for changes to the agenda setting process in this case.

However, actor centred models have proved useful in explaining some elements of the success of the anti-roads groups. The direct action campaigns at Twyford Down and Newbury, for example, were instrumental in opening the transport problem to a completely new arena – the media – through which the public perception of transport was transformed from that of a dull, technical and routine issue to a dynamic and emotive one. The increasing interest of the media was very important in opening up more effective communication for the anti-groups, enabling them to raise the profile of transport as a policy 'problem', and thus further eroding its policy image (Chapter 5). But in evaluating the impact of the anti-roads groups on the political handling of the transport issue it is important not to over-exaggerate their importance. While it is true that the strategies of these groups gained significant media attention, and generated considerable embarrassment – not to mention financial cost – for government policy makers, they were only peripherally responsible for the increasing political salience of the transport issue.

The apparent impact of these groups was highly conditional on a number of external developments, outside their control, from which they were able to benefit. Firstly, transport increasingly came to be seen as a policy problem (Chapter 4). Secondly, their impact was conditional on electoral politics (see Kingdon, 1995, Chapter 7 for a discussion of the impact of changes in the politics stream). Major's small majority resulted in a number of sitting Conservative MPs, particularly in the South East of England, opposing road proposals within their constituencies in order to strengthen their electoral fortunes (Chapter 5). Thirdly, changes to the focus of macro-economic policy based on reduced state spending left infrastructure projects particularly vulnerable to cuts in periods of economic austerity (Chapter 6). Finally, the impact of the roads protests was conditional on what may be termed 'regional political culture'. The 'success' of the protests was largely restricted to the South East of England, with a considerable number of road schemes in the Midlands and North proceeding without opposition. There are two reasons for this. Attitudes of the local populace to proposed road schemes shows considerable regional variation, with the South East being more concerned with the environmental implications of new road schemes than either the Midlands or the North. In addition, these latter areas are still strongly influenced by the historical importance of the motor industry to the regional economy. Local (typically Labour) centres of power remain convinced of the link between well developed transport infrastructure and economic growth in the geographical periphery (Chapter 5).

The impact of the activity of the anti-roads groups on the coherence of the core, pro-roads, policy community was also limited. The advocacy coalition framework shows that coalitions of actors can develop based on deep (normative) core beliefs, near (policy) core beliefs or secondary beliefs. Advocacy coalitions themselves develop and maintain their coherence based on the deep core beliefs of actors. According to Sabatier, 'an actor (or coalition) will give up secondary aspects of a belief system before acknowledging weakness in the policy core' (1993, p. 33). This has proved to be true in the transport case, with the result that the deep divisions between pro- and anti-roads groups, however 'moderate', still remain intact.

In the first place, the construction interests have pragmatically reoriented their priorities towards road maintenance and 'environmental improvements' to the existing road network, in a strategy which enables them to continue to utilise their traditional expertise and to benefit from considerable government spending (i.e. this change is to the secondary aspects of their beliefs only). Secondly, the new perception of transport as a policy problem by the user groups is only superficially linked to the similar views of the anti-roads groups. According to the user groups, the transport problem is primarily a problem of congestion. Although, like the anti-roads groups, the user groups now acknowledge that the idea of 'providing' for predicted traffic growth by an expanded roads programme is unsustainable, they use congestion as an argument for a reduction on the load on the network (through, for example, road pricing) only in order to increase mobility, and thus continue the essence of the 'roads for prosperity' orthodoxy (i.e. their deep core beliefs remain intact).

In contrast, the anti-roads groups view the end of the 'predict and provide' model as a mandate for the promotion of an alternative model of economic development which focuses on local sustainability, regionalised production and low mobility (i.e. their deep core beliefs). Thus, although the transport 'problem' is characterised in a similar way by both the road users and anti-roads groups the resulting implications for policy are very different, with the anti-groups arguing for policy outcomes which conflict with the operation of the capitalist system.

Overall, therefore the increasing political salience of the transport issue is only superficially explained by a focus on actor centred accounts of agenda setting. While such accounts are useful in explaining the conflict over the policy image of the car which has been conducted through the media, they overstate both the 'fragmentation' of the road lobby and the extent to which the rationale of policy changed as a result of the activities of the outsider groups in this period.

Problem Centred Models of Agenda Setting

Problem centred models provide a particularly important aspect of any explanation of the increase in political salience of the transport issue in the Major era. As Kingdon argues (1995), problems tend to develop as a result of events which are independent of the actions of either insider or outsider groups. This has proven to be true in the transport case. According to this research, problems have developed due to systemic developments (such as the internationalisation of environmental policy following the Rio Earth Summit) or the actions of what I have termed 'unwitting policy entrepreneurs' (such as central government, through the publication of its *National Road Traffic Forecasts* which 'unwittingly' politicised the 'predict and provide model') (Chapter 4). However, although problems initially develop independently, intensive conflict subsequently develops between the pro- and anti-roads groups over their implications, while central government once more aims to manage the implications of these transport problems and thus insulate the pro-roads groups against widespread policy change.

Congestion   The SACTRA report was extremely important in clarifying a general understanding that the capacity of government to cater for rising traffic levels by continuously building more roads was limited. Until this point an expanded roads programme, *Roads for Prosperity*, had been justified in response to the government's 1989 *National Road Traffic Forecasts*, with the opponents of the roads programme having very little success in arguing that this expanded programme would fail to cater for the projected traffic increases (Chapter 4). The SACTRA report served to undermine the *Roads for Prosperity* orthodoxy.

The impact of the SACTRA report was in fact based on a misperception of its contents. SACTRA was widely perceived as arguing that extensions to the road programme generate additional traffic, when actually it argued that while the impact of induced traffic would be marginal in most cases, DTp modelling ought to incorporate this impact into their calculations of the costs and benefits of road schemes.

In spite of this, the effect of the SACTRA report was to irreconcilably damage the predict and provide orthodoxy (and hence the rationale of the road programme itself), and to instigate conflict over what 'ought' to replace it, with the road user groups arguing for restrictions on access to the network and provisions of alternatives ('the restrict and provide' model) and the anti-roads groups demanding a model based on sustainable development and reduced levels of mobility (Chapter 4).

Environmental Problems   In the Major era transport increasingly came to be seen as a problem in environmental terms. In the past twenty years the nature, and magnitude, of the problems associated with transport have changed significantly. The environmental problems associated with transport have 'moved from concern with local, and especially urban, environmental effects such as noise, vibration and emission of pollutants such as lead and black smoke, to the contribution that transport makes to transboundary environmental problems, such as acid rain, and to global environmental change, and especially its share of carbon dioxide emissions' (Button, 1995, p. 173).

In the period with which the preceding part of this book is concerned the increased political salience of the transport issue came as a response to both the local and trans-national nature of the transport problem. At a local level, concern with the health effects of vehicle emissions became intense and a series of technical measures were invoked to lower the impact of vehicle emissions on local air quality, thus 'solving' the policy problem. In contrast, transboundary problems associated with transport were managed off the agenda by policy makers who rejected the lifestyle changes which their resolution would demand.

Emotive Issues Environmental problems, such as vehicle emissions, have also been very important in creating a new negative policy image for the motor car. Problems such as vehicle emissions came to be blamed for deteriorating public health, with a number of emotive campaigns linking them, for example, to increasing incidences of childhood asthma (Chapter 4).

The vehicle emissions example is particularly instructive in illustrating the cyclical nature of the impact of problems which rely on high levels of public emotion. As Downs' 'issue attention cycle' demonstrates, problems frequently emerge which independently project an issue onto the agenda, generating a public reaction which demands a solution. However, the impact of concerns over the link between rising vehicle emissions and deteriorating public health has not been sustained. On the one hand, the UK government's *National Air Quality Strategy*, together with the development of an EU framework to tighten emissions standards, has actually dealt with the problem: ambient air quality is scheduled to improve considerably as a result (Chapters 4 and 6). These technical solutions reduced public concern with the environmental effects of transport, deflated the policy agenda and enabled the government to manage the policy cycle (Chapter 4). On the other hand, however, the 'resolution' of this problem prevented more significant questions about the lifestyle implications of transport decisions being raised: transport will thus remain a significant source of environmental problems in the future.

Lifestyle Issues   A number of environmental problems associated with transport are simply not amenable to technical solutions, instead requiring fundamental changes to lifestyle. For example, government proposals to tighten regulations of vehicle emissions have no effect on transport's contribution to the problem of global warming. Consequently, although at a local level ambient air quality is improving, at a global level the problems caused by transport remain.

This study argues that the primary reason for this is that the problem of greenhouse gas emissions can only be solved by policies designed to change behaviour. But as a consideration of the failed proposal for an EU carbon-energy tax has illustrated, policies designed to directly interfere with the operation of the market for transport were strongly opposed by the Major government, leaving both the UK government and EU with no significant policy instruments with which to tackle the problems associated with global warming (Chapter 6).

This failure to develop policies to reduce greenhouse gas emissions is paralleled by the failure to develop policies which affect lifestyle in other ways. For example, Chapter 4 argues that land-use planning initiatives such as PPG 13 had only a limited impact on the culture of deregulated land-use planning, which remains inextricably linked to the demands for access and freedom which are central to the orthodoxy of central government.

Overall, we have seen that transport problems which demand widespread changes to lifestyle have been managed from the policy agenda rather than being allowed to challenge the central tenets of the system. De-regulated planning and unrestricted mobility are both closely related to the free-market ideology of the UK state. Consequently, measures which seek to alter the nature of the regulatory framework governing land-use planning are seen as draconian, going against the emphasis of the market driven transport tradition in the UK.

Agenda Management and the Autonomy of Central Government

A number of scholars have reacted to the prevailing networks orthodoxy by arguing that central government and the state can exercise considerable autonomy in their dealings with policy networks. Thus, the priorities of government are not simply a reflection of the demands of interest groups, social classes or general societal pressures; instead it can formulate policy and hold objectives which reflect its own interests (see for example Skocpol, 1985, p. 9 and Nordlinger, 1981, and Dowding, 1991, pp. 124-25). This study shares this view of the relative autonomy of government.

We have seen that central government has tended to play an extremely important role in providing a supportive external environment for the pro-roads groups. The UK government has a strong interest in the outcomes of policy in the transport sector, favouring a policy framework which conforms to the 'Anglo-Saxon' model with its emphasis on commercial considerations (Chapter 6). Under this approach the government is seen to be concerned with maximising transport efficiency in order to facilitate economic development, historically seen by government as synonymous with increased road building (Chapter 3).

In addition, the Major government was able to act with significant autonomy in defending its interests against the increasing opposition of the anti-roads groups. As the transport issue rose in political salience, central government successfully defended its position through a process of managing the policy agenda.

First, central government supported a series of technical solutions to transport problems which mitigated against widespread policy change involving lifestyle (Chapter 4). For example, government support of improvements to catalytic converters to reduce vehicle emissions enabled them to manage aspects of the problem associated with road transport, invoke an issue attention cycle and thus protect the positive policy image associated with motoring. However, these solutions have themselves created a number of problems which are now becoming manifest. In particular, technical solutions to improve vehicle emissions do not reduce the impact of transport on global warming or land-use planning, both problems which can only be solved by broader changes to lifestyle (Chapter 4).

Second, central government managed the political agenda by transferring the responsibility for solving a number of transport problems onto local government. Local authorities were charged with implementing a number of politically unpalatable decisions, such as urban road pricing and residential and town-centre parking restrictions, which restrict motorists in accordance with the government's sustainable mobility aims. Although local authorities had some success in building financial coalitions with EU and private investors in order to exert pressure on central government to develop public transport alternatives, these did not offset the political costs resulting from central government's management of the policy agenda (Chapter 7).

As well as defending its autonomy through agenda management, central government has also benefited from the lack of alternative arenas open to the anti-roads groups (Baumgartner and Jones, 1991). This study rejects Dudley and Richardson's (1995 and 1996a) view that the EU has undermined the autonomy of national government in the UK by providing an alternative arena which domestic opponents of the road programme can infiltrate (Chapter 6). In fact, the opposite has proved true: the EU has served to increase the autonomy of national government in its conflict with the anti-roads groups. For example, the development of EU emissions regulations through the 'Auto-Oil' framework strengthened the autonomy of the UK government, as it supported the market orientation of national policy. Although in a technical sense the rise in EU regulatory policy restricted the autonomy of UK policy makers, the commonality of focus between the UK government and the EU's objectives had the opposite effect in practical terms, with the prioritisation of technical solutions to the transport problem helping to insulate the pro-roads groups from the challenges to lifestyle raised by the opponents of roads. In addition, the EU supported building public-private partnerships for infrastructure funding and emphasised the strategic role of infrastructure links for developing the regions. All of these developments strengthened the autonomy of central government and the road lobby and weakened the influence of the anti-roads groups (Chapter 6).

Although central government was effective in retaining high levels of relative autonomy in the Major era in the face of the increasing political salience of the transport issue, two important trends emerged which suggest that in the long term central government autonomy will undergo relative decline. Firstly, the increasing concern that existing policy was unsustainable led to division between the Department of Transport and Department of Environment over the priority of policy. The effect of this was to weaken the coherence of the 'government interest' and, in consequence, the support which the pro-roads groups derived from central government (Chapter 4).

Secondly, the technical solutions supported by government in order to manage the policy agenda in fact failed to solve a number of the problems associated with transport in the long term. Although ambient air quality has considerably improved (with a consequent reduction in many of the associated health risks), the impact of transport on global warming shows no sign of diminishing. And congestion itself has come to be seen as an even greater policy problem as transport operators have gained knowledge of its regressive effect on economic development. The government's acknowledgement that congestion cannot be contained by providing ever greater levels of infrastructure has only exacerbated the situation. Thus the only available solution available to policy makers is traffic restraint, in order to force road users to use alternatives, which will result in considerable opposition from those effected (Chapter 4).[2]

Overall, although we have seen that central government was instrumental in restricting the impact of the anti-roads groups in the Major era, its continued ability to do so is in relative decline. Presently, central government remains the most important actor in the policy process; it can insulate the core policy community from conflict and manage the policy agenda when its interests are threatened. However, its ability to manage the policy agenda will decline as it proves unable to reconcile popular demands for unrestricted mobility with the problems which such demands create.

Providing a Multi-Faceted Explanation of Political Change: Some Reflections from the Advocacy Coalition Framework

This study has argued that the operation of the agenda setting dynamic in the transport case illustrates aspects of a number of models of agenda setting. I have looked at the role of actors, problems, external events and non-decision making and argued that, in part, they all make a useful contribution to the study of political change in the Major era. However, I have also argued that different models of agenda setting apply in different circumstances and that a model which may provide a useful explanation of situation *A* may provide a less satisfactory explanation of situation *B*. It is the task of these concluding comments to explain this finding.

Transport is a multifaceted issue, which affects mobility, the environment, economic development, and issues of lifestyle and personal freedom; the priorities which central government attaches to transport policy outcomes reflect this diversity. These different aspects of the transport issue are affected by different agenda setting processes, depending on the extent to which they challenge the dominant policy imperatives of the state. For example, in a situation in which the policy imperatives of the state are threatened, the agenda setting process will be highly constrained and proponents of change will find it very difficult, if not impossible, to alter the agenda. In such a case, the models of non-decision making will be an important, often the dominant, explanation of the agenda setting process. Overall, this study argues that the transport agenda setting process operates in, and is constrained by, a policy making environment which is dominated by the policy imperatives of the state.

Sabatier's work on the role of beliefs in the policy process provides an overarching framework through which we can evaluate the extent of agenda dynamism. He argues that all actors have core, near core and secondary beliefs and that they will organise themselves into advocacy coalitions on the basis of their core (deeply held) beliefs. Sabatier's framework argues that 'shared beliefs provide the principal "glue" of politics'; that core beliefs are 'quite resistant to change'; and that the 'line up of allies and opponents [in rival advocacy coalitions] tends to be rather stable over periods of a decade or so' (1993, p. 27). This study shares these views.

Sabatier's framework explains the motives for coalition building and emphasises that a supportive external environment is vital for the stability of the core policy community. However, a weakness of Sabatier's model is that it ignores the impact of state policy imperatives on the operation of the agenda setting process. Therefore, Sabatier's framework needs to be applied to the state as an 'interest' in order to measure its core, near core and secondary policy imperatives, and to explain their effect on the process of agenda setting.

The argument of this study is that the agenda setting process operates against a framework in which the policy imperatives of the state are dominant. These policy imperatives help to explain why policy change is possible in some areas and not in others. I have argued that the conflict over the transport issue is multifaceted, with implications for both core and secondary policy imperatives. However, as Figure 8.1 on the following page illustrates, the agenda has only been open to significant change in areas which have not challenged the core policy imperatives of the state.

Looking at Figure 8.1, issues or proposals which have been compatible with the policy imperatives of the state have encountered limited opposition. In such circumstances actor centred models, problem centred accounts or dynamic (external) models all provide useful explanations of the agenda setting process in the transport case. Rail privatisation and bus deregulation provide two examples of policies which, in spite of the opposition of the many of the affected operators, were raised up the political agenda and subsequently implemented, due to their compatibility with the policy imperatives of the state (Chapter 3).

Figure 8.1   Classification of state policy imperatives and their effect on the process of agenda setting

		RELATIONSHIP OF ADVOCATES OF POLICY CHANGE TO STATE POLICY IMPERATIVES	
		Compatible	**Incompatible**
S T R E N G T H O F O P P O S I T I O N	T O P R O P O S A L	**Weak** — Proponents of change can alter the agenda relatively easily (e.g. proponents of bus deregulation)	Proponents of change will find it very difficult if not impossible to alter the agenda (e.g. widespread restrictions of road transport usage)
		Strong — Proponents of change can alter the agenda but they will encounter considerable difficulty. (e.g. proponents of strengthening emissions controls on motor vehicles)	Proponents of change will find it impossible to alter the agenda (e.g. banning all future motor car production)

In cases in which an issue or proposal affects only 'secondary' policy imperatives of the state, problem centred accounts of agenda setting are very important. Proposals to tighten the regulatory framework for vehicle emissions, for example, have been supported by the UK government even though they have, on the surface, challenged the auto-centric nature of national policy. The development of this framework has protected the pro-roads groups (and the government) from the lifestyle implications of policy; the core policy imperatives of the state have thus been protected although a secondary imperative has been sacrificed.

The agenda setting process is much less fluid in cases in which a near core imperative has been challenged. In such circumstances, a combination of exogenous (systems) changes, the activity of actors and the conceptualisation of transport as a policy problem have been vital to the success of the opponents of roads in altering the agenda. This reflects Kingdon's account of the policy process, in which the coming together of streams of problems, policy and politics is a vital precondition for policy change (1995). The conflict over the 'roads for prosperity' programme provides an example of a situation in which conflict has occurred over a near core imperative. The government has acknowledged that in its old form the 'predict and provide' orthodoxy was failing to maintain network efficiency in the face of rising congestion, and it has revised its policy priorities accordingly. Hence, the government has altered its emphasis from expansion of the network to an increase in its efficiency.

Finally, in cases in which the opponents of existing policy have attempted to challenge the core policy imperatives of the state the agenda setting dynamic is dominated by non-decision making. This is most clearly illustrated in the divide between the pro- and anti-road groups on their perception of the link between mobility and capitalism: the pro-roads groups believe that this link is intuitive and the anti-roads groups argue for an alternative development model based on local sustainability and reduced mobility (Chapter 5). Aspects of the transport agenda which concern greenhouse gas emissions, land-use planning and mobility generally have only limited potential impact due to their incompatibility with the core policy imperatives of the state (Chapter 4).

Overall, different aspects of the transport issue are affected by different agenda setting processes, depending on the extent to which they challenge the dominant imperatives of the state. In cases in which the core imperatives of the state are not affected by a proposed change the process of agenda setting can be explained by one (or a combination) of the dynamic models of political change. The strategies of actors, the conceptualisation of transport as a policy problem and developments in the external environment can destabilise the status quo. However, agenda setting shows considerable rigidity when a proposed change challenges the core policy imperatives of the state. In particular, the state views the link between economic development and mobility as intuitive. Thus, proponents of an alternative discourse of development are unable to challenge the agenda; the process remains dominated by non-decision making.

Notes

1   These changes were played out within government, which had to balance conflicting priorities between environmental concerns over transport and the importance of transport as a generator of economic development. In spite of the increasing emphasis on the environmental aspect of transport policy, I argue that in areas in which conflict between these objectives was intense the economic priorities of policies tended to dominate.

2   This is a key theme of the analysis within Chapter 9 of the politics of the car in the Blair era.

9 Postscript: New Labour and the Politics of Transport

Introduction

Transport policy under the Blair government represents a paradox. On the surface, the agenda has been much more stable than in the Major era. In the Major era, transport, and most particularly the motor car, emerged as an issue of high political salience as it increasingly was blamed for a combination of environmental and economic problems such as rising congestion and deteriorating public health. In contrast, the Blair government has confronted a quite different pattern of policy making as the car was already established as a policy problem requiring a policy response. The principal focus of the Blair government has, in fact, been on the formulation of policy alternatives designed to accommodate the car whilst reducing its impact, attending to the problem of the car rather than simply managing the policy agenda as was the pattern in the Major era. The Labour government has thus attempted to formulate policy to 'solve the transport problem' on the basis of a consensus between pressure groups, expert opinion, the EU and the public.

The principal argument within this chapter is that, when examining the transport issue in detail, it can be seen that the Blair government's attempts to build consensus have been only partially successful. It has successfully built a consensus which has incorporated groups, experts and the European Union, but has had less success in incorporating the wishes of 'middle England'. While a group-led consensus has emerged around the need for a package of transport measures including both greater public transport provision and restricting usage of the private car, the public still reject the view that the car needs to be restricted at all. In part, the manifestation of public opposition reflects economic self-interest; but it also reflects deeper structural factors which are linked to the structural imperatives of the state. The conflict over policies such as road pricing thus reflects a deeper conflict over values which are core to the capitalist state such as liberty, individuality and freedom: challenges to such values

248

are challenges to the structural imperatives of the state which, as I have argued earlier, are highly resistant to change.

In part one, I provide a model of governance in the Blair era. In this section, I argue that a principal preoccupation of the Blair government has been to govern on the basis of consensus: between groups, expert opinion, the public and in relations with the EU. On the one hand such consensus is largely pragmatic: the government seeks to seize the middle ground of British politics in order to win further elections, and to build confidence that it is 'fit to govern' after 18 years of opposition through using expert advice in order to devise policy. On the other hand, however, there is an important philosophical dimension to the Blair government's desire for consensus: they seek to reverse the individualistic thrust of Thatcherism and to redevelop a sense of society through an emphasis on communitarianism.

In part two, I apply this model of governance to the case study of the politics of the car, arguing that the Blair government has attempted to build consensus in three key ways. Firstly, there has been a significant change in the nature of group conflict surrounding the car. Mainstream transport groups such as Transport 2000 have been more formally incorporated into the policy process, thus shifting their status further towards policy insiders, while in response to the cuts to the road programme and the perception that the government is genuinely trying to solve the transport problem, both moderate conservation groups such as the National Trust and the RSPB and the direct action movement have scaled back their campaigning. Secondly, the government has tried to build consensus on the basis of expert advice, aiming for policy which reflects the majority opinion within the scientific/expert community rather than partisan party politics. Its most significant policy initiative to this end has been centred on the formation of the Commission for Integrated Transport, reflecting a genuine desire to depoliticise the politics of the car as far as possible. Thirdly, the politics of consensus has been demonstrated in a change to the policy style of the government towards constructive engagement with the EU. This change has been largely at a rhetorical level; the actual pattern of policy making between the Blair and Major eras is virtually indistinguishable. In Chapter 6, I argued that although the Major government did try to make political capital out of opposition to EU initiatives, it was in fact accommodating towards the broad thrust of policy in the transport case; the Blair government has continued this trend. They have continued to use the Auto-Oil framework in order to develop environmental regulation for the road transport sector; they remain committed to the Community's infrastructure plans, emphasising the same priority projects and a continued commitment to financing them through a partnership between the public and private sectors, and they have continued to reject Community proposals for the development of EU wide fiscal instruments such as carbon-energy taxes on the basis of sovereignty.

In part three, I argue that in spite of the efforts to build consensus, the government has had significant problems with realising its objectives due to an inability to build a consensus which includes the interests of the public. When the Blair and Major eras are compared, I argue that public opinion displays considerable 'schizophrenia'. In the Major era, it was a source of considerable pressure on the government's control of the agenda, emphasising environmental concerns with the car. However, in the Blair era, public opinion has become a brake on radical change, resisting proposals to restrict the use of the car. In order to explore the impact of the changing nature of public opinion on the political handling of the transport issue this section focuses on a discussion of the conflict over road pricing.

In part four, I look at the nature of this conflict through the model of agenda setting which I have constructed throughout this book. I argue that the division over road pricing is in fact symptomatic of a more significant conflict which centres on the importance of rules of structure formation. I argue that road pricing (in part) threatens a number of core values which are held by the capitalist state such as liberty, individualism and freedom; as such there are likely to be significant levels of political conflict over its introduction.

Models of Governance in the Blair Era

In contrast to the wealth of theoretical literature on the Thatcher era, there is relatively little on the Blair period. In part, this is explained by the relatively recent election of the Blair government in May 1997 but principally reflects a common conception in the literature that the Blair government is a product of two legacies: Thatcherism, and a reluctance to be seen as 'old labour' (on the former see Hay, 1994; on the latter see for example Jones, 1996, pp. 135-9). There has thus been little attempt to formulate a theory of 'Blairism' or indeed of governance in the Blair era more generally – the inference being that there are high levels of policy continuity between the Thatcher and Blair era (See Kenny and Smith, 1997 for a review. For a critique see Driver and Martell, 1998, pp. 164-7).

However, in spite of this theoretical ambiguity, I argue that a number of trends can be identified which enable us to construct a broad model of governance in the Blair era, and thus to explain the processing of the transport issue since the election of the Labour government. In constructing this model, useful insights can be drawn from the work of Driver and Martell who suggest that New Labour is in fact a 'post-Thatcherite' party:

> It has left behind the pre-Thatcher days of Old Labour and accepted much of the terrain left by Lady Thatcher. Yet it takes this as a starting point beyond which there are elements which make New Labour different from and beyond Thatcherism. (1998, p. 165)

One key difference between New Labour and Thatcherism is its focus on communitarianism, developed as 'an antidote to Thatcherite individualism' (p. 167). Driver and Martell argue that while communitarianism does accept that the market economy should have a key role it is 'hostile to what Blair has called "the politics of the self"' (p. 167). They go on to say:

> Communitarianism is about rebuilding the social cohesion and moral fabric undermined by years of Tory individualism and *laissez faire*. Much of Labour's economic and social policies are about communitarian inclusion. Divisions must be replaced by the inclusion of all in one nation: government for 'the many and not the few'. Communitarianism gives Labour a tone which differentiates it from that of its Thatcherite predecessors, and provides a framework for policies which in intent aim to bring about greater social inclusion. (p. 168)

A key argument within this chapter is that New Labour's desire to govern for 'the many and not the few' has had important implications for the policy process, with the Blair government aiming to construct a coalition of interests surrounding the 'centre ground' of British politics in order to govern on the basis of consensus. This focus by the Blair government on consensus indicates a significant shift in policy style in comparison to the Thatcher and Major eras and is demonstrated in four main ways (see Richardson, Gustafsson and Jordan, 1982, for a discussion of the concept of policy style. See Jordan and Richardson, 1982 for an application of policy style to the UK case).

Firstly, the emphasis of the Blair government on consensus is shown by its desire to increase consultation with pressure groups. This marks a significant break with the Thatcher government which, as Holliday argues, was ideologically opposed to any dealings with organised interests, feeling that they undermined the capacity of government to govern in the national interest and contributed to governmental overload (1993, pp. 311-13). On the one hand, the change of policy style by the Blair government is indicative of the importance of communitarianism, illustrating, as it does, a desire to accommodate groups in the pursuit of greater social cohesion and consensus. On the other hand, however, it is indicative of a pragmatic approach to policy by New Labour, which was keen to reverse the propensity to policy mistakes which had been a feature of the later years of the Thatcher government (see Marsh and Rhodes, 1992b, for examples such as education and health; see also Dunleavy, 1995, for a general discussion of the concept of policy disasters).

Secondly, the importance of consensus to the Blair government is illustrated by the widespread usage of committees of inquiry designed to offer policy prescriptions on the basis of expert advice for both ideological and pragmatic reasons (see Cartwright, 1975, for a balanced overview of the role of committees of inquiry in the policy process). In ideological terms, it is connected to the focus on communitarianism and consensus which is integral to the New Labour ideal; while at a pragmatic level committees of inquiry have been used to increase the perception that Labour is using non-partisan experts to devise policy and is thus competent to govern following 18 years in opposition. Once more the approach of New Labour is quite different to that of the Thatcher government, which as Hennessy argues, felt that committees of inquiry, with their focus on consensus, undermined political conviction: consequently a focus on government by committee was rejected by the Thatcher government (1990, pp. 581-6).

Thirdly, Sanders suggests that the importance of consensus is also demonstrated by the relationship between New Labour and the electorate. He argues that New Labour's programme for government was targeted directly at 'middle England', with a focus on fiscal prudence and with 'policies on crime, defence and the trade unions [which] were, with minor exceptions, virtually indistinguishable from the Conservatives' (1997, p. 72). Sanders argues that New Labour's success at the polls reflects the decline of traditional party identification and the fact that 'voters have become much more consumer-like in their voting decisions' (p.73). But such electoral volatility is unlikely to affect traditional Labour voters who, although increasingly marginalised within the party, will continue to support it as they have no electable alternative. Thus, New Labour's strategy of targeting the 'middle ground' is further evidence of the desire to build policy consensus – but it is consensus with 'middle England' rather than with its traditional supporters.

Finally, the emphasis of the Blair government on building consensus is shown by the changing nature of the relationship between Britain and the EU, which now prioritises constructive engagement. This is a further break with the pattern of the Thatcher and Major eras in which Britain was frequently 'at odds with Europe' (Wallace, 1997) with widespread conflict across a number of issues (see Peterson, 1997, pp. 24-29). In particular, following the conflict over BSE 'many of Britain's EU partners were so bitterly disappointed with the Major government that they simply stopped negotiating on many vital issues within the IGC until Labour was in power' (Peterson, 1997, p. 30). In part, this response was pragmatic as the EU member states realised 'that the IGC would make little progress' while the Conservative government remained in power (Dinan, 1999, p. 298); but the EU did anticipate a change in policy emphasis in the event of a Labour victory towards a more conciliatory style of policy making. Hazell and Sinclair suggest that there was some justification for such a view: in contrast to the Maastricht bill, the ratification of the Treaty of Amsterdam demonstrated a 'more relaxed attitude to matters European' (1999, p. 174). The desire of the Blair government to work within the established mechanisms of the EU in November 1999 to resolve the beef ban is further indication of a desire for constructive engagement, showing a marked contrast with the pattern of policy making in the Major era on the same issue. According to Holden this change in focus is unsurprising, reflecting the importance of the European dimension as a catalyst for internal reform of the Labour party in the 1980s. Europe then 'provided both a context and primer for change' by focusing the leadership on the impact of globalisation, the need for changes to economic policy and the importance of the EU as a source of trans-national social regulation (Holden, 1999, p. 103). However, it would be wrong to suggest that New Labour has fully embraced EU integration. Driver and Martell describe New Labour's approach as 'constructive Euroscepticism' (1998, p. 146), with continued opposition to the development of a federal Europe but a much more conciliatory tone in its day-to-day dealings with the EU.

Overall, I have argued that New Labour is best seen as a post-Thatcherite political party, emphasising communitarianism and consensus which have manifested themselves in both ideological and pragmatic terms. The focus on consensus has manifested itself in four key ways: in the changing nature of the government's dealings with groups; in the widespread usage of committees of inquiry; in the targeting of policy initiatives at 'middle England', and in the focus on constructive engagement within the EU. In the next section, I look at the effect of this pattern of governance on the political handling of the transport issue in the Blair era, arguing that although the government has attempted to govern on the basis of consensus, this has proven to be very difficult to achieve. I will argue that this is because tensions have emerged between the priorities of 'middle England' and the other interests involved in the transport coalition: the overwhelming consensus within both the pressure groups and scientific communities centres on the need to restrict the usage of the car, while the electorate, in particular 'middle England', remains strongly opposed to such a focus.

New Labour and Transport: Towards a Politics of Consensus

As the introduction to this chapter made clear, between the Major and Blair eras the nature of the transport issue has changed considerably. While in the Major era transport, and particularly the motor car, was still emerging as an issue of high political salience, by the Blair era the car had become established as a policy problem. Thus, in the Blair era, the government's principal concern has been with processing policy alternatives designed to ameliorate the effects of the car rather than responding to a new policy problem.

But there are also clear differences between the Blair and Major governments in terms of their genuine desire to 'solve the transport problem'. An important contention within this book has been that the Major government did not have any real desire either to solve the problem of transport generally, or in particular, to develop policies to ameliorate the effects of the car. For example, I have argued in Chapter 5 that the primary motivation for the launching of the consultation process surrounding the 'Great Debate' was to retain control over the agenda setting process prior to the General Election which was due in 1997: the government instigated the consultation process with a clear sense of both its own objectives and the parameters within which the debate would be conducted, thus reducing the likelihood of significant policy change (pp. 134-38).

In contrast, the Blair government has undertaken consultation designed to build a consensus between experts, the public, the EU and pressure groups in order to reach genuine solutions to transport problems. The remainder of this chapter explores the efforts of the Blair government to build consensus in the transport field, arguing that while it has had some success in building a consensus between organised interests, the scientific community and the EU, it has had much less success in accommodating the wishes of the public.

At the level of building consensus with groups, the shift in the policy priorities of the Labour government away from those of the road lobby and towards those of the moderate anti-roads groups have served to significantly change the nature of the transport policy network in three key ways. The moderate anti-roads groups have been formally incorporated within the decision making process, moving towards specialist insider status; the pro-roads groups have been increasingly marginalised, moving towards peripheral insider status, while the direct action movement has reduced the intensity of its activity in response to the reduction in the scale of the road programme.

Figure 9.1 Location of actors on a policy network continuum (Blair period)

Insiders   **Outsiders**

◄───►

core insiders	specialist insiders	peripheral insiders	outsider by goal	outsider by choice
CfIT	T2000	road haulage sector		Direct Action
	RSPB	FoE		Movement
		BRF	ALARM UK	
	National Trust			
	SMMT	Construction interests		
	AA/RAC			

Figure 9.1 provides a diagrammatic representation of the transport policy network following these changes, and shows significant change from the pattern which existed in the Major era (for comments referring to the Major era see pp. 117-22). Moderate anti-roads groups such as Transport 2000 and the CPRE have become increasingly incorporated within the core policy community, enjoying frequent contact with ministers and serving on a number of Department of the Environment, Transport and the Regions (DoETR) advisory committees: the incorporation of these two groups, in particular, within the newly formed Commission for Integrated Transport (CfIT) being an important symbol of the changing status afforded to them.

Outside the core policy community are the pro-roads groups which have much less access to government than they enjoyed in the Major era. The creation of the DoETR has served to reduce the links between the pro-roads groups and what was historically their client department (see Dudley, 1983 for an overview). In an interview in 1996, Paul Everitt of the BRF outlined the potential threat which a merger between the two departments would have for the operational autonomy of the road lobby:

> I'm sure the Department of the Environment would like Transport to be back. I think we would be very concerned by that and we would be lobbying as hard as we could to ensure that it didn't [become merged within the DoE] ... I think we would be concerned that it would, within the DoE, lose the ability to recognise the commercial, or the industrial importance, of transport ... The DoE don't recognise or don't seem to recognise how important transport is to the economy, because that's not their primary role, and the people who are involved perhaps are, in our view, tending more to the environmental line that says, 'well economic growth is something that goes on over there and really we're not really bothered whether it happens or not' ... if it was subsumed within the DoE, I think it would change things, I think we would struggle even more to get attention. Transport would just become just one other thing that the DoE handled. (Interview, 21st August 1996)

In Chapter 5 I suggested that during the Major era, with the decline of the predict and provide model, that groups such as the road haulage sector shifted from being core insiders to specialist insiders, seen as an authoritative source of knowledge on a much narrower niche of policy. During the Blair era, the hitherto dominant road user groups have become even further marginalised. In an interview in 1996, Sydney Balgarnie of the Road Haulage Association (RHA) argued that groups such as his would never get involved in 'extremist' activity such as direct action through blockading the roads:

> Our organisation, which has a very long history, we are not an extremist organisation. We don't resort to sensationalist, publicity type things. We lobby quietly, we can get in and to put it bluntly, if we want a question asked in Parliament – it will be asked, and we won't pay for it. (Interview, 21st August 1996)

However, following the change of government there seems to have been a significant change: the road haulage sector has increasingly resorted to direct action tactics (blockading roads, go-slows etc.) in order to lobby for reductions in fuel duties and vehicle excise levels. This is illustrative of the increasing isolation of these groups from central government decision making.

At the same time, the direct action movement has also come to exert much less influence on the agenda. The cancellation of a number of road schemes has enormously reduced the objects to campaign against; the media has lost interest in the novelty of the protests, and the movement has tended to change the focus of its protests towards 'new' issues such as Genetically Modified foods and the protests against the World Trade Organisation (WTO), part of a broadening of their campaigning against capitalism more generally (Aufheben, 1998, pp. 102-03):

> That's the real strength of Newbury and all the 90s counter-culture protests – we're not fighting one thing we don't like; we have a whole vision of how good life could and should be, and we're fighting anything that blocks it. This is not just a campaign, or even a movement; it's a whole culture. (Merrick, road protester cited in McKay, 1998, p. 2)

This change suggests that, in part, the direct action movement can be described as 'protest mercenaries', but also that the anti-roads protests were important in building a broader protest movement through links with groups such as 'Reclaim the Streets' and 'This Land is Ours' (on building links with the latter see Monbiot, 1998, pp. 179).

This shift in the nature of the policy network reflects the different beliefs of the Labour government, which in terms of transport are much closer to the moderate anti-roads groups than they are to the pro-roads groups. Thus, the change of government has served to destabilise the policy network; the moderate anti-roads groups have derived their insider status because of their links to the policy objectives of the Blair government. Thus, as has been the case throughout the post-war era, the pattern of the policy network, and the status of groups as insiders or outsiders, has reflected the priorities of the government: but while it was the case that until the Major era government priorities favoured the pro-roads groups, in the Blair era the changed government priorities have favoured the interests of the moderate anti-roads groups above those of its opponents.

At the level of building consensus on the basis of scientific understanding two observations can be made. First, in contrast to the Major era, there have been no new scientific findings which have destabilised the agenda in the Blair period. Under Major, scientific reports served to undermine the stability of the policy process on three key levels: public health, congestion and lifestyle. Scientific research increasingly implicated the car in damaging human health, particularly in connection with asthma and the effects of PM10s (in the latter case, PM10s were actually discovered during the Major era and were thus a new problem. See above, pp. 81-88). On congestion, reports such as the SACTRA report destabilised the policy process by providing quasi-governmental authorisation for the view that road building could not successfully accommodate predicted growth in traffic (SACTRA, 1994). Thus the predict and provide orthodoxy which had hitherto been the dominant orthodoxy used to rationalise transport infrastructure investment was undermined (see above pp. 96-100). In terms of lifestyle, an important development was the growth of the sustainable development discourse in response to the discovery of global warming. As transport is the fastest growing source of CO_2 emissions (the principal greenhouse gas), a car-based lifestyle was increasingly questioned (pp. 100-01). At another level, policy experts expressed growing concern about planning for both town centres and housing allocation, arguing that a legacy of deregulated planning was reducing the vitality of urban areas, while deregulated housing planning was increasing the propensity for travel, with a number of local authorities proposing extensive developments out-of-town on green-field sites (pp. 107-08).

In contrast, the Blair era has not witnessed any comparable changes to the knowledge base; thus unlike the Major era in which policy makers had to respond to a changing sense that transport was a policy problem, the Blair government has seen transport consolidated as a policy problem. This shift in emphasis is well illustrated by the Royal Commission report, *Transport and the Environment: Developments since 1994*, which reviewed both changes to knowledge of the environmental effects of transport and the policy proposals by government designed to reduce such effects. Unlike the Commission's 1994 report, *Transport and the Environment*, this report neither identified nor clarified any new policy problems but merely served to consolidate and re-emphasise those already in existence. (Cm 3752. See Chapter 1 for an overview; paras 4.5-4.9 for the discussion of car dependence; paras 8.1-8.5 on the continuing effect of transport on CO_2 emissions; and para. 7.26 for discussion of ongoing failure of the planning system, especially surrounding the implementation of PPG13).

The Blair government, then, has overwhelmingly accepted as fact that cars cause fundamental damage, and in contrast to the Major era, has aimed to use science in order to formulate its strategy for responding to that problem. Thus, there has been an attempt to build policy along the lines practised in the Netherlands, where the government devises a long-term national transport plan on the basis of expert advice which is largely *apolitical* (The *Guardian*, 14 December 1999, p. 3). In the Major era, because much of the science surrounding issues such as global warming was disputed, it had little effect on the formation of policy, which was governed instead by the predefined ideological thrust of the government. Policy formulation under Major was thus heavily political and largely *ascientific*, in sharp contrast to the focus of the Blair government (see for example pp. 134-38 above for the importance of ideology in constraining the parameters of the 'Great Debate' in the Major era).

At the level of British-EU relations, the Blair government has sought to establish consensus, here largely continuing the approach of the Major government which, as discussed in Chapter 6, belied the theory as outlined within the awkward partner thesis (see pp. 161; 166-67; 172-75; 179-87). The Blair government has continued to utilise the EU level in formulating environmental regulation, continuing involvement with the Auto-Oil programme and its focus on technical solutions for managing transport impacts (this is particularly well illustrated in DoETR 1999a, paras 62-4). Legislative activity in the transport sphere relating to the single market initative has also continued to have an important effect on the UK, serving to increase autonomy rather than reduce it as the priorities of UK transport providers match the deregulatory thrust of EU policy, such as the proposed regulations on railway track access within the EU and the further deregulation of the road haulage and air transport sectors (for developments in the Major era see above pp. 163-67). For proposals for the liberalisation of the railway sector in the Blair era see CEC, 1998, para. 10; on the Road Haulage and Airline sectors see for example, CEC, 1998, Annex 1). Activist infrastructure policy is also largely unchanged (for an overview of the Major era see above pp. 176-87). The EU has continued to prioritise the same fourteen priority projects of which three are in the UK (CEC, 1998, para. 13). While the government has shifted focus slightly by down-scaling the support for the Benelux road link and channelling most of the funds from the EU into the West Coast Main Line and Channel Tunnel rail link, these projects still remain dependent on a private/public sector partnership for most of their finance, with the principal investor being Railtrack (DoETR, 1999c). Finally, the development of activist environmental policies continues to meet hostility from the UK government, particularly EU-wide fiscal instruments such as carbon taxes. As in the Major era, opposition remains driven by a concern that policy should not formally constrain sovereignty in the area of tax granting powers (see above pp. 188-89). That this is so is clearly illustrated in the Blair era, as in early 1999 the government actually proposed a carbon-energy tax as part of domestic policy (DoETR, 1999d). Thus, it is not the tax itself which is opposed, but rather the principle that its operation should be undertaken by the EU. Overall, therefore, the relationship between Britain and the EU remains unchanged: the pattern of constructive engagement identified in Chapter 6 has continued to be the norm under Blair.

Overall, the efforts by the Labour government in building consensus between organised interests, expert opinion and the EU have largely been successful, resulting in a significant change of emphasis between the Major and Blair administrations. This change of emphasis can be seen in three key ways. Firstly, the Blair government has accepted that transport is a public policy problem. The 1998 White Paper, *A New Deal for Transport*, provides one such example of the government's view:

> Our quality of life depends on transport. Most of us travel every day, even if only locally. And we need an efficient transport system to support a strong and prosperous economy. But in turn, the way we travel is damaging our towns and cities and harming our countryside. As demand for transport grows, we are even changing the very climate of our planet ... The mood is for change. Business is concerned about the costs of congestion. People want the existing transport system to work better. They want more choice and a new emphasis on protecting the environment and their health. (Cm 3950, paras 1.2-1.4)

Secondly, the Labour government has accepted that the car is the principal cause of the transport problem, with the government advancing proposals to restrict the use of the car for the first time. In 1998, the government published a consultation document, *Breaking the Logjam*, which outlined the nature of this change:

> Cars in particular have revolutionized the way we live. But the way we use our cars has a price – for health, the economy and for the environment ... Traffic jams cost time and money, create pollution and take the pleasure out of driving. On recent trends, things are going to get much worse ... Unless something is done, this means more traffic jams, not just in cities but in country towns too. Rush hours will become longer. The tranquillity of the countryside will be further eroded. Driving will become less of a pleasure and the costs to the business will soar. There will be more damage to the environment and our health will suffer. (DoETR, 1998a, paras 1.2-1.3; see para. 2.6 for the view that measures such as road pricing are needed to restrict the car)

Finally, in response to this change of emphasis the Labour government has focused on developing a policy framework which is designed to 'solve the problem of transport'. This framework, developed within the transport White Paper, contains the following key measures:

- the creation of a *Strategic Rail Authority* to work alongside the rail regulator to strengthen regulation of both Railtrack and the train operators (for an overview of the SRA's proposed functions see Cm 3950, paras 4.12-4.37; for the legal text outlining its role see HC Bill 8 (99-00), Part IV, Chapter 1),

- the creation of the *Commission for Integrated Transport*, a 'new independent body' to 'provide independent advice to Government on the implementation of integrated transport policy, to monitor developments across transport, environment, health and other sectors and to review progress towards meeting our [i.e. the Labour government's] objectives' (Cm 3950, para. 4.4;. for an overview of it's programme of work see CfIT, 1999a),

- a strengthening of the framework for *environmental appraisal* (for an overview see Cm 3950, paras 4.193-4.211; for the changes with respect to the road programme see DoETR 1998b, Annex B),

- a review of the previous government's *National Air Quality Strategy* designed to further tighten air quality targets for the 8 primary pollutants (for an overview of the role of the NAQS in the Major era see pp. 89-94 above; for an overview of the Labour government's proposed changes see DoETR, 1999a),

- the continued utilisation of the EU's *Auto-Oil framework* to reduce vehicle emission levels (for an overview of the Major era see pp.167-75 above; for the importance of the Auto-Oil Programme to the Blair government see DoETR, 1999a, paras 62-64 and Technical Annex),

- a strengthening of the *mechanisms for transport planning* including a review of local planning guidance for transport (for an overview see Cm 3950, paras 4.156-4.176; for the proposed revisions to PPG13 see DoETR, 1999b),

- the development of enabling legislation designed to allow local authorities to implement *hypothecated urban road pricing and work-based parking charges*, with the revenues retained by the authority for the development of local transport projects (for an overview of the proposals see DoETR, 1998a, Chapter 3-7; for the legal text outlining these changes see HC Bill 8 (99-00), Part III),

- finally, a number of changes to *the nature of the road programme* shifting the overall emphasis of policy away from road building and towards road maintenance and small scale improvements such as bypasses and local traffic management schemes (see DoETR, 1998b, Section 1.6-1.7); detrunking approximately 40% of the existing national trunk road network, shifting control from the Highways Agency to local authorities thus increasing co-ordination of regional planning and integration (DoETR, 1998b, Section 2.2-2.3); changes to the nature of the appraisal system for roads to emphasise environmental and social factors alongside economic considerations (DoETR, 1998b, Annex B).

Thus there is considerable consensus that improvements to the alternatives to the car are crucial and that the car is a principal source of the problem of transport. But this consensus is far from complete. As I show in the next section, when the government has attempted to formulate policy designed to restrict the usage of the car, such as road pricing, attempts to build a consensus have largely ended in failure: while the majority of pressure group, EU and expert opinion acknowledge that measures to restrict the car are vital if the problem of transport is to be solved, the public remain strongly resistant to such measures, rejecting any attempts to restrict the usage of the car.

Restricting the Car in the Blair Era: a Failure of Consensus?

In this section I explore the difficulties which the Blair government has had in building a consensus which accommodates the public. In it I argue that the public have played an important role in agenda change in both the Blair and Major eras; however, the manner in which they have interacted with the agenda has been very different.

In the Major era public pressure manifested itself in a general concern over the environmental effects of further road building and the effects of cars on human health and quality of life, both in relation to the contribution of vehicle emissions to increasing levels of asthma and the effects of increasing congestion. Such concerns manifested themselves in three key ways. First, Conservative MPs responded to the concerns of their constituents over the effects of road building on the environment by actually opposing the government's road building plans which affected their constituencies. These essentially NIMBY based campaigns were influential in stalling the proposed M25 widening and the widening of the M62 along with a number of minor schemes in areas such as Buckinghamshire and Oxfordshire (see above pp. 144-48). Second, the public played an important role in legitimising the activities of the direct action movement. On the one hand, formal links between middle class NIMBY campaigners and the direct action movement were successfully developed at a number of nationally significant road protests, particularly at Twyford Down and Newbury, if not through a meeting of minds then through an acknowledgement and acceptance that the two groups could help each other to realise their objectives in important ways. The direct action movement needed the legitimacy at a symbolic level which association with the voting classes gave it, while the middle class NIMBY groups benefited from the tactics and energy of the direct action movement who were willing to risk their lives in order to try to prevent the construction of the road. On the other hand, the linkage between these groups was important in symbolic terms. Chapter 5 showed that these groups did not in fact have values which were compatible with one another, but the media reporting of the protests characterised the direct action movement and middle class NIMBY groups as being closely linked, helping to further legitimise the activities of the direct action movement (pp. 132-33; 140-44). Thirdly, the growing public disquiet about road building and the environmental effects of the car encouraged groups such as the National Trust and RSPB to enter the conflict over roads. This was enormously important, as these groups not only command significant membership, but also contain within that membership the key electoral constituency of 'middle England' (pp. 114 and 118).

In the Blair era, public concern has remained an important factor in the politics of the car, but it has manifested itself in a very different way. In this period the principal concern has been that government proposals to change patterns of transport behaviour will be overly restrictive, constraining the public's freedom to use their cars. In particular, public concern has led to widespread opposition to the proposed introduction of urban road pricing and work-based parking charges, which the government outlined in its transport White Paper, and will seek to implement in the transport bill slated for the year 2000 parliamentary session.

The public, and the newspapers appealing to the centre right of British politics such as the *Daily Telegraph* and the *Daily Mail*, have reacted strongly to the proposals. The Conservative party in turn have sought to use this shift in public opinion as the basis for attacks on the government, arguing that it is 'pursuing a vicious vendetta against the motorist' and suggesting instead a return to an expanded roads programme in order to accommodate projected congestion (John Redwood, then Shadow Transport Secretary, cited in the *Guardian*, 30th November 1999, p. 13. For an overview of Conservative proposals to return to an expanded roads programme see the *Guardian*, 13th July 1999, G2, p. 2).

As a result, some commentators have suggested that the government has been forced to amend its plans, both in terms of restricting their scope and in pushing back the timetable for implementation (*Guardian*, 30th November 1999, p. 13). But close analysis of both the original proposals and legislation shows that these limitations were in fact always present; Dowding's 'law of anticipated reactions' is once again applicable. The government, despite the public reaction, has at no point sought to develop policies which are 'too contrary to their [the public's] interests' (Dowding, 1991, p. 137).

The Blair government, anticipating the public's reaction to proposals such as road pricing and work-based parking charges, has thus developed a number of political strategies designed to remove the conflict from the responsibility of central government by displacing it to local government. On the surface, the pattern of policy making is similar to that in the Major era in which central government sought to manage the agenda in a similar way (see pp. 219-27 above for an overview of the Major era).[1] But unlike the Major era, the desire to manage the policy agenda is not the principal motive behind government strategy in the Blair era.

Firstly, central government has designed road pricing in such a way that it will only be undertaken if local authorities want to introduce it. The 1998 consultation document, *Breaking the Logjam*, provides an illustration of the Blair government's view:

> The Government believes that the decision on whether or not to implement a road user charging scheme should be one for local traffic authorities to take ... The government does not propose that an authority should be compelled to introduce a charging scheme in its area since the Government's view is that the decision to implement a scheme needs to be taken locally in light of individual circumstances and needs. (DoETR, 1998a, paras 3.3-3.4)

Road pricing is thus not a national policy initiative and will only take on the appearance of a national initiative if most urban areas choose to implement it (DoETR, 1998a, para. 1.12). At a pragmatic level, the decision to grant local authorities the powers to implement road pricing if they wish to will effectively shift the blame for an unpopular measure from central government to local government, thus minimising its national electoral impact. But while the desire to manage the policy agenda was the principal motivation in the Major era, this can be shown not to be the case in the Blair era. For where the Conservative government explicitly rejected any possibility of the revenues raised from local road pricing schemes being hypothecated, and hence spent by the local authority on local transport projects of its own choosing, the Labour party has ensured that revenue hypothecation is integral to any road pricing proposal. Local authorities will still lose out in terms of the electoral impact of road pricing, but under Blair they will be able to gain by using the revenue stream to invest in public transport alternatives in compensation (see pp. 222-27 above for a discussion of the Major era; see Cm 3950, para. 4.94 and DoETR 1998a, paras 1.6-1.10 for acknowledgment by the Blair government of the importance of revenue hypothecation to the successful implementation of road pricing).

Furthermore, the political impact of the proposed introduction of urban road pricing ought to be further reduced by the fact that local authorities will be able to borrow and invest in public transport schemes such as rail, light rail and measures to enhance the efficiency and quality of the bus services on the basis of the anticpated revenue streams from road pricing:

> It's quite clear that the revenues could be derived [for investment in public transport projects] perhaps on some PFI deal just from the forward view of what those revenues might be – all of that would be perfectly deliverable. I don't think that's a problem. I don't think the actual logistics of which comes first the charge or the investment need detain us, unduly. (Interview, Steven Norris, former Minister for Public Transport, Traffic Safety and Transport in London, 29th June 1996. See also DoETR, 1998a, para. 4.11)

Thus, the public will be able to see the benefits of road pricing (in the form of improved public transport) on the ground, and get used to using them, before pricing mechanisms are introduced which are designed to reduce the usage of the private car.

However, there are four important restrictions which the government has imposed on local authorities which will reduce their enthusiasm for local road pricing. Firstly, revenues raised can only be used for transport improvements, and not for the promotion of a more wide-ranging urban renaissance. In its transport White Paper, *A New Deal for Transport*, the Labour government made its position clear, stating that they would 'not permit their use as a general revenue raising device' (Cm 3950, para. 4.111).

However, in its submission to the House of Commons Select Committee inquiry into urban road pricing in 1995, much of Lothian Regional Council's enthusiasm for road pricing stemmed from its feeling that such a revenue stream could be used to fund a variety of projects, many of which had no transport aspect. Lothian council's aim was thus to provide a whole raft of civic improvements which would be designed to reinvigorate the city of Edinburgh, providing a much larger range of compensation for those priced out of their cars, and hence increasing the attractiveness of road pricing as a policy option (See Memorandum from Lothian Regional Council, to HCTSC in HC 104-II, pp. 72-75 and Memorandum from Professor May, to HCTSC in HC 104-II, pp. 75-83). As I emphasised in Chapter 7, central government retains very powerful levers of political control over local government in the UK polity, most importantly through the funding mechanisms which are used by central government to maintain control over local government. If local authorities had been permitted to spend the proceeds of urban road pricing as they wished then this would have marked an important change in the nature of central-local relations, with a significant shift away from central government and towards increasing the autonomy of local government. At a practical level, this would have enormously increased the scope for local authorities to build financial advocacy coalitions in a whole number of areas, thus accessing greater levels of EU and private sector funds (see pp. 209-19 for a discussion of the concept of financial advocacy coalitions). As it is such coalitions will remain restricted to transport schemes, thus significantly restricting the growth of local government autonomy.

Secondly, the revenues which accrue from road pricing can only be retained 'provided that there are worthwhile transport-related projects to be funded', after which point the revenues will revert to the Exchequer as part of general taxation (DoETR, 1998a, para. 3.13). Such a restriction poses significant problems for local authorities. At its extreme it suggests that central government will retain significant control over the nature of central-local relations, with local authorities denied the opportunity to devise schemes as they would wish. Might it for example, restrict the capacity of a city such as Edinburgh to design a network of light rail schemes? Could the government argue that the level of investment required is prohibitive? Also the transport bill makes it clear that enabling legislation will only be granted to local authorities alongside the endorsement of an approved plan of transport investments (HC Bill 8

(99-00), para. 140 (2). See also DoETR, 1998a, paras 4.24-4.26). With the government imposing such stringent restrictions on the nature of the schemes which local authorities can develop it further reduces the attractiveness of such schemes to them, increasing the suspicion that while the government is allowing local authorities considerably more freedom than they gained in the Major era, the key motive of this policy is in fact still to manage the agenda and not reduce the level of car use.

Thirdly, the government has tightened the conditions which local authorities must meet if they are to be granted the legal entitlement to implement road pricing, making it more difficult for the enabling legislation to apply to each individual local authority and pushing back the date at which any road pricing scheme is likely to be formally introduced until 2005 (*Guardian*, 30th November 1999, p. 13). In the first place, the government suggested that each city will have to have the required public transport improvements in place before it is able to introduce congestion charging. Although it is not completely clear exactly how stringent such requirements are, it does seem to suggest either that the government does not envisage local authorities building capital intensive schemes such as light rail schemes, or that even the date of 2005 is unlikely for the introduction of congestion charging. A city such as Edinburgh, which proposes two interconnected light rail schemes, may well not be ready by 2005 (HC 104-II, p.74, para. 10). The second condition is that the local authority has an efficient, fully-trialled electronic charging mechanism in place. This further suggests that policy implementation will be highly incremental, with only Leeds, Edinburgh and (possibly) Bristol in the first wave of local authorities (DoETR, 1999e).

The final condition suggested by the *Guardian* report is that the local authority 'would have to consult the electorate, through a referendum if necessary, before introducing congestion charging'. (30th November 1999, p. 13. See also CfIT, 1999b, paras 29-35 for the CfIT's view that public consultation ought to be comprehensive, encompassing all stages of the policy formulation process). But unless such a requirement is specifically imposed on local authorities, it seems likely that they would rely on a more limited form of 'consultation', using a combination of conventional public meetings and their electoral mandate to legitimise the introduction of road pricing (see HC Bill 8 (99-00), para. 146, which makes it clear that there is no compulsion on local authorities to undertake a referendum before introducing road pricing).

Aside from the restrictions which the government's own framework will impose on the development of road pricing schemes, market competition itself will restrict its scope. In an interview, Jeremy Vanke of the RAC pointed out that road pricing proposals would face major problems if implemented on an *ad hoc* basis with no regional strategy. From Vanke's point of view, it would be necessary for local authorities to agree on a regional strategy for charging; otherwise there would be an incentive for a neighbouring authority to reject road pricing and encourage the public (in the form of employers and shoppers) to use their town/city at the expense of their neighbour (Interview, 26th May 1996. This view is also articulated by Prof. May in his submission to the HCSC inquiry into 'urban road pricing', HC 104-II, p. 88). According to reports in the *Guardian* such concerns are already affecting the pre-planning stage, with Manchester in particular being reluctant to proceed with road pricing unless action is taken on a regional basis involving all of its neighbouring authorities (30th November 1999, p. 13).

The focus of the government on highly localised implementation of road pricing is in fact a significant policy oversight which could undermine its entire strategy of regional planning for transport. The Blair government has increasingly emphasised that local authorities need to devise regional plans for the provision of roads – detrunking roads for example so that local authorities can better integrate them with their other public transport provision (see DoETR 1998b, paras 2.1-2.3, for an overview of the proposals for detrunking). Thus it has acknowledged that the co-ordination of the 'carrot' or incentive aspect of policy is best realised regionally. But it is not developing the disincentives on a similar basis: there is no co-ordination of the 'stick' with the 'carrot'. This imbalance of policy instruments could be extremely detrimental to the development of integrated regional solutions to public transport problems.

There are three possible explanations for the development of policy on this inconsistent basis. First, that policy makers have simply made a policy mistake, not thinking the nature of the policy through fully. Second, that policy has been developed in this way for political reasons. From this perspective, if the 'carrot' (of improvements) is co-ordinated regionally, because there is no regional government in the UK then the centre is likely to get much of the credit; but if the 'stick' (of the charging regime) is implemented locally then the local authority will be clearly associated with the policy proposal and will be blamed for it, thus losing out electorally. Assuming such a rationale for the formulation of policy then the government's motivation for the imbalance of policy instruments is largely explained by a desire to manage the agenda for political reasons. The third possible explanation for the *ad hoc* implementation of road pricing schemes on a city by city basis reflects a desire by the government to continue to develop policy on the basis of the market mechanism. From this perspective, government emphasises that transport consumers still retain choices – being able to shop or work in a place which has charging or one which does not. Thus, the market in the form of the price mechanism will serve to regulate the provision of road space and also the access to city centres.

Overall, this discussion of road pricing has illustrated the nature of the conflict between the electorate on the one hand and the pressure group and expert community on the other. It has also revealed that the government's desire to build policy on the basis of consensus has to confront some very real policy problems which are serving to reinvigorate the conflict over the politics of the car. Thus, consensus is extremely difficult to achieve; falling victim to the schizophrenic nature of public opinion which has lurched from preoccupation with the environmental effects of the car (i.e. a collective focus) to preoccupation with ensuring that everyone retains the right to use a car as they wish (i.e. an individualist perspective).

The Model of Agenda Setting and the Blair era

In the last section of this chapter I argue that the pattern of political conflict in the Blair era – centred as it is on balancing the rights of people to use their cars with managing the detrimental environmental effects of the car – can be explained by the model of agenda setting developed in the earlier part of this book, which emphasises that policy makers are constrained by rules of structure formation which constrain the policy agenda.

It is worth reminding the reader very briefly of the implications of the model of agenda setting developed in the book (see Chapter 8 for an overview):

- that agenda setting is constrained by deep rules of structure formation which constrain the free movement of the agenda dynamic
- that policy networks are a useful descriptive device but have little analytical value

In terms of the different models of agenda setting:

- If a policy objective which is promoted by a change to the agenda is compatible with the structural imperatives of the state (e.g. privatisation/bus deregulation) then any of the surface models of agenda setting (i.e. group theory/problem theory etc) will be able to account for change

- However, if the issue challenges the near core values so, in part the structural imperatives of the state are challenged (e.g. a change in the dominant orthodoxy from predict and provide to restrict and provide), then a combination of:
  actor + problem + exogenous models will be needed

- Finally, if it totally challenges the structural imperatives of the state (e.g. proposals to ban the car) then only models of non-change are of use.

The conflict over road pricing in the Blair era, symbolising as it does a conflict over measures to restrict the usage of the car can, I argue, be explained with reference to this framework. In the Major era, the old 'predict and provide' orthodoxy was fundamentally challenged, leading policy makers to acknowledge that it was simply impossible to continue to provide for all of the anticipated growth in traffic (see above pp. 98-99). In the earlier chapters of this book I have argued that the response of the Conservative government to this challenge was centred on policy inertia and agenda management: for the first time the Conservatives acknowledged that access to the road network would have to be rationed, but it was to be rationed not by charging but by congestion (pp. 95-96). At one level, such a focus is easy to achieve in policy terms, being fully compatible with the structural imperatives of the state with its acceptance that every one retains a right to use a car, providing they are willing to wait in line with everyone else. However, it was clearly a pragmatic orthodoxy designed to stall decision making until after the next election, being totally unsustainable in the long term due to the significant costs in terms of congestion and environmental damage.

Following the election of the Labour government there has been a significant change in orthodoxy. The government has acknowledged that access to the most congested elements of the road network must be rationed through the operation of the price mechanism (DoETR, 1998a, para. 2.13; DoETR 1998b, para. 5.4). At one level, the focus on 'restrict and provide' seeks to maintain a free-flowing road network into the next century with benefits for both the economy and the environment (DoETR 1998b, para. 5.1). Thus, it acknowledges the SACTRA report's conclusion that it is simply not possible for government to provide the levels of construction which are needed to meet pace with projected traffic growth; from this perspective restriction is the only policy option (DoETR 1998b, para. 5.4). In addition, restrict and provide is integral to the government's desire that transport consumers should pay the full external costs of their transport decisions (i.e. to further integrate market mechanisms in to the transport sector) (Cm 3950, paras 4.118-4.120). A considerable body of expert opinion suggests that car users, especially in urban areas, do not come close to paying the full costs of their transport actions: urban road pricing is part of a drive to redress this imbalance and to reduce market distortions which have historically skewed the transport market in favour of the car and away from public transport. (For a summary of expert opinion on the former see SACTRA, 1999, para. 7.13-7.21; on the latter see SACTRA, 1999, para. 7.28).

The transport orthodoxy has further changed following the election of the Blair government with their replacement of the hitherto dominant predict and provide orthodoxy on decisions concerning public transport investment with a new orthodoxy in the form of 'encourage and provide'. This is an important shift. As I have argued elsewhere in this book, before the Blair era reduced investment in public transport was repeatedly rationalised as a response to falling demand: predictions of reduced demand justified reductions in expenditure (pp. 53-55). The Blair government's new ethos of encourage and provide instead seeks to offer incentives in the form of better integration, lower fares, and an improved service, moves explicitly designed to encourage changes in consumer behaviour (Cm 3950, Ch. 3). Thus the government, significantly, is manipulating the transport market to try to encourage public transport use while discouraging the use of private transport.

In this context, the difficulties with implementing road pricing can be explained with reference to the agenda setting framework which I have developed in this book. Road pricing is designed to restrict the usage of the car, imposing charges on all road users which reduce the demand for car travel and hence increase the demand for a substitute form of travel (be it walking, cycling or public transport). One key element of road pricing, however, is that it is likely to price the marginal motorist off the roads, for a number of individual journeys if not completely (see above pp. 225-26; DoETR, 1998a, para. 2.12).

The proposals to implement road pricing are thus meeting strong hostility because, to an unprecedented degree, they challenge the structural imperatives of the state. As I have argued elsewhere, the car in the UK has come to be associated with a number of iconic values which are directly related to the perceived virtues of capitalism. At its most fundamental level, car ownership has important aspirational values, being associated with coming of age and the satisfaction of one's basic material needs. It is thus an important element of the perceived material development of many citizens: when they own a car they are well on the way to economic emancipation.

However, car ownership also contains deeper values: values which are connected to the core values of the capitalist state. As I have argued earlier, in the UK the car has become interlinked with core values such as liberty, freedom and self-realisation (see Chapter 3). Such values are not merely those of advertising executives and car enthusiasts but are ingrained in the structural imperatives of the state. The problem for road pricing is that it is seen as an attack on such core values. It poses a fundamental challenge to the right of certain citizens (i.e. marginal motorists) to own a car, forcing them away from individualistic solutions towards collectivist ones in the form of public transport.

Ironically, the perception that road pricing is an attack on personal liberty and challenges the structural imperatives of the state is only enhanced by the proposal to hypothecate road pricing to public transport investment. The link of the imposition of the charge with investment in public transport sends two clear signals to transport consumers: you are being forced out of your car, and you are being forced onto public transport. The latter could not be provided without the former, so it appears that the attack on individuality and freedom is being mounted in order to promote a collectivist approach to policy (such a view is particularly well articulated in Mawhinney, 1995).

This is not to suggest that the popular opposition to road pricing has been motivated by such structural imperatives; they may indeed just be motivated by self-interest. But a policy such as road pricing which poses an unprecedented challenge to the near core imperatives of the state will, I suggest, always meet real difficulties in being successfully implemented.

Conclusion

In this chapter I have argued that a primary motive of the Blair government has been to try to reduce the conflict over transport policy which characterised the Major era in order to build policy on the basis of a consensus between actors, experts, the EU and 'middle England'. This claim has been substantiated in several ways. Firstly, a general model of governance in the Blair era has been constructed in order to argue that the government has attempted to build consensus at all levels of policy making. In part this has been pragmatically based, but it also marks a genuine desire to build a communitarian settlement and reverse the pattern of conflict which permeated policy making under Thatcher. Secondly, this chapter has shown that the government has experienced considerable difficulties in realising such an approach in the case of the politics of the car: while they have successfully been able to build consensus within the pressure group and expert communities, and continued to accommodate the EU within decision making, there has been a significant fissure with the public. This split has focused on the issue of restricting the use of the private car, through proposals such as those for road pricing. Finally, I have argued that the reason that such conflict is so deep-seated is that it reflects a conflict over the structural imperatives of the state. Road pricing and associated proposals to restrict the use of the car are, for those affected, a threat to their 'right' to own and use a car. The car, I have argued elsewhere in this book, is closely synonymous with a number of core values of the capitalist state such as freedom, liberty and individualism; road pricing, which restricts the use of the car, is thus part of a fundamental attack on such values. This conflict is the first step in a reversal of the pattern of agenda setting which has hitherto characterised policy making in the Blair era. Whilst it has so far been stable, the future suggests a return to the volatility and widespread conflict over the politics of the car which characterised the Major era.

Note

1   Although I focus in this section on a discussion of road pricing, these comments are equally applicable to other proposals (such as work-place parking charges) which are explicitly designed to restrict the usage of the car, shifting transport users towards public transport.

Bibliography

Allen, D. (1996), 'Cohesion and Structural Adjustment' in H. Wallace and W. Wallace, *Policy-Making in the European Union* (Oxford: Oxford University Press), 3rd edition, pp. 209-33.

Andersen, S.S. and Eliassen, K.A. (1993), *Making Policy in Europe: The Europeification of National Policy-Making* (London: Sage).

Anderson, A. (1997), *Media, Culture and the Environment* (London: UCL Press).

Aspinwall, M. (1996), 'Planes, Trains and Automobiles: Governance of Transport Policy in the European Union', paper presented to the European Consortium for Political Research, March 29th to April 3rd (ECPR: Oslo).

Association of Metropolitan Authorities (1995), *Local Government on the Move: A New Agenda for Local Transport* (London: Association of Metropolitan Authorities).

Atkinson, M.M. and Coleman, W.D. (1989), 'Strong States and Weak States: Sectoral Policy Networks in Advanced Capitalist Economies', *British Journal of Political Science*, vol. 19, pp. 47-67.

Atkinson, M.M. and Coleman, W.D. (1992), 'Policy Networks, Policy Communities and the Problems of Governance', *Governance: An International Journal of Policy and Administration*, vol. 5, pp. 154-80.

Aufheben (1998), 'The Politics of Anti-road Struggle and the Struggles of Anti-road Politics: the Case of the NO M11 Link Road Campaign', in G. McKay (ed.), *DiY Culture: Party and Protest in Nineties Britain* (London: Verso), pp. 100-28.

Bachrach, P. and Baratz, M. (1970), *Power and Poverty: Theory and Practice* (London: Oxford University Press).

Baker, S. (1994), 'Travelling Fast to Get Nowhere: Transport Policy in the European Union', *Politics*, vol. 14, pp. 67-73.

Baker, S., Kousis, M., Richardson, D. and Young, S. (1997a), 'Introduction: The Theory and Practice of Sustainable Development in EU Perspective' in S. Baker et al (eds), *The Politics of Sustainable Development: Theory, Policy and Practice in the European Union* (London: Routledge), pp. 1-40.

Baker, S., Kousis, M., Richardson, D. and Young, S. (eds) (1997b), *The Politics of Sustainable Development: Theory, Policy and Practice in the European Union* (London: Routledge).

Barker, T., Baylis, S. and Maben, P. (1993), 'A UK Carbon-Energy Tax: The Macroeconomic Effects', *Energy Policy*, vol. 21, pp. 296-308.

Barker, T. and Gerhold, D. (1993), *The Rise and Rise of Road Transport, 1700-1990* (Basingstoke: Macmillan).

Baumgartner, F.R. and Jones, B.D. (1991), 'Agenda Dynamics and Policy Subsystems', *The Journal of Politics*, vol. 53, pp. 1044-74.

Baumgartner, F.R. and Jones, B.D. (1993), *Agendas and Instability in American Politics* (Chicago: University of Chicago Press).

Benson, J.K. (1982), 'A Framework for Policy Analysis' in D.L. Rogers and D.A. Whetten and Associates, *Interorganizational Coordination: Theory, Research and Implementation* (Ames: Iowa State University Press), pp. 137-76.

Bonefeld, W., Brown, A. and Burnham, P. (1995), *A Major Crisis: The Politics of Economic Policy in Britain in the 1990s* (Aldershot: Dartmouth).

British Broadcasting Corporation (1994), *Panorama: Nose to Tail.*

Bryant, B. (1996), *Twyford Down: Roads, Campaigning and Environmental Law* (London: E & FN Spon).

The Buchanan Committee (1963), *Traffic in Towns: A Study of the Long-Term Problems of Traffic in Urban Areas – Report of the Working Group* (London: HMSO).

Buller, J. (1995), 'Britain as an Awkward Partner: Reassessing Britain's Relations with the EU', *Politics*, vol. 15, pp. 33-42.

Button, K.J. (1984), *Road Haulage Licensing and EC Transport Policy* (London: Gower).

Button, K.J. (1995), 'UK Environmental Policy and Transport', in T.S. Gray (ed.), *UK Environmental Policy in the 1990s* (Basingstoke: Macmillan), pp. 173-88.

Cartwright, T.J. (1975), *Royal Commissions and Departmental Committees in Britain: A Case-Study in Institutional Adaptiveness and Public Participation in Government* (London: Hodder and Stoughton).

Castle, B. (1984), *The Castle Diaries: 1964-70* (London: Weidenfeld and Nicolson).

CBD Research Limited (1996), *Directory of British Associations and Associations in Ireland*, Edition 13 (Beckenham: CBD Research).

Cd 3080 (1906), Royal Commission on Motor Cars, *Report of the Royal Commission on Motor Cars, Volume 1* (London: HMSO).

Centre for Economics and Business Research (1994), *Roads and Jobs: The Economic Impact of Different Levels of Expenditure on the Roads Programme*, (London: British Road Federation).

Centro (1993), *Keeping the West Midlands Moving: A 20 Year Strategy for Public Transport – Summary Document* (Birmingham: WMPTA).

Centro (1994a), *Annual Review and Accounts: 1993-1994* (Birmingham: WMPTA).

Centro (1994b), Transport and our Environment: Moving with the Times (Birmingham: WMPTA).

Chartered Institute for Transport (1990), *Paying for Progress* (London: Chartered Institute for Transport).

Christiansen, T. (1996), 'A Maturing Bureaucracy? The Role of the Commission in the Policy Process', in J. Richardson (ed.), *European Union: Power and Policy-Making* (London: Routledge), pp. 77-95.

Christophersen Group (1994), 'Trans-European Networks: Interim Report of the Chairman of the Group of Personal Representatives of the Heads of State or Government to the Corfu Council (Christophersen Group)', *Bulletin of the European Communities*, Supplement, 2/94 (Luxembourg: Office for Official Publications of the European Communities).

Christophersen Group (1995), *Trans-European Networks: Report of the Group of Personal Representatives of the Heads of State or Government* (Luxembourg: Office for Official Publications of the European Communities).

Church, C. and Phinnemore, D. (1994), *European Union and European Community: A Handbook and Commentary on the Post-Maastricht Treaties* (London: Harvester Wheatsheaf).

City Research Project (1993), *Meeting the Transport Needs of the City: A Report for the City Research Project* (London: City of London).

Cm 693 (1989), *Roads for Prosperity* (London: HMSO).

Cm 1200 (1990), *This Common Inheritance: Britain's Environmental Strategy* (London: HMSO).

Cm 2068 (1992), *This Common Inheritance: Britain's Environmental Strategy – The Second Year Report* (London: HMSO).

Cm 2426 (1994), *Sustainable Development: The UK Strategy* (London: HMSO).

Cm 2427 (1994), *Climate Change: The UK Programme* (London: HMSO).

Cm 2674 (1994), *Royal Commission on Environmental Pollution, Eighteenth Report – Transport and the Environment* (London: HMSO).

Cm 3188 (1996), *This Common Inheritance: UK Annual Report 1996* (London: HMSO).

Cm 3206 (1996), *Transport: The Government's Expenditure Plans, 1996-97 to 1998-99* (London: HMSO).

Cm 3234 (1996), *Transport – The Way Forward: The Government's Response to the Transport Debate* (London: HMSO).

Cm 3587 (1997), *The United Kingdom National Air Quality Strategy* (London: HMSO).

Cm 3752 (1997), *Royal Commission on Environmental Pollution, Twentieth Report – Transport and the Environment: Developments since 1994* (London: HMSO).

Cm 3950 (1998) *A New Deal For Transport: Better for Everyone – The Government's White Paper on the Future of Transport* (London: HMSO).

Cmnd 3057 (1966), *Transport Policy* (London: HMSO).

Cmnd 4369 (1970), *Roads for the Future: The New Inter-Urban Plan for England* (London: HMSO).

Cmnd 7132 (1978), *Policy for Roads: England 1978* (London: HMSO).

Cmnd 8852 (1983), *Royal Commission on Environmental Pollution, Ninth Report – Lead in the Environment* (London: HMSO).

Cobb, R.W. and Elder, C.D. (1972), *Participation in American Politics: The Dynamics of Agenda-Building* (Baltimore & London: John Hopkins University Press).

Cohen, M.D., March, J.G. and Olsen, J.P. (1972), 'A Garbage Can Model of Organizational Choice', *Administrative Science Quarterly*, vol. 17, pp. 1-25.

Commission for Integrated Transport (1999a), *Work Programme 1999-2001* (London: Commission for Integrated Transport).

Commission for Integrated Transport (1999b), *Guidance on Provisional Local Transport Plans – Advice by the Commission for Integrated Transport* (London: Commission for Integrated Transport).

Commission of the European Communities (1979), 'A Transport Network for Europe: Outline of a Policy', *Bulletin of the European Communities*, Supplement, 8/79 (Luxembourg: Office for Official Publications of the European Communities).

Commission of the European Communities (1985), *Completing the Internal Market: White Paper from the Commission to the European Council*, COM (85) 310 Final (Luxembourg: Office for Official Publications of the European Communities).

Commission of the European Communities (1990a), *European File: European Community Transport Policy in the Approach to 1992* (Luxembourg: Office for Official Publications of the European Communities).

Commission of the European Communities (1990b), 'Declaration by the European Council on the Environmental Imperative', *Bulletin of the European Communities*, vol. 23, no. 6 (Luxembourg: Office for Official Publications of the European Communities), pp. 17-20.

Commission of the European Communities (1993a), 'The Future Development of the Common Transport Policy: A Global Approach to the Construction of a Community Framework for Sustainable Mobility', *Bulletin of the European Communities*, Supplement, 3/93 (Luxembourg: Office for Official Publications of the European Communities).

Commission of the European Communities (1993b), *Trans-European Networks: Towards a Master Plan for the Road Network and Road Traffic* (Luxembourg: Office for Official Publications of the European Communities).

Commission of the European Communities (1993c), 'Growth, Competitiveness, Employment: The Challenges and the Ways Forward into the 21st Century', *Bulletin of the European Communities*, Supplement, 6/93 (Luxembourg: Office for Official Publications of the European Communities).

Commission of the European Communities (1994a), *The Trans-European Transport Network* (Luxembourg: Office for Official Publications of the European Communities).

Commission of the European Communities (1994b), *Europe 2000+: Cooperation for European Territorial Development* (Luxembourg: Office for Official Publications of the European Communities).

Commission of the European Communities (1995a), 'Address by Jacques Santer, President of the Commission, to the European Parliament on the Occasion of the Investiture Debate of the New Commission', *Bulletin of the European Communities*, Supplement, 1/95 (Luxembourg: Office for Official Publications of the European Communities), pp. 5-17.

Commission of the European Communities (1995b), 'The Citizens' Network: Fulfilling the Potential of Public Passenger Transport in Europe', *Bulletin of the European Communities*, Supplement, 4/95 (Luxembourg: Office for Official Publications of the European Communities).

Commission of the European Communities (1996), 'Towards Fair and Efficient Pricing in Transport: Policy Options for Internalizing the External Costs of Transport in the European Union', *Bulletin of the European Communities*, Supplement, 2/96 (Luxembourg: Office for Official Publications of the European Communities).

Commission of the European Communities High Level Group: 'The European High-Speed Train Network', in (1995), *High Speed Europe* (Luxembourg: Office for Official Publications of the European Communities).

Commission of the European Communities (1998), *The Common Transport Policy – Sustainable Mobility: Perspectives for the Future* (Luxembourg: Office for Official Publications of the European Communities).

Confederation of British Industry (1995a), *Missing Links: Settling National Transport Priorities - A CBI Discussion Document* (London: CBI).

Confederation of British Industry (1995b), *Moving Forward: A Business Strategy for Transport* (London: CBI).

Council for the Protection of Rural England (1995), *The Great Transport Debate: A Submission by the CPRE* (London: CPRE).

Cram, L. (1993), 'Calling the Tune Without Playing the Piper? Social Policy Regulation: the Role of the Commission in European Community Social Policy', *Policy and Politics*, vol. 21, pp. 135-46.

Cram, L. (1994), 'The Commission as a Multi-Organisation: Social Policy and IT Policy in the EU', *Journal of European Public Policy*, vol. 1, pp. 195-217.

Crenson, M.A. (1971), *The Un-Politics of Air Pollution: A Study of Non-Decision Making in the Cities* (Baltimore: John Hopkins Press).

Dahl, R.A. (1961), *Who Governs? Democracy and Power in an American City* (London: Yale University Press).

Dearlove, J. (1973), *The Politics of Policy in Local Government: The Making and Maintenance of Public Policy in the Royal Borough of Kensington and Chelsea* (Cambridge University Press).

Department of Environment (1993), *Planning Policy Guidance Note 6 (Revised): Town Centres and Retail Developments* (London: DoE).

Department of Environment (1994), *Vital and Viable Town Centres: Meeting the Challenge* (London: HMSO).

Department of Environment and Department of Transport (1994), *Planning Policy Guidance Note 13: Transport* (London: DoE/DTp).

Department of Environment, Transport and the Regions (1997), *Transport Statistics: Great Britain, 1997* (London: HMSO).

Department of Environment, Transport and the Regions (1998a), *Breaking the Logjam: The Government's Consultation Paper on Fighting Traffic Congestion and Pollution through Road User and Workplace Parking Charges* (London: DoETR).

Department of Environment, Transport and the Regions (1998b), *A New Deal for Trunk Roads in England* (London: DoETR).

Department of Environment, Transport and the Regions (1999a), *The Air Quality Strategy for England, Scotland, Wales and Northern Ireland: a Consultation Document* (London: DoETR).

Department of Environment, Transport and the Regions (1999b), *Revision of Planning Policy Guidance Note (PPG) 13: Transport (Public Consultation Draft)* (London: DoETR).

Department of Environment, Transport and the Regions (1999c), 'UK to Receive £32 Million from Europe for Transport Trans European Networks', *DoETR Press Release: 754*, 27th July 1999 (London: DoETR).

Department of Environment, Transport and the Regions (1999d), 'Prescott: Good News for the Environment, Public Transport, Business and the Motorist', *DoETR Press Release: 1074*, 9th November 1999 (London: DoETR).

Department of Environment, Transport and the Regions (1999e), 'Leeds to Host Trials of Electronic Road User Charging Equipment', *DoETR Press Release: 618*, 28th June 1999 (London: DoETR).

Department of Health (1995a), *Asthma: An Epidemiological Overview* (London: HMSO).

Department of Health (1995b), *Asthma and Outdoor Air Pollution* (London: HMSO).

Department of Transport (1989a), *National Road Traffic Forecasts (Great Britain) 1989* (London: HMSO).

Department of Transport (1989b), *Section 56 Grant for Public Transport: DoT Circular 3/89* (London: DTp).

Department of Transport (1993), *Transport Policies and Programme Submissions for 1994-95: Local Authority Circular 2/93* (London: DTp).

Department of Transport (1994), *Trunk Roads in England: 1994 Review* (London: HMSO).

Department of Transport (1995a), 'National Transport Policy Should Not Ignore Individual Choice', *DTp Press Release: 90*, 28th March 1995 (London: DTp)

Department of Transport (1995b), 'Local Authorities Must Play Leading Part in Developing Transport Solutions says Mawhinney', *DTp Press Release: 113*, 10th April 1995 (London: DTp)

Department of Transport (1995c), 'Mawhinney Shows the Way Ahead', *DTp Press Release: 176*, 12th June 1995 (London: DTp)

Department of Transport (1995d), 'UK Gets £22 Million from Europe for Trans-European Networks', *DTp Press Release*, 26th October 1995 (London: DTp).

Department of Transport and The Highways Agency (1995), *Managing the Trunk Road Programme* (London: HMSO).

Dinan, D. (1999), 'Treaty Change in the European Union: The Amsterdam Experience', in L. Cram, D. Dinan and N. Nugent (eds), *Developments in the European Union* (Basingstoke: Macmillan), pp. 290-310.

Doherty, B. (1997), 'Direct Action Against Road-Building: Some Implications for the Concept of Protest Repertoires', in J. Stanyer and G. Stoker (eds), *Contemporary Political Studies, 1997*, vol. 1 (Nottingham: The Political Studies Association of the United Kingdom), pp. 147-55.

Döhler, M. (1991), 'Policy Networks, Opportunity Structures and Neo-Conservative Reform Strategies in Health Policy', in B. Marin and R. Mayntz (eds), *Policy Networks: Empirical Evidence and Theoretical Considerations* (Boulder, Colorado: Westview Press), pp. 235-96.

Dowding, K. (1991), *Rational Choice and Political Power* (Aldershot: Edward Elgar).

Dowding, K. (1994), 'Policy Networks: Don't Stretch a Good Idea too Far', in P. Dunleavy and G. Stanyer (eds), *Contemporary Political Studies, 1994*, vol. 1 (Belfast: The Political Studies Association of the United Kingdom), pp. 59-77.

Dowding, K. (1995), 'Model or Metaphor? A Critical Review of the Policy Network Approach', *Political Studies*, vol. 43, pp. 136-71.

Downs, A. (1973), 'The Political Economy of Improving Our Environment', in J. Bains, *Environmental Decay: Economic Causes and Remedies* (Boston: Little Brown), pp. 59-81.

Driver, S. and Martell, L. (1998), *New Labour: Politics After Thatcherism* (Cambridge: Polity Press).

Dudley, G.F. (1983), 'The Road Lobby: A Declining Force ?', in D. Marsh (ed.), *Pressure Politics* (London: Junction Books), pp. 104-28.

Dudley, G.F. and Richardson, J.J. (1995), 'Explaining Policy Change: Adversarial Communities, Policy Arenas, and the Development of UK Trunk Roads Policy Since 1945', *unpublished paper*.

Dudley, G.F. and Richardson, J.J. (1996a), 'Why does Policy Change over Time? Adversarial Policy Communities, Alternative Policy Arenas, and British Trunk Roads Policy 1945-95', *Journal of European Public Policy*, vol. 3, pp. 63-83.

Dudley, G.F. and Richardson, J.J. (1996b), 'Promiscuous and Celibate Ministerial Styles: Policy Change, Policy Networks, and UK Roads Policy', *Essex Papers in Politics and Government*, No. 107.

Dudley, G.F. and Richardson, J.J. (1998), 'Arenas Without Rules and the Policy Change Process: Outsider Groups and British Roads Policy', *Political Studies*, vol. 46, pp. 727-47.

Dunleavy, P. (1980), *Urban Political Analysis: The Politics of Collective Consumption* (London: Macmillan).

Dunleavy, P. (1995), 'Policy Disasters: Explaining the UK's Record', *Public Policy and Administration*, vol. 10, pp. 52-70.

Durant, R.F. and Diehl, P.F. (1990), 'Agendas, Alternatives and Public Policy: Lessons from the U.S. Foreign Policy Arena', *Journal of Public Policy*, vol. 9, pp. 179-205.

Earnshaw, D. and Judge, D. (1996), 'From Co-operation to Co-decision: The European Parliament's Path to Legislative Power', in J. Richardson (ed.), *European Union: Power and Policy Making* (London: Routledge), pp. 96-126.

Eastman, C. (1969), *Work Accidents and the Law* (New York: Arno and New York Times).

Elton, B. (1991), *Gridlock* (London: Sphere Books).

European Programme on Emissions, Fuels and Engine Technologies (1995), *Executive Summary, July 1995* (Brussels: ACEA and Europia).

Evans, P.B., Rueschmeyer, D. and Skocpol, T. (eds) (1985) *Bringing the State Back In* (Cambridge: Cambridge University Press).

Festing, S. (1997), 'Friends of the Earth and the Direct Action Movement', paper given at *Conference on Direct Action and British Environmentalism*, University of Keele, 25th October 1997.

Finer, S.E. (1958), 'Transport Interests and the Road Lobby', *Political Quarterly*, vol. 29, pp. 47-58.

Freund, P. and Martin, G. (1993), *The Ecology of the Automobile* (London: Black Rose Books).

Gamble, A. (1994), *The Free Economy and the Strong State: The Politics of Thatcherism* (Basingstoke: Macmillan), 2nd edition.

Gaventa, J.P. (1980), *Power and Powerlessness: Quiescence and Rebellion in an Appalachian Valley* (Oxford: Clarendon Press).

George, S. (1996), *Politics and Policy in the European Union* (Oxford: Oxford University Press), 3rd edition.

George, S. (1999), *An Awkward Partner: Britain in the European Community* (Oxford: Oxford University Press), 3rd edition.

Grant, M. (1986), 'The Role of the Courts in Central-Local Relations', in M. Goldsmith (ed.), *New Research in Central-Local Relations* (Aldershot: Gower), pp. 191-204.

Grant, W. (1995), *Autos, Smog and Pollution Control: The Politics of Air Quality Management in California* (Aldershot: Edward Elgar).

Grant, W. (1997), 'BSE and the Politics of Food', in P. Dunleavy, A. Gamble, I. Holliday and G. Peele (eds), *Developments in British Politics 5* (Basingstoke: Macmillan), pp. 342-54.

Greenwood, J., Grote, J.R. and Ronit, K. (eds) (1992), *Organised Interests in the European Community* (London: Sage).

Haas, P.M. (1992), 'Introduction: Epistemic Communities and International Policy Co-ordination', *International Organisation*, vol. 46, pp. 1-36.

Haigh, N. (1996), 'Climate Change Policies and Politics in the European Community', in T. O'Riordan and J. Jager (eds), *Politics of Climate Change: A European Perspective* (London: Routledge), pp. 155-85.

Hamer, M. (1987), *Wheels Within Wheels* (London: Routledge and Kegan Paul).

Hampton, W. (1987), *Local Government and Urban Politics* (London: Longman).

Hantrais, L. (1995), *Social Policy in the European Union* (Basingstoke: Macmillan).

Hay, C. (1994), 'Labour's Thatcherite Revisionism: Playing the Politics of Catch-up', *Political Studies*, vol. 42, pp. 700-7.

Hazell, R. and Sinclair, D. (1999), 'The British Constitution in 1997-98: Labour's Constitutional Revolution', *Parliamentary Affairs*, vol. 52, pp. 161-78.

HC (376-I) House of Commons Transport Committee, Fifth Report Session 1993-94, *Charging for the Use of Motorways* (London: HMSO).

HC (376-II) House of Commons Transport Committee, Fifth Report Session 1993-94, *Charging for the Use of Motorways: Minutes of Evidence* (London: HMSO).

HC (506-I) House of Commons Transport Committee, Sixth Report Session 1993-94, *Transport-Related Air Pollution in London* (London: HMSO).

HC (104-I) House of Commons Transport Committee, Third Report Session 1994-95, *Urban Road Pricing* (London: HMSO).

HC (104-II) House of Commons Transport Committee, Third Report Session 1994-95, *Urban Road Pricing: Minutes of Evidence* (London: HMSO).

HC Bill 8 (1999), *Transport Bill*, Session 1999-2000 (London: HMSO).

Heclo, H. (1978), 'Issue Networks and the Executive Establishment', in A. King (ed.), *The New American Political System* (Washington DC: American Enterprise Institute for Public Policy Research), pp. 87-124.

Held, D. (1989), *Political Theory and the Modern State: Essays on State, Power and Democracy* (Oxford: Polity Press).

Hennessy, P. (1990), *Whitehall* (London: Fontana Press).

Hillman, M. (1992), 'Reconciling Transport and Environmental Policy Objectives: The Way ahead at the End of the Road', *Public Administration*, vol. 70, pp. 225-34.

HL (50-I) House of Lords Select Committee on the European Communities, Eighth Report Session 1993-4, *Common Transport Policy – Sustainable Mobility* (London: HMSO).

HL (50-II) House of Lords Select Committee on the European Communities, Eighth Report Session 1993-4, *Common Transport Policy – Sustainable Mobility: Minutes of Evidence* (London: HMSO).

HM Treasury and Department of Employment (1993) 'Growth, Competitiveness and Employment in the European Community', in CEC (1992) (ed.), 'Growth, Competitiveness, Employment: The Challenges and the Ways Forward into the 21st Century', *Bulletin of the European Communities*, 6/93 – Part B (Luxembourg: Office for Official Publications of the European Communities), pp. 272-93.

Holden, R. (1999), 'Labour's Transformation: Searching for the Point of Origin – The European Dynamic', *Politics*, vol. 19, pp. 103-08.

Holliday, I. (1993), 'Organised Interests After Thatcher', in P. Dunleavy, A. Gamble, I. Holliday and G. Peele (eds), *Developments in British Politics 4* (Basingstoke: Macmillan), pp. 307-20.

Jenkins-Smith, H.C. and St. Clair, G.K. (1993), 'The Politics of Offshore Energy: Empirically Testing the Advocacy Coalition Framework', in P.A. Sabatier and H.C. Jenkins-Smith (eds), *Policy Change and Learning: An Advocacy Coalition Approach* (Boulder, Colorado: Westview Press), pp. 149-75.

Jones, T. (1996), *Remaking the Labour Party: from Gaitskill to Blair* (London: Routledge).

Joppke, C. (1991), 'Social Movements During Cycles of Issue Attention: The Decline of the Anti-nuclear Movements in West Germany and the USA', *British Journal of Sociology*, vol. 42, pp. 43-60.

Jordan, A. and O'Riordan, T. (1995), 'The Precautionary Principle in UK Environmental Law and Policy', in T.S. Gray (ed.), *UK Environmental Policy in the 1990s* (Basingstoke: Macmillan), pp. 57-84.

Jordan, G. (1990), 'Sub-Governments, Policy Communities and Networks: Refilling the Old Bottles?', *Journal of Theoretical Politics*, vol. 2, pp. 319-38.

Jordan, G. and Richardson, J.J. (1987), *British Politics and the Policy Process: An Arena Approach* (London: Allen and Unwin).

Jordan, G. and Richardson, J. (1982), 'The British Policy Style or the Logic of Negotiation?', in J. Richardson (ed.), *Policy Styles in Western Europe* (London: George Allen and Unwin), pp. 80-110.

Judge, D. (1993), *The Parliamentary State* (London: Sage Publications).

Kassim, H. (1996), 'Air Transport', in H. Kassim and A. Menon (eds), *The European Union and National Industrial Policy* (London: Routledge), pp. 106-31.

Kassim, H. and Menon, A. (1996a), 'The European Union and State Autonomy', in H. Kassim and A. Menon (eds), *The European Union and National Industrial Policy* (London: Routledge), pp. 1-10.

Kassim, H. and Menon, A. (eds) (1996b), *The European Union and National Industrial Policy* (London: Routledge).

Kenny, M. and Smith, M. (1997), '(Mis)understanding Blair', *Political Quarterly*, vol. 63, pp. 220-30.

Kersbergen, K.V. and Verbeek, B. (1994), 'The Politics of Subsidiarity in the European Union', *Journal of Common Market Studies*, vol. 32, pp. 215-36.

King, A. (1975), 'Overload: Problems of Governing in the 1970s', *Political Studies*, vol. 23, pp. 284-96.

King, D. (1993), 'Government Beyond Whitehall: Local Government and Urban Politics', in P. Dunleavy, A. Gamble, I. Holliday and G. Peele (eds), *Developments in British Politics 4* (Basingstoke: Macmillan), pp. 194-218.

Kingdon, J.W. (1984), *Agendas, Alternatives and Public Policies* (New York: Harper Collins).

Kingdon, J.W. (1995), *Agendas, Alternatives and Public Policies* (New York: Harper Collins), 2nd edition.

Krause, F., Bach, W. and Kooney, J. (1990), *Energy Policy in the Greenhouse* (London: Earthscan).

Laffin, M. (1986), *Professionalism and Policy: The Role of the Professions in Central-Local Relations* (Aldershot: Gower).

Lange, P. (1993), 'Maastricht and the Social Protocol: Why Did they Do It?', *Politics and Society*, vol. 21, pp. 5-36.

Lee. N. (1994), 'Transport Policy', in M. Artis and N. Lee (eds) *The Economics of the European Union* (Oxford: Oxford University Press), pp. 202-37.

Leibfreid, S. and Pierson, P. (1996), 'Social Policy', in H. Wallace and W. Wallace (eds), *Policy-Making in the European Union* (Oxford: Oxford University Press), 3rd edition, pp. 185-207.

Levin, P.H. (1979), 'Highway Inquiries: A Study in Governmental Responsiveness', *Public Administration*, vol. 57, pp. 21-49.

Ludlum, S. (1996), 'The Spectre Haunting Conservatism: Europe and Backbench Rebellion', in S. Ludlum and M.J. Smith (eds), *Contemporary British Conservatism* (Basingstoke: Macmillan), pp. 98-120.

Lukes, S. (1974), *Power: A Radical View* (Basingstoke: Macmillan).

McCormick, J. (1991), *British Politics and the Environment* (London: Earthscan).

McGough, R. (1992), *Defying Gravity* (London: Penguin).

McGowan, F. (1994), 'EC Transport Policy', in A.M. El-Agraa (ed.), *The Economics of the European Community* (London: Harvester Wheatsheaf), 4th edition, pp. 247-64.

McKay, G. (1998), 'DiY Culture: Notes Towards an Introduction', in G. McKay (ed.), *DiY Culture: Party and Protest in Nineties Britain* (London: Verso), pp. 1-53.

McLaren, D.P. and Higman, R. (1993), 'The Environmental Implications of Congestion on the Inter-urban Network in the UK', paper given to *21st PTRC Summer Annual Meeting*, 1993.

Machiavelli, N. (1513), 'The Prince', translation by L. Ricci, revised by E.R.P. Vincent in *The Prince and Discourses* (New York: The Modern Library).

Maddison, D. and Pearce, D. (1995), 'The UK and Global Warming Policy', in T.S. Gray (ed.), *UK Environmental Policy in the 1990s* (Basingstoke: Macmillan), pp. 123-43.

Majone, G. (1991a), 'Cross-National Sources of Regulatory Policymaking in Europe and the United States', *Journal of Public Policy*, vol. 11, pp. 79-106.

Majone, G. (1991b), 'Regulatory Federalism in the European Community', paper given to *American Political Science Association Annual Conference*, August-September, 1991.

Majone, G. (1993), 'The European Community Between Social Policy and Social Regulation', *Journal of Common Market Studies*, vol. 31, pp. 153-70.

Majone, G. (1996), 'Which Social Policy for Europe?', in Y. Mény, P. Muller and J.L. Quermonne (eds), *Adjusting to Europe: the Impact of the European Union on National Institutions and Policies* (London: Routledge), pp. 123-36.

Maloney, W.A., Jordan, G. and McLaughlin, A.M. (1994), 'Interest Groups and Public Policy: The Insider/Outsider Model Revisited', in *Journal of Public Policy*, vol. 14, pp. 17-38.

Marks, G. (1992), 'Structural Policy in the European Community', in A. Sbragia (ed.), *Euro-Politics: Institutions and Policymaking in the "New" European Community* (Washington: The Brookings Institute), pp. 191-224.

Marsh, D. (1983), 'Introduction: Interest Groups in Britain', in D. Marsh (ed.), *Pressure Politics: Interest Groups in Britain* (London: Junction Books), pp. 1-19.

Marsh, D. and Rhodes, R.A.W. (eds.), (1992a) *Policy Networks in British Government* (Oxford: Oxford University Press).

Marsh, D. and Rhodes, R. (1992b), *Implementing Thatcherite Policies: Audit of an Era* (Buckingham: Open University Press).

Mawhinney, B. (1995), *Transport: The Way Ahead* (London: HMSO).

Mawson, J. and Gibney, J. (1985), 'English and Welsh Local Government and the European Community', in M. Keating and B. Jones (eds), *Regions in the European Community* (Oxford: Oxford University Press), pp. 133-59.

Mazey, S. and Richardson, J. (eds) (1993), *Lobbying in the European Community* (Oxford: Oxford University Press).

Mazey, S. and Richardson, J. (1996), 'The Logic of Organisation: Interest Groups', in J. Richardson (ed.), *European Union: Power and Policy-Making* (London: Routledge), pp. 200-15.

Menon, A. and Hayward, J. (1996), 'States, Industrial Policies and the European Union', in H. Kassim and A. Menon (eds), *The European Union and National Industrial Policy* (London: Routledge), pp. 267-90.

Ministry of Transport (1962), *Roads in England and Wales: Report by the Minister of Transport for the Year 1961-2* (London: HMSO).

Ministry of Transport (1972), *Roads in England: Report by the Secretary of State for the Environment for the Year Ended 31st March 1971* (London: HMSO).

Monbiot, G. (1998), 'Reclaim the Fields and Country Lanes! The Land is Ours Campaign', in G. McKay (ed.), *DiY Culture: Party and Protest in Nineties Britain* (London: Verso), pp. 174-86.

Moravcsik (1991), 'Negotiating the Single European Act: National Interests and Conventional Statecraft in the European Community', *International Organisation*, vol. 45, pp. 19-56.

Nader, R. (1965), *Unsafe at any Speed: The Designed in Dangers of the American Automobile* (New York: Grossman). √

Naess, A. (1997), 'Sustainable Development and the Deep Ecology Movement', in S. Baker, M. Kousis, D. Richardson and S. Young (eds), *The Politics of Sustainable Development: Theory, Policy and Practice within the European Union* (London: Routledge), pp. 61-71.

Newbury, D. (1995), *Reforming Road Taxation, Report Commissioned by the Automobile Association* (London: Automobile Association).

Nieburg, H.L. (1962), 'The Threat of Violence and Social Change', *American Political Science Review*, vol. 56, pp. 865-73.

Nordlinger, E. (1981), *The Autonomy of the Democratic State* (Cambridge, Massachusetts: Harvard University Press).

Page, E. and Robinson, N.T. (1995), 'Future Generations, Ethics and Transport Policy', *PAIS Working Paper*, no. 122 (Coventry: Department of Politics and International Studies, University of Warwick).

Painter, M. (1980), 'Whitehall and Roads: A Case Study of Sectoral Politics', *Policy and Politics*, vol. 8, pp. 163-86.

Parsons, W. (1995), *Public Policy: An Introduction to the Theory and Practice of Policy Analysis* (Cheltenham: Edward Elgar).

Paterson, M. (1996), *Global Warming and Global Politics* (London: Routledge).

Paterson, M. (1997), 'Swampy and the Tabloids', paper given at *Conference on Direct Action and British Environmentalism*, University of Keele, 25th October 1997.

Peters, B.G. and Hogwood, B.W. (1985), 'In Search of an Issue Attention Cycle', *Journal of Politics*, vol. 47, pp. 238-53.

Peterson, J. (1997), 'Britain, Europe and the World', in P. Dunleavy, A. Gamble, I. Holliday and G. Peele (eds), *Developments in British Politics 5* (Basingstoke: Macmillan), pp. 20-42.

Plowden, W. (1971), *The Motor Car and Politics: 1896-1970* (London: Bodley Head).

Polsby, N. (1963), *Community Power and Political Theory* (New Haven: Yale University Press).

Polsby, N. (1980), *Community Power and Political Theory* (New Haven: Yale University Press), 2nd edition.

Pross, P. (1992), *Group Politics and Public Policy* (Toronto: Oxford University Press), 2nd edition.

Putnam, R. (1988), 'Diplomacy and Domestic Politics: The Logic of Two-Level Games', *International Organisation*, vol. 12, pp. 427-60.

Rhodes, R.A.W. (1986), *National World of Local Government* (London: Allen and Unwin).

Rhodes, R.A.W. (1988), *Beyond Westminster and Whitehall* (London: Allen and Unwin).

Rhodes, R.A.W. (1990), 'Policy Networks: A British Perspective', *Journal of Theoretical Politics*, vol. 2, pp. 293-317.

Rhodes, R.A.W. and Marsh, D. (1992), 'New Directions in the Study of Policy Networks', *European Journal of Political Research*, vol. 21, pp. 181-205.

Richardson, D. (1997), 'The Politics of Sustainable Development', in S. Baker, M. Kousis, D. Richardson and S. Young (eds), *The Politics of Sustainable Development: Theory, Policy and Practice in the European Union* (London: Routledge), pp. 43-60.

Richardson, J.J. (1993a), 'Doing Less By Doing More: British Government 1979-93', *European Public Policy Institute Occasional Papers,* 93/2 (Coventry: Department of Politics and International Studies, University of Warwick).

Richardson, J.J. (1993b), 'Interest Group Behaviour in Britain: Continuity and Change', in J.J. Richardson (ed.), *Pressure Groups* (Oxford: Oxford University Press), pp. 86-99.

Richardson, J.J. (ed.) (1996a), *European Union: Power and Policy-Making* (London: Routledge).

Richardson, J.J. (1996b), 'Eroding EU policies: Implementation Gaps, Cheating and Re-Steering', in J. Richardson (ed.), *European Union: Power and Policy-Making* (London: Routledge), pp. 278-94.

Richardson, J.J. (1996c), 'Policy-making in the EU: Interests, Ideas and Garbage Cans of Primeval Soup', in J. Richardson (ed.), *European Union: Power and Policy-Making* (London: Routledge), pp. 3-23.

Richardson, J.J., Gustafsson, G. and Jordan, G. (1982), 'The Concept of Policy Style', in J. Richardson (ed.), *Policy Styles in Western Europe* (London: George Allen and Unwin), pp. 1-16.

Richardson, J.J. and Jordan, A.G. (1979), *Governing Under Pressure: The Policy Process in a Post-Parliamentary Democracy* (Oxford: Basil Blackwell).

Riddel, P. (1994), 'Major and Parliament', in D. Kavanagh and A. Seldon (eds), *The Major Effect* (London: Macmillan/Papermac), pp. 46-63.

Roberts, J., Cleary, J., Hamilton, K. and Hanna, J. (eds) (1992), *Travel Sickness: The Need for a Sustainable Transport Policy in Britain* (London: Lawrence & Wishart).

Robinson, M. (1992), *The Greening of British Party Politics* (Manchester: Manchester University Press).

Robinson, N. (1997a), 'The Student-Supervisor Relationship', in P. Burnham (ed.), *Surviving the Research Process in Politics* (London: Pinter), pp. 71-82.

Robinson, N. (1997b), 'Still the Great Green Saviour? Transport, the Environment and the European Union', *2nd UACES Research Conference*, University of Loughborough, September 10-12, 1997.

Ross, J.F. (1994), 'High Speed Rail: Catalyst for European Integration?', *Journal of Common Market Studies*, vol. 32, pp. 194-214.

Ross, J.F. (1995), 'When Co-operation Divides: Öresünd, the Channel Tunnel and the New Politics of European Transport', *Journal of European Public Policy*, vol. 2, pp. 115-46.

Royal Automobile Club (1995), *Car Dependence: A Report for the RAC Foundation for Motoring and the Environment* (London: RAC).

Royal Society for the Protection of Birds (1995), *Breaking Point: The RSPB's Policy on Transport and Biodiversity* (Sandy, Bedfordshire: RSPB Publications).

Sabatier, P.A. (1988), 'An Advocacy Coalition Framework of Policy Change and the Role of Policy-Orientated Learning Therein', *Policy Sciences*, vol. 21, pp. 129-68.

Sabatier, P.A. (1993), 'Policy Change Over a Decade or More', in P.A. Sabatier and H.C. Jenkins-Smith (eds), *Policy Change and Learning: An Advocacy Coalition Approach* (Boulder, Colorado: Westview Press), pp. 13-39.

Sabatier, P.A. (1998), 'The Advocacy Coalition Framework: Revisions and Relevance for Europe', *Journal of European Public Policy*, vol. 5, pp. 98-130.

Sabatier, P.A. and Jenkins-Smith, H.C. (eds) (1993a), *Policy Change and Learning: An Advocacy Coalition Approach* (Boulder, Colorado: Westview Press).

Sabatier, P.A. and Jenkins-Smith, H.C. (1993b), 'The Advocacy Coalition Framework: Assessment, Revisions, and Implications for Scholars and Practitioners', in P.A. Sabatier and H.C. Jenkins-Smith (eds), *Policy Change and Learning: An Advocacy Coalition Approach* (Boulder, Colorado: Westview Press), pp. 211-35.

Sanders, D. (1997), 'Voting and the Electorate', in P. Dunleavy, A. Gamble, I. Holliday and G. Peele (eds), *Developments in British Politics 5* (Basingstoke: Macmillan), pp. 45-74.

Sbragia, A. (1996), 'Environmental Policy: The "Push-Pull" of Policy-Making', in H. Wallace and W. Wallace (eds), *Policy-Making in the European Union* (Oxford: Oxford University Press), pp. 235-55.

Schattschneider, E.E. (1960), *The Semisovereign People: A Realist's View of Democracy in America* (Illinois: The Dryden Press).

Seldon, A. (1997), *Major: A Political Life* (London: Phoenix).

Sharpe, L.J. (1985), 'Central Co-ordination and the Policy Network', *Political Studies,* vol. 33, pp. 361-81.

Skjaerseth, J.B. (1994), 'The Climate Policy of the EC: Too Hot to Handle?', *Journal of Common Market Studies*, vol. 32, pp. 25-45.

Skocpol, T. (1985), 'Bringing the State Back in: Strategies of Analysis in Current Research', in P.B. Evans, D. Rieschmeyer and T. Skocpol (eds), *Bringing the State Back In* (Cambridge: Cambridge University Press), pp. 3-37.

Smith, A. (1776), *An Enquiry into the Nature and the Causes of the Wealth of Nations* (Harmondsworth: Penguin/Pelican books), 1981 reprint.

Smith, M. J. (1993), *Pressure, Power and Policy: State Autonomy and Policy Networks in Britain and the United States* (London: Harvester Wheatsheaf).

Society of Motor Manufacturers and Traders (1964), *The Motor Industry of Great Britain 1964* (London: Society of Motor Manufacturers and Traders).

Society of Motor Manufacturers and Traders (1990), *The Motor Industry and the Greenhouse Effect* (London: Society of Motor Manufacturers and Traders).

Spicker, P. (1991), 'The Principle of Subsidiarity and the Social Policy of the European Community', *Journal of European Social Policy*, vol. 1, pp. 3-14.

Standing Advisory Committee on Trunk Roads Assessment (1994), *Trunk Roads and the Generation of Traffic* (London: HMSO).

Standing Advisory Committee on Trunk Roads Assessment (1999), *Trunk Roads and the Economy* (London: HMSO).

Steering Group of the Buchanan Committee (1963), *Traffic in Towns: A Study of the Long-Term Problems of Traffic in Urban Areas – Report of the Steering Group* (London: HMSO).

Stone, D.A. (1989), 'Casual Stories and the Formation of Policy Agendas', *Political Science Quarterly,* vol. 104, pp. 281-300.

Stringer, J.K. and Richardson, J.J. (1980), 'Managing the Political Agenda: Problem Definition and Policy Making in Britain', *Parliamentary Affairs,* vol. 33, pp. 23-39.

Thain, C. and Wright, M. (1995), *The Treasury and Whitehall: The Planning and Control of Public Expenditure, 1976-1993* (Oxford: Clarendon Press).

Thatcher, M. (1993), *The Downing Street Years* (New York: Harper Collins).

Tolley, R.S. and Turton, B.J. (1995), *Transport Systems, Policy and Planning: A Geographical Approach* (Harlow: Longman).

Tsoukalis, L. (1996), 'Economic and Monetary Union: The Primacy of High Politics', in H. Wallace and W. Wallace (eds), *Policy-Making in the European Union* (Oxford: Oxford University Press), pp. 279-99.

Tyme, J. (1978), *Motorways versus Democracy* (Basingstoke: Macmillan).

UNICE (1991), 'Position on a Number of Basic Principles for the Formulation of a Community Action Strategy on the Greenhouse Effect', *UNICE press release,* 25th June 1991 (Brussels: UNICE).

Vogel, D. (1986), *National Styles of Regulation: Environmental Policy in Great Britain and the United States* (London: Cornell University Press).

Walker, J.L. (1977), 'Setting the Agenda in the U.S. Senate: A Theory of Problem Selection', *British Journal of Political Science,* vol. 7, pp. 423-45.

Wallace, H. (1997), 'At Odds with Europe', *Political Studies,* vol. 45, pp. 677-88.

Wallace, H. and Young, A.R. (1996), 'The Single Market: A New Approach to Policy', in H. Wallace and W. Wallace (eds), *Policy-Making in the European Union* (Oxford: Oxford University Press), 3rd edition, pp. 125-55.

Wallace, W. (1996), 'Government Without Statehood: The Unstable Equilibrium', in H. Wallace and W. Wallace (eds), *Policy-Making in the European Union* (Oxford: Oxford University Press), 3rd edition, pp. 439-60.

Ward, S. (1995), 'The Politics of Mutual Attraction? UK Local Authorities and the Europeanisation of Environmental Policy', in T.S. Gray (ed.), *UK Environmental Policy in the 1990s* (Basingstoke: Macmillan), pp. 101-22.

Weale, A. (1992), *The New Politics of Pollution* (Manchester: Manchester University Press).

Webb, C. (1983), 'Theoretical Perspectives and Problems', in H. Wallace, W. Wallace and C. Webb (eds), *Policy Making in the European Community* (Chichester: John Wiley), 2nd edition, pp. 1-41.

Whitelegg, J. (1988), *Transport Policy in the EEC* (London: Routledge).

Wilks, S. and Wright, M. (1987), 'Conclusion: Comparing Government-Industry Relations: States, Sectors, and Networks', in S. Wilks and M. Wright (eds.), *Comparative Government-Industry Relations* (Oxford: Clarendon Press), pp. 274-313.

Wilson, D. (1984), *Pressure: The A to Z of Campaigning in Britain* (London: Heinemann).

Wilson, D. and Game, C. (1994), *Local Government in the United Kingdom* (Basingstoke: Macmillan).

Wise, M. and Gibb, R. (1993), *Single Market to Social Europe: The European Community in the 1990s* (Harlow: Longman).

Wolman, H. and Goldsmith, H. (1992), *Urban Politics and Policy: A Comparative Approach* (Oxford: Blackwell).

Young, K. (1994), 'Local Government', in D. Kavanagh and A. Seldon (eds), *The Major Effect* (London: Macmillan Papermac), pp. 83-98.

Young, S. (1993), *The Politics of the Environment* (Manchester: Baseline Books).